Early Cinema in Scotland

Dedicated to the memory of Karel Dibbets, 1947–2017

Early Cinema in Scotland

Edited by John Caughie, Trevor Griffiths
and María A. Vélez-Serna

EDINBURGH
University Press

Edinburgh University Press is one of the leading university presses in the UK. We publish academic books and journals in our selected subject areas across the humanities and social sciences, combining cutting-edge scholarship with high editorial and production values to produce academic works of lasting importance. For more information visit our website: edinburghuniversitypress.com

© editorial matter and organisation John Caughie, Trevor Griffiths and María A. Vélez-Serna, 2018
© the chapters their several authors, 2018

Edinburgh University Press Ltd
The Tun – Holyrood Road
12 (2f) Jackson's Entry
Edinburgh EH8 8PJ

Typeset in Ehrhardt by
Servis Filmsetting Ltd, Stockport, Cheshire

A CIP record for this book is available from the British Library

ISBN 978 1 4744 2034 1 (hardback)
ISBN 978 1 4744 2035 8 (webready PDF)
ISBN 978 1 4744 2036 5 (epub)
ISBN 978 1 4744 5223 6 (paperback)

The right of contributors to be identified as authors of this work has been asserted in accordance with the Copyright, Designs and Patents Act 1988 and the Copyright and Related Rights Regulations 2003 (SI No. 2498).

Contents

List of Figures and Tables		vii
Acknowledgements		ix
Notes on the Contributors		xi
1	Introduction *John Caughie, Trevor Griffiths and María A. Vélez-Serna*	1
2	Travelling Bioscopes and Borrowed Spaces *María A. Vélez-Serna*	14
3	Fixed-site Cinemas and the First Film Renters *María A. Vélez-Serna*	33
4	Cinema and Cinema-going in Small Towns *John Caughie*	52
5	Making a Living at the Cinema: Scottish Cinema Staff in the Silent Era *Trevor Griffiths*	68
6	Early Municipal Cinema *Julia Bohlmann*	91
7	*Rob Roy*: Britain's First Feature Film *Caroline Merz*	110
8	Local Films for Local People: 'HAVE YOU BEEN CINEMATOGRAPHED?' *John Caughie and Janet McBain*	130
9	Depicting Scotland: Scotland in Early Films *John Caughie*	147

10	The Talkies Triumphant: Scottish Cinema and the Coming of Sound *Trevor Griffiths*	166
11	Filmography of Scottish-themed Fiction Films *John Caughie*	188

Bibliography 239
Index 250

Figures and Tables

Figures

2.1	Fairground shows travelled on roads using traction engines	18
2.2	Traction engines could also be fitted with a dynamo to generate electricity for a moving picture show	18
3.1	Previous uses of cinema venues operating before 1910	38
3.2	Adapted venues and new cinema construction, 1910–14	39
3.3	Release patterns for a sample of programmes showing in Scottish cinemas during the second week of January 1913	44
4.1	Copy postcard. Exterior of the Hippodrome Cinema, Bo'ness	58
5.1	Workers from the Hillfoot Picture House, Alva, on a staff outing	72
5.2	Staff of the Gaiety Theatre, Clydebank, later the Bank Cinema, c.1910	73
6.1	Kirkintilloch Town Hall, c.1937	97
6.2	Advertisement for Kirkintilloch Municipal Pictures, 1914	100
6.3	Advertisement for Kirkintilloch Pavilion Picture House, 1917	103
6.4	Advertisement for Kirkintilloch Municipal Pictures, 1917	104
6.5	Advertisement for Kirkintilloch Pavilion Picture House & Town Hall, 1923	105
7.1	The only surviving fragment of United Films' 1911 *Rob Roy*	116
7.2	Full-page advertisement for *Rob Roy*, 1911	120
7.3	Queue for *Rob Roy* outside the Picture Salon, Sauchiehall Street, Glasgow	121
8.1	People leaving church in a still from local topical 'Great Western Road 1922'	144
8.2	Territorial Army parade in a still from 'Arrival at Whitehart Hotel, Campbeltown' (1914)	144
8.3	Still from 'Lochgelly Old Age Pensioners' Drive to Crook O'Devon' (c.1928)	144
8.4	Still from 'Lochgelly Old Age Pensioners' Drive to Crook O'Devon' (c.1928)	144

9.1 Locations of scenic films given in trade reviews 152
9.2 Places mentioned in Samuel Johnson's *Journey to the Western Islands of Scotland* (1775) 154
9.3 Places mentioned in Dorothy Wordsworth's *Recollections of a Tour Made in Scotland, A.D. 1803* 155
10.1 'Looking for the man who invented the "talkies"', *The Musicians' Journal*, July 1929 171

Tables

3.1 Cinema capacity in 1914 41
9.1 Examples of early Scottish scenic films 151
10.1 Torry Cinemas Ltd: expenditure on films and wages, 1926–33 178
10.2 Business at two Aberdeen cinemas, 1928–9 to 1933–4 182
10.3 Torry Cinemas Ltd: accounts, 1928–9 to 1933–4 182

Acknowledgements

We gratefully acknowledge the support of the Arts and Humanities Research Council whose Research Grant (AH/I020535/1) funded the three-year project, 'Early Cinema in Scotland, 1896–1927'.

We are also grateful for the active support of our International Advisory Board: Professor Robert C. Allen (University of North Carolina, USA), Dr Karel Dibbets (University of Amsterdam), Professor Richard Maltby (University of Flinders, Australia), Dr Luke McKernan (British Library), Professor Kevin Rockett (Trinity College, Dublin). Their advice and contributions to our symposium and to our final project conference were invaluable in placing our local history in an international context.

Similarly, we acknowledge the significance for international work on cinema history of the HoMER (History of Moviegoing, Exhibition and Reception) Network, and we are grateful for its collaboration in organising the conference 'What Is Cinema History?', held in Glasgow in June 2015.

More locally, we are grateful to Alison Strauss and the Hippodrome Cinema in Bo'ness (a restored jewel of the original 1912 cinema), and their annual Silent Cinema Festival for the opportunity to bring our research to local audiences.

Locally also, we are grateful to our Steering Group for their advice and support: Professor Adrienne Scullion, Professor Karen Lury, Dr Janet McBain, Dr Paul Maloney, Gordon Barr, Martin Bellamy. We acknowledge the contribution of Matt Barr and Mark Herraghty for their technical support of our digital systems.

We are particularly grateful to Jeanette Berrie at Glasgow University for her wise and efficient financial administration.

We acknowledge the contribution to our research of the Moving Image Archive of the National Library of Scotland, an invaluable resource for the history of Scottish cinema and for the social history of Scotland, and are grateful for the assistance of its curators, Ruth Washbrook and Kay Foubister.

We owe a particular debt of gratitude to Janet McBain, then founding

Curator of the Scottish Screen Archive (now the Moving Image Archive), and David Bruce, former Director of the Scottish Film Council, who, in 2010, originally proposed the idea of a research project on early Scottish cinema.

Notes on the Contributors

Contributors were associated with the research project, 'Early Cinema in Scotland, 1896–1927'. This was a three-year collaborative project between the Universities of Glasgow and Edinburgh, supported by an Arts and Humanities Research Council Research Grant.

Julia Bohlmann was a PhD student at Glasgow University on the project, successfully submitting a thesis entitled 'Regulating and Mediating the Social Role of Cinema in Scotland, 1896–1933'.

John Caughie was Principal Investigator on the project, primarily researching cinema in small towns in Scotland. He is Professor Emeritus and Honorary Research Professor in Film & Television Studies at Glasgow University.

Trevor Griffiths was Co-Investigator on the project, primarily researching both the role of cinema staff in the social role of cinema, and the arrival of sound. He is a Reader in Economic and Social History at the University of Edinburgh.

Janet McBain was a member of the Steering Committee for the project. She was formerly the founding Curator of the Scottish Screen Archive (now the Moving Image Archive in the National Library of Scotland).

Caroline Merz was a PhD student at the University of Edinburgh, successfully submitting a thesis entitled 'Why Not a Scots Hollywood? Fiction film production in Scotland, 1911–1928'.

María Vélez-Serna was Postdoctoral Researcher on the project, primarily researching early distribution and exhibition in Scotland and the mapping of cinema development. She is now a Leverhulme Fellow at the University of Stirling.

CHAPTER 1

Introduction

John Caughie, Trevor Griffiths and María A. Vélez-Serna

For film is the only art whose birthday is known to us – the beginnings of all the others are lost in the fog of antiquity.

Béla Balázs, *Theory of the Film*, 1945[1]

The project on which this collection of essays is based was an attempt to bring together systematically a range of resources and archive records in order to produce a rounded account of the beginnings of cinema in Scotland from the first screenings in 1896 to the arrival of sound at the end of the 1920s: a period which also marks the development of the cinema from its origins as a supplementary side-show in variety theatres and fairground booths through its emergence in dedicated fixed-site venues from around 1908 to its maturation in the majestic picture palaces of the 1920s.

The three-year project, which was funded by the Arts and Humanities Research Council, brought together five researchers, and it began with three primary research questions:

- What are the distinctive features of the early development of cinema and cinema-going in Scotland?
- Given the well-documented popularity of cinema-going in Scotland in the period, what were the factors which inhibited the development of feature film production?
- How does research on the circulation and reception of cinema in Scotland in the early years of the twentieth century add to wider debates about what Francesco Casetti has called 'the popularisation of modernity and the modernisation of popularity'?[2]

Underlying these questions was a sympathy for the argument articulated by Richard Maltby and Melvyn Stokes in their introduction to the collection *Going to the Movies: Hollywood and the Social Experience of Cinema*, that Film Studies cannot simply be the study of film texts but must also be the study of the social, economic, and political history of a cultural institution which is central to an understanding of the early twentieth century. 'We are proposing', they say, 'a distinction between what might be called film history and cinema history: between an aesthetic history of textual relations between individuals and individual objects, and the social history of a cultural institution.'[3] This distinction is reflected in the essays collected here not as a stark dichotomy but as a mediating principle: if the project is on cinema-going in the context of a nation, then national representation in films becomes part of the social experience of cinema – whether that experience be the embarrassment that many Scottish audiences quite clearly felt about being represented in kilts and tam-o-shanters, or the identification which the same audiences may have felt with their own national romance and mythology. While the project is sympathetic to the claims of a history of the social experience of cinema as a cultural institution and a product of concrete economic activities, it is also sympathetic to the claims of a history of representation as central to that experience. Local topicals, scenics, 'Scottish films for Scottish people' and American as well as British romances of a mythological Highlands were part of the experience of early cinema for Scottish audiences.

Three characteristics of the original project proposal may be worth noting briefly here. The first is that the project was intended to be not simply a history of early cinema in Scotland but also a geography. Using Geographical Information Systems it mapped the location of venues in which early cinema was experienced, from village halls, town halls, temperance halls, drill halls and music halls to purpose-built cinemas and picture palaces. It also mapped, where possible, the locations used for filming local topicals, scenic or interest films, and the relatively few fiction films that used Scottish locations. This process of mapping was intended to move history away from the dominant histories of metropolitan cinema to a history which emphasised the diversity of locations in which cinema was experienced or the scenes which constituted the actual or imagined Scotland. Significantly, this moves the history away from a 'national' history in which differences are elided towards a more local history which recognises the regional diversities which characterise the demography of Scotland. We believe that this emphasis is preserved in this collection of essays.

Secondly, and distinctively, a website was proposed as the primary output of the project. This was not simply an identification with fashionable technology but a recognition that the fascination of early cinema was, precisely, the diversity, complexity and particularity of the structures, objects and understandings of early cinema and its development, and that the best way of representing this complexity may not be the synoptic monograph. The website was intended to capture the diversity of data and experience of early cinema before it had been properly institutionalised or became fully subject to forces of globalisation and standardisation. The website may provide a useful background reference for this book.[4] While we welcome the opportunity to develop some of the arguments and analyses that the digitisation of data sometimes misses, this collection of essays is selective and representative in its focus rather than comprehensive. It reflects the diversity of topics and approaches of the project rather than reducing them to a single synoptic narrative, following the contours of the landscape rather than retracing the crest-line.

Thirdly, while the project, in its initial formation, could claim to be one of the first academic accounts of early cinema in Scotland, it was anticipated almost before it began by Trevor Griffiths's *The Cinema and Cinema-going in Scotland, 1896–1950*, published in 2012.[5] As a researcher on the project, Trevor Griffiths brought a great deal of prior research, both economic and social, to the project and his book was a constant point of reference. In many senses, this present book may usefully be considered as complementary to his overview of the trajectory of cinema's development across Scotland.

The popularity of cinema in Scotland is enshrined in both popular mythology and popular history. It is certainly the case that by 1929 Glasgow had 127 cinemas, and by 1939 it claimed more cinema seats per capita than any other city in the world. Green's Playhouse, opening in 1927, had a seating capacity of 4,368, and was, by repute, the largest cinema in the world outside the USA at the time of its construction. Glasgow, like many other European cities, claimed the title of 'Cinema City' and a later generation of Glaswegians would be acknowledged as the most inveterate cinema-goers in Britain and, by extension, the world. The roots of this popularity here and elsewhere across Scotland were laid in the years immediately following the debut of moving pictures. The cinematograph and animated pictures were widely shown throughout the country in public venues of every description, and, by the outbreak of the First World War, a 'purpose-built' cinema was evidence that a small town was 'modern' and 'up-to-date'. Cinema's social and geographical reach continued to expand into the 1920s. The fund set up to provide welfare facilities across mining areas and financed out of a tax on each ton of coal raised was enthusiastically mobilised across both the western and eastern parts of the Scottish coalfield to build institutes most of which were not complete without their installations for the showing of moving pictures.[6] No community appeared truly complete without its own means of accessing the movies. The ubiquity and popularity of cinema was further enshrined in popular memory. Managers became the stuff of legend, memorialised for their geniality or their sourness, distributing either sweets or clips around the ear to maintain order in the front rows, and children, it is claimed, paid for admission by 'jeely jars' (jam jars). While jars and bottles could indeed be sold back to retailers, it is difficult to find the kind of hard documentary evidence needed to satisfy sceptics for them being used as currency over the counter of the cinema box office. If anecdotal approaches are open to challenge, and some scepticism may be healthy, taken together popular memories and personal reminiscences provide significant evidence of the social and cultural appeal of cinema in Scotland at the beginning of the twentieth century.

The question which the project proposed of the material and definitive distinctiveness of Scottish cinema within the world history of cinema is more elusive. Many of the patterns of development are familiar. The networks of itinerant exhibitors and many of the early rental and distribution chains were regional rather than national, and many of the early showmen and entrepreneurs in Scotland had their roots in the North of England. They did not necessarily recognise the notional boundary between England and Scotland. Many of the processes of institutionalising cinema were familiar across national, European and world cinemas, and the movements of globalisation and the dominance of Hollywood were common across frontiers. Westerns seem to have been as popular among Scottish audiences as they were everywhere else, and romantic melodramas and 'screaming' comedies knew no boundaries, except, perhaps, between men and women. The star system was a common currency, minted primarily in the United States, and the arrival of Charlie Chaplin and serials in the mid-1910s subverted the centrality of the exhibitor and instituted a system of block-booking which applied wherever your field of operation happened to lie, this side of the Atlantic or that. A shared chronology can be applied to the movement from fairgrounds and fixed-site venues, to purpose-built cinemas and to luxurious picture palaces across nations and continents. Much of the history of early cinema in Scotland, then, is continuous with the world history of early cinema.

Yet, much as Scotland was influenced by broader global forces, it also contributed materially to the way those forces worked out in practice, shaping industrial trends within the United Kingdom. In the later 1920s, central figures behind the increasingly corporate nature of the British cinema industry and the promotion of a viable British production base were Scots: John Maxwell and Thomas Ormiston, for example.[7] Equally, while we must be sensitive to the playing out of broader global trends, it is also important to recognise that there are certain characteristics which seem to be distinctive within Scotland, and which may inflect its history of early cinema in particular ways.

In the first place, there is a distinctive demography and a particular geographical and cultural distribution of the audience. This is by no means unique, and Scotland shares some of the characteristics of other northern European countries with small populations, concentrated around a geographically limited core. Sweden, at the beginning of the twentieth century, had a population of just over five million, Norway one of just over two million, and Ireland, which became a Free State only from 1922, had a population then of around three million. Each had an area of high concentration (a third of the Irish population lived in Dublin) and a substantial land mass in which population density was very low and was highly dispersed. Scotland, with a population in the 1911 census of 4,760,904, shared this profile. Distinctively, however, Scotland's central industrial belt, ranging, at the beginning of the twentieth century, from the Clyde shipbuilding industry to the jute manufactories of Dundee, was not only densely populated but was also economically a world force. The Clyde shipyards at that time produced around twenty per cent of the world's shipping. Alongside it were extractive, heavy industries like coal and steel, and a vigorous and varied engineering sector which covered everything from railway engines to sewing machines. At the same time, the material context within which cinema emerged in Scotland was not as obviously propitious as it sometimes seems. Per capita incomes were lower than south of the border, and, while textile manufacture offered a degree of financial independence to a key cinematic demographic, young unmarried women, the predominance elsewhere of heavy industry produced a distribution of domestic resources that disadvantaged precisely those groups who would flock to picture houses from around 1910. For the male working class the contest between the pub and the pictures was an ongoing theme for social reformers throughout the period. Nevertheless, a taste for cinema had been fostered, particularly in Glasgow, by repeated recourse to cheap concerts mounted by charitable bodies and the city corporation. The marked reduction in the price of an evening's entertainment signalled by the replacement of most or all live performers with film shows unlocked demand among this audience, and effectively launched Glasgow's career as 'Cinema City'. The years from 1914 worked to consolidate that trend as the demands of the war economy ensured full-time work for those at home, while separation allowances paid to the dependants of those who chose or were called up to serve in the armed forces diffused spending power among the new generation of cinema enthusiasts. With certain living costs, those relating to housing especially, controlled from 1915, money available for spending on recreations became marginally more predictable. By the end of the war, loyalty to the cinema, engendered further by marketing devices such as stars and serials, was deeply ingrained among urban working-class Scots.[8]

Yet alongside this familiar metropolitan narrative, the emergence and consolidation of cinema in smaller, more dispersed settlements must also be considered. Cinema in small towns reached out to an audience which comprised more than fifty per cent of the population of Scotland, and ranged from townships bordering on the industrial belt and culturally identified with it, to townships in agricultural areas, market towns, towns and fishing villages on the East Coast, remote townships like Kirkwall, Lerwick and Stornoway on the itinerant North Atlantic pelagic fishing routes, and a few towns where Gaelic was still a significant or dominant language. Cinema was widespread and competitive; in a town with a population of 14,000 there could be three or four venues. While cultural diversity may have been common in the development of cinemas in rural and non-metropolitan areas in a number of countries, it is important to note its distinctive characteristics in Scotland.

There was also, as in Sweden and Norway, a significant Scottish land mass in the Western Highlands and Islands where a population of around 350,000 was so dispersed that it provided no firm footing for fixed-site cinemas. Except for the Lewis Cinema in Stornoway, there were no cinemas west of a line very roughly from Lerwick to Oban or from Oban to Campbeltown. Popular mythology has laid this at the door of the Presbyterian Church. While the Church, however, may have become a more active regulatory force in the 1920s and 1930s when cinema became a global entertainment industry and was seen to reflect the decadent ways of Hollywood or 'tinseltown', there is little evidence, as is argued in Chapter 4, of the Church as an energetic or effective regulator of cinema in its early period. Rather it was a facilitator, as much of the initial contact with cinema in rural Highland communities was through the Church and its Christmas treats for local children. The evidence from the early years of cinema is that it was the low population density rather than Presbyterian censorship that inhibited the development of cinema in the Highlands and Islands.

This points to another distinctive feature of the development of cinema in Scotland: the mechanisms of regulation and control. Although, from the later nineteenth century, parliamentary authority was vested in the Secretary (later Secretary of State) for Scotland and the Scottish Office at

Westminster, local authority was exercised by local magistrates and local Town or Rural Councils. This constitutional arrangement embodied the autonomy of local communities which had been a principle of government in Scotland at least since the battles of the Covenanters for the autonomy of the church parish. It meant that Acts of Parliament such as the 1909 Cinematograph Act became part of the law of the land, as did such earlier regulations as the Disorderly Houses Act, but that much significant day-to-day administration was devolved on to local authorities. Significantly for the regulation of cinema, the interpretation of the Scottish Office and the courts was that the Cinematograph Act applied only to licensing cinemas as secure and safe from such common hazards as fire, and could not be used to determine what could be shown or when. The showing of films on Sundays, or the showing of such controversial films as *The Life of Christ* (aka *From the Manger to the Cross*) (1912) or *Sapho* (1913 – banned in Leeds, but shown successfully in Edinburgh), were regulated by local authorities on the basis of their understanding of the culture and forbearance of their local population.

Some national normalisation of censorship standards was introduced by the British Board of Film Censors (BBFC), which was founded in 1912. The BBFC, however, was a non-governmental body, founded with the active support of the Cinematograph Exhibitors' Association (CEA) in their attempt both to ensure the respectability of cinema and to avoid the imposition of centralised state censorship. Even then, licensing authorities largely ignored the advisory role adopted by the BBFC until, in 1920, it was generally agreed by all exhibitors who were members of the CEA that no film would be shown which had not been certificated by the BBFC without the permission of the local authority, and this was broadly seen as a move towards a common standard of regulation. However, as membership of the CEA was weak in many rural and non-metropolitan areas, many local exhibitors did not recognise the agreement, and relied instead on whatever regulation there might be from local magistrates and councils. Even Dundee did not fall into line until 1929.

An interesting case in point is the exhibition of *The End of the Road* (1918). This was an American narrative film, sponsored by the American Social Hygiene Association, intended as a warning against syphilis which was perceived as a growing health threat after the war. The film depicted quite graphically the descent into the disease, presented as the result of a carefree attitude by a careless woman.[9] Though the film had been approved as educational by the Ministry of Health, it was refused a certificate by the BBFC and could therefore be shown by CEA members only with the co-operation of the licensing authority. It had been given a private showing in Motherwell in 1919, in the Pavilion Picture House 'to a large audience', and it was noted that since the scheme to combat the disease had begun there had been nine hundred cases in Lanarkshire.[10] Given such circumstances, it remained a commercially attractive subject, remaining in circulation into the early 1920s. It was shown in Buckie in 1921 and in Inverness in 1922. In Aberdeen, in 1921, 'The Greatest Sex Picture Ever Shown' was billed as a 'Great Moral Lesson' and shown in the Music Hall, a prestigious venue, with a separate matinee performance for ladies only. It was so successful that it was brought back for another three-day screening. Its appearance in Coatbridge and Airdrie in 1923, provoked a threatening comment in the Scottish Section of *The Bioscope*:

> There are some members of the exhibiting side of the Scottish cinema trade whose chief aim and object seems to be to provide the advocates of local censorship with ammunition to fire at the Trade. Probably it is a charitable view of the matter to think that economic circumstances may force them to do so, but in view of the fact that the whole Trade gets besmirched with their actions, it is scarcely creditable to find one hall in Coatbridge and another in Airdrie showing uncensored films this week. *The End of the Road* and *Morality* may help them to show a better financial result on the week, and allow them to slip across their fellow exhibitors who support a 'clean screen' programme, but it is not playing the game, and if they remain in the business their present-day actions may cause them many regrets in the days to come.[11]

Despite the disapproval of the CEA, always sensitive to any threats to cinema's respectability, it was local regulation that applied rather than the recognition of the British Board of Film Censors. *The End of the Road* is thus indicative of the limits of the authority of 'national' regulatory agencies. This would be further demonstrated at the end of the silent era by the widespread exhibition of Herbert Wilcox's *Dawn* (1928), denied a BBFC certificate in the face of government disapproval but endorsed by all but one licensing authority in Scotland.[12] If cultural stereotypes based around Presbyterian rectitude provide an imperfect guide to the forces shaping cinema's growth, other supposed national characteristics, in particular the determined pursuit of profit, appear to have proved enduringly influential.

Despite the persistent attempts by, in particular, the Glasgow Education Authority to introduce local and then national regulation and censorship schemes to protect children, regulation throughout the period remained local, and consistently recognised the authority of local councils and magistrates to regulate cinema. Local diversity in regulating when films were shown, to whom and what was shown was recognised not simply culturally but also constitutionally. In many ways, this localisation makes it more difficult to speak of a national history of early Scottish cinema and brings to the foreground the geography of the development of early cinema, and the mapping of diversity across the landscape.

One problem loomed quite large in our original formulation of the research proposal: given the evident popularity of cinema-going in Scotland, and given the wealth of stories which Scottish history and literature contributed to international cinema, why was it that Scotland had not successfully established a sustainable industry for the production of films? In retrospect, this may have been an invented problem and the answer may be more familiar than we had originally assumed. Scotland was a small country with a low population in the increasingly competitive English-language market. Other northern European countries like Sweden could establish a fragile industry to meet the demands of the national language, but, by the 1930s, Britain could not appeal to the national language, and was finding it difficult to sustain a film industry against the dominance of Hollywood without such protective measures as the quota system. While it is tempting to compare Scotland and Ireland, it may be Ireland that is the exception rather than Scotland, sustained by its national history, by the particularities of its diaspora and by the somewhat eccentric decision of the Kalem Company in the 1910s, inspired by the diasporic Irishman, Sidney Olcott, to invest in film production in Ireland and to found the series of films known as the O'Kalems. The problem for Scotland is pragmatic rather than principled: it is very difficult indeed for countries with a population base too small to support national films to found a sustainable national film industry.

Caroline Merz, in her chapter here and in her PhD thesis, has considerably expanded our knowledge of the context of film production in Scotland, and both she and Trevor Griffiths in *The Cinema and Cinema-going in Scotland* have shown that, against the odds, films were being produced, and, in at least one instance – *Fitba Daft* (1921) – were meeting with some success. United Films' *Rob Roy* (1911) stands out as the earliest three-reel feature film produced in Britain, and it was seen as far afield as New Zealand and Australia. From the evidence, however, it does not seem to have been widely distributed in Scotland, may not have reached England and made no impact in the USA. From the evidence, other films produced in the 1920s noted in the filmography seem also to have been restricted in their distribution and exhibition. The problem is one that became recurrently familiar in Britain across the twentieth century. Without a large enough domestic audience to pay for the costs of production, and without access to a larger international market, one film could not produce sufficient surplus to be reinvested in the next film. Production, therefore, tended to be a series of one-off films in which each production was an isolated and risky speculative venture. However enterprising the early producers may have been, they do not seem to have been able to establish a sustainable footing for reinvestment in a programme of production.

Where Scotland is distinctive, however, and where it may even be unique, is that it is difficult to think of a small country without its own film industry which is so much represented in film. This is discussed in Chapter 9 and is illustrated by the feature filmography at the end of the book. Here, the significance of Walter Scott as a major figure in world literature becomes obvious. What Scott achieved was the transformation of Scotland into a historical and mythical border territory, marking a boundary on the edge of Europe between the advance of modernisation and the resistance of tradition: Frances Osbaldistone and Rob Roy or, later, the Little Minister and Babbie. In various ways and at various times, like the West in the United States, Scotland, and the romance of the Highlands in particular, could be used to mark the meeting of modernity and tradition. And where this was not tragic or romantic, it could be comic, with the kilted Highlander as a figure for humour from the very early days of Edison's cinematograph (e.g. *Sandy McPherson's Quiet Fishing Trip* (Edison, 1908)) to Chaplin's fancy-dress ball in *The Idle Class* (1921). It is in this sense that the history of early cinema in Scotland cannot simply be a social history of the institution of cinema, but must also be a history of representation.

Finally, there is Francesco Casetti's resonant phrase: 'the popularization of modernity and the modernization of popularity'. The processes captured in this formulation seem fundamental to this book, and, however much the stories of Scotland may be rooted in the eighteenth and nineteenth centuries, the mechanisms by which they circulate are modern in their economy and their mode of circulation. The early chapters of the book consider the institutional development of cinema, the structures it evolved and the relationships both within and beyond the business that sustained it. The movement that María Vélez-Serna discusses from travelling exhibition to fixed-site cinemas reinvented the skills and networks of fairground, lantern and variety entertainment in the formation of cinema as a modern institution. Purpose-built and architect-designed cinemas became an emblem of modernisation in small towns. However much the treats offered to tenants and children by the land-owning gentry and the Church may have echoed with the benevolent paternalism of a declining aristocracy and a Church keen to engage its congregation in new ways, the engagement with the novelty of the cinematograph is a recognition of the new, the modern and, indeed, the enlightening. As the novelty of the technological marvel wore off, the continuing appeal of cinema depended on its entanglement with the everyday, its ability to embed its cosmopolitan attractions in the rhythms of local life. This articulation between particular audiences and a rapidly changing international production sector was steered by many hands, including the regional distributors who brokered Scotland's place in the global film market. Chapter 3 explores the role of these pioneer film renters in mediating between the local needs of individual cinema managers and the forces of consolidation reshaping the industry from above.

The tension between continuity and modernity carried over into the everyday operation of cinema, examined by Trevor Griffiths in Chapter 5. Those who found work in the picture houses that dotted the urban and rural landscape were subject to precisely the same forces as industrial workers elsewhere and, from the second decade of the twentieth century in particular, began to organise in collective self-defence. Yet the forces of class which coloured Clydeside red were here muted by the internal dynamic of career patterns and a managerial culture firmly rooted in older paternalist traditions. This by no means exhausted cinema's political importance, as it was seen to offer a new solution to enduring social and economic problems, particularly those associated with drink. Municipal government had long been involved in the provision of entertainments designed to ensure a morally uplifting alternative to the public house. As has been noted, many had encountered moving pictures for the first time in the concerts mounted from the later nineteenth century by Glasgow Corporation. Their success and the profitability of early picture houses before 1914 encouraged the initiation by local councils of municipal cinemas. The most prominent and long-lived of these, in Kirkintilloch, is documented in Chapter 6 by Julia Bohlmann and represented the most sustained attempt to incorporate modern entertainment within the remit of civic responsibility.

The chapters that follow centre on themes of production. In Chapter 7, Caroline Merz identifies the challenges which modern business and economy pose to the production of feature films in the silent era. Although an air of commercial failure hangs over Scottish efforts in this period, this should not obscure their importance in considering representations of Scotland on celluloid, as they were concerned more often than not to root their subjects in a sense of the authentic. In this regard, it is significant that the film *Rob Roy*, which she discusses in her chapter, produced by an aspiring modern film industry, is precisely a story set in the eighteenth century, first written in the early nineteenth century, and celebrated as 'the national drama' in endless productions and touring companies in the late nineteenth and early twentieth centuries. Given this, its failure should not be taken for granted. Rather, as this chapter argues, its fortunes must be viewed and interpreted in the context of the time. The scenics, lyrical adaptations and romances that John Caughie considers are again appropriations of the past in popular song and literature, often adapting earlier theatrical adaptations of literature, into the modern form of cinematic narrative and description. Finally and surprisingly, the local topicals which John Caughie and Janet McBain describe, glimpses of an intimate social history, may be the most modern forms in early Scottish cinema: designed by modern marketing techniques to draw the audience into the cinema, they share with modernist art and literature a focus on the everyday and on participants who shatter the illusion of the cinema by gazing back at the screen.

As the final chapter indicates, the tension between the modern and the traditional extended across the silent era and worked to shape Scotland's transition into the age of sound. New technology called fundamentally into question existing modes of film presentation and the cinema-going experience as a whole. To contemporaries the appeal of sound appeared anything but inevitable, with the result that importance continued to attach to maintaining the element of the 'local' in the programme, primarily through the presence of live performers. The trend towards standardisation of the cinema-going experience was, as a result, never absolute. In one sense, however, the coming of sound would align Scottish production efforts more firmly with the modern, focusing as they did increasingly on the making of documentaries that were informed by a very mid-twentieth-century vision of the state as an active social democracy.

The history of early cinema in Scotland then, from its diverse and unruly beginnings in the 1890s and 1910s to its increasing standardisation and globalisation throughout the 1920s, and from the 'attractions' and novelties of the fairground to the sophistication of classical narrative in the 1920s, is precisely about this: the processes of modernising popularity and popularising modernity, shared across world cinema but articulated in particular ways by the culture, geography and politics of Scotland.

Notes

1. Balázs, *Theory of the Film: Character and Growth of a New Art*, 21.
2. Casetti, 'Filmic Experience', 58.

3. Maltby, Stokes, and Allen, *Going to the Movies*, 2.
4. Early Cinema in Scotland Research Project, 'Early Cinema in Scotland 1896–1927'. See http://earlycinema.gla.ac.uk.
5. Griffiths, *The Cinema and Cinema-going in Scotland, 1896–1950*.
6. Parl. Papers 1919, xi (359), Coal Industry Commission, Interim reports, p. ix; *Scotsman*, 19 November 1922, p. 11; 9 June 1923, p. 7; 27 October 1924, p. 5; 9 November 1925, p. 9; NRS, IRS21/1934, Cleland Miners' Welfare Society, Abstract of Cash Transactions for year ending 31 May 1928; IRS21/2018, Standburn Miners' Welfare Society, Balance Sheet, 31 December 1927.
7. For both, see Dickinson and Street, *Cinema and State: The Film Industry and the British Government, 1927–84*, 23, 35.
8. Lee, 'Scotland, 1860–1939: Growth and Poverty'; Walker, *Juteopolis: Dundee and Its Textile Workers, 1885–1923*; Wright, 'Juteopolis and After: Women and Work in Twentieth-Century Dundee'; Bakker, *Entertainment Industrialised: The Emergence of the International Film Industry, 1890–1940*, chs 3 and 4.
9. Colwell, '*The End of the Road*: Gender, the Dissemination of Knowledge and the American Campaign against Venereal Disease in World War 1'; Kuhn, *Cinema, Censorship and Sexuality, 1909–1925*, 49–74.
10. *Motherwell Times*, 19 November 1919.
11. *The Bioscope*, 12 April 1923, p. 62.
12. Griffiths, *The Cinema and Cinema-going in Scotland, 1896–1950*, 67.

CHAPTER 2

Travelling Bioscopes and Borrowed Spaces

María A. Vélez-Serna

MILLIE'S PARK, PATHHEAD. TWO DAYS ONLY – **John Manders' Combined Shows**, ROYAL WAXWORK, American Museum, and the Great Electric Cinematograph Living Pictures, worked by Electricity, by means of a Magnificent Engine.[1]

The second entertainment for the season under the auspices of the Turriff Cricket Club, in aid of a fund for a new practice ground, was given on Friday in the Parish Church Hall . . . the audience were treated to a cinematograph exhibition, depicting scenes both humorous and pathetic with all the realism of life.[2]

In Scotland, as elsewhere, moving pictures met their first audiences in borrowed or temporary spaces. Films appeared in places such as fairgrounds, public halls and music halls which were already used for other purposes and imbued with social meaning. Sharing their spaces connected the new medium into existing 'cultural series', from which cinema adapted patterns of circulation and, in some cases, forms of social conduct and expectation.[3] Without taking into account these settings, it is easy to overestimate the novelty of moving pictures when they first encountered general audiences. The apparent modernity of the new medium can be found in its use of cutting-edge engineering, mechanical reproduction, and vivid action as its aesthetic premise. However, the contexts in which films were shown to Scottish audiences absorbed the shock of the new.[4] Moving pictures built their popularity on shared stages that integrated the novelty of mechanically reproduced movement within familiar practices in familiar spaces.

In the context of early cinema, intermediality refers to the appearance of the moving image as a part of other, pre-existing cultural series, like nineteenth-century theatre, music-hall sketches, magic lantern lectures, fairground sideshows, parlour songs or scientific photography.[5] The protocols offered by these pre-existing cultural series came to define the expectations that people brought to their experience of moving pictures.[6] But even before the encounter with the projected image, the audience's experience was shaped by their socially grounded knowledge of the spaces and contexts in which they were situated. The borrowed spaces of travelling exhibition lent the new medium a connection to existing audiences, a repertory of practices to engage those audiences and an evolving template for industrial organisation. As Calvin Pryluck argues, '[a]s long as touring exhibition was the mode of operation, it continued to be – no matter how obscure – a part of traditional show business. Movies became a distinct industry when a fixed-location movie show became the dominant choice'.[7]

Embedding moving pictures within 'traditional show business' was crucial to the eventual emergence of cinema as the defining entertainment form of the twentieth century. As Vanessa Toulmin argues in her influential 1994 article on fairground bioscopes, 'the moving picture industry was shaped in its initial years by the travelling showmen'.[8] Historians have been slow to recognise this influence, in part because the cinema trade, in its later drive for respectability, was keen to forget it too. Fairground and music-hall showpeople accommodated film into a landscape of leisure that was changing rapidly, and used it to industrialise aspects of their trade.[9] Besides this connection to a thriving, modern entertainment business, moving pictures also found a role in non-commercial or para-commercial forms of social gathering, from Sunday schools to Co-operative meetings. Films first reached Scottish audiences thanks to a growing number of entertainment caterers who worked across these different circuits, using skills from their previous trades to invent the new showmanship required by moving pictures.[10]

Understanding the regularity of entertainment provision before permanent cinemas adds nuance to Robert C. Allen's description of the 'eventfulness of the experience of cinema' as being 'poised between the everyday and the extraordinary'.[11] Scotland had a highly developed commercial and non-commercial entertainment trade, and its annual cycles meant that cinema shows quickly became a *regular* occurrence. Taking place mostly within established and traditional cycles, the periodic presence of moving pictures was less destabilising, as a social force, than the permanent availability of cinema in its second decade, particularly outside the main cities. Hence, the temporality of film exhibition, appearing only occasionally, but on a regular and recognised schedule, was important for the acceptance of cinema in Scottish communities, and a topic for debate as it gradually gave way to more permanent availability.

The amusements available to audiences in Scottish towns and villages fluctuated according to the rhythms of work, weather and calendar customs. Since the middle of the nineteenth century, these patterns had become more established, and often crystallised in built infrastructure for leisure. The distinction between the summer and winter touring seasons is a long-standing feature of Scottish entertainment, and it corresponded to a division of spaces: the fairgrounds in the warmer months; the theatres and public halls in the autumn and spring; the seaside pavilions in summer; and the Christmas and New Year holiday carnivals in large urban halls. The cinematograph found a role in all of these circuits, and people working with film crossed over between different forms of exhibition in order to keep business active throughout the year. It is a dense, organic network of practices that needs to be understood as an emergent system, but each part of it had its own history.

The Scottish fairground season was considered officially open around Easter, when showpeople converged at Kirkcaldy for Scotland's oldest fair and, to this day, one of the largest.[12] Mechanical rides, sideshow tents and hook-a-duck stalls arrived, with the families that owned them, in hundreds of wagons. Around the turn of the century, horses were being replaced by steam-powered traction engines to drag the wagons. These engines could not only pull the increasingly heavy loads on the road and move the roundabouts and other rides, they could also generate electricity for lights and power a dynamo for the film projector.[13] Particularly heavy loads could be packed for railway transport, although the rates charged by railway companies were high and to be avoided if possible.[14] To give an idea of the scale and diversity of the amusement on offer, in 1899 the Kirkcaldy Links Market featured, amongst other attractions, two kinematograph booths, two Mutoscope displays, a ghost illusion, a Wild West show and three 'athletic concerns' (probably boxing), while the machines included gondolas, swinging boats, gallopers and roundabouts. There were also rifle saloons, 'bottle smashers' and cokernut (*sic*) stalls 'in almost bewildering variety'.[15] Over the following years, the number of film shows kept growing, as did their capacity and the luxuriousness of their ornate frontages, with parading stages, big lights and mechanical organs. By 1905, it was not uncommon to find six or more bioscope shows at the same fair.

The first kinematograph or 'bioscope booths' to operate in Scotland were portable theatres that had been used for ghost shows, a type of melodramatic stage performance incorporating visual effects.[16] In Scotland, ghost shows had been operated by showmen like George Biddall, Henry Codona and John McIndoe.[17] With their mobile infrastructure, their experience with Victorian visual technologies, their sensational patter and openness to novelty, fairground entertainers were in a good position to take up the new attraction of the cinematograph. Most of them came from fairground families and were well acquainted with a business that relied extensively on family bonds and shared understandings. As Vanessa Toulmin has argued, '[t]he fair may move with the times and technology, but the society that operates it is basically a village on wheels tied by kinship and existing under a swathe of regulations'.[18] The annual round of fairs, central both to the business model and to the social life of the fairground, is arranged around fixed dates that often go back to medieval Royal Charters. Initially tied to feeing fairs, where farm labourers and maids would seek new employment for a year, some of the fair dates were associated with legal term days, evolved from Celtic quarter days.[19] Once redefined around leisure rather than commerce, the 'Scottish Round' went from March to December and was loosely structured around a few points of convergence, including Kirkcaldy, the Races at Paisley and Ayr, and several Common Ridings in the Borders.[20] Around those points, regional circuits of fairs were clustered, and different routes could be arranged.

The annual 'round' was thus not a fixed path but a layout of possibilities that needed to be negotiated by each travelling family according to their resources, connections and experience. In the paper collections of the Moving Image Archive of the National Library of Scotland there is a fascinating bundle of letters sent by Peter Swallow to George Green at the point where Green was only becoming established in the Scottish entertainment trade. Swallow managed bioscope shows for Green as Green had more than one outfit on the road. In the archived correspondence Swallow informs his employer about who has a lease for a particular ground – 'I hear that Jimmy Wilmot is going to Girvan' – and suggests a route: 'Jimmy is nearly sure to go to Maybole the week before Girvan. Girvan is on the first Monday in April & you can usually open the Friday & Saturday before it'.[21] This insider's knowledge was shared and updated within the business and family bonds of the travelling community, making the yearly round of fairs a flexible and evolving network.

For most places, fairground cinema was a once- or twice-a-year attraction. Had it remained that way, that avid everyday audience that sustained the development of cinema on a global scale would not have emerged.[22] However, a change was taking place in the cities. In the second half of the nineteenth century the spaces where shows used to appear, such as market squares and commons, were being built upon as urban populations increased. In other cases, use of public spaces became restricted by local councils that objected to the carnivalesque goings-on of the fairgrounds. Facing up to this encroachment, some of the more affluent showpeople started leasing or acquiring grounds, either as a yearly arrangement with local authorities or as a permanent lease. They could then control and organise the fairground (ensuring, for instance, an appropriate mix of amusements that did not compete against their own machines), and sub-let spaces to other showpeople.

Figure 2.1 Fairground shows travelled on roads using traction engines. In June 1908, the engine pulling Wilson's Austrian Electric Colosseum crashed through the parapet at Wooler Bridge, Northumberland. Photo courtesy of the National Library of Scotland's Moving Image Archive.

Figure 2.2 Traction engines could also be fitted with a dynamo to generate electricity for a moving picture show. Note the engine next to Green's Cinematograph booth, c.1908. Photo courtesy of the National Library of Scotland's Moving Image Archive.

George Green controlled the Old Barracks carnival grounds in the East End of Glasgow, contiguous to the Vinegarhill fields where several fairground families had long had their winter quarters. During Glasgow Fair in 1897, a penny would grant admission to the grounds including an outdoor circus, several bands and variety entertainment on the main stage, besides rides and sideshows owned by other showmen who leased their space from Green at so much per foot.[23] A more centralised model was developed by William Codona, who opened Fun City in Portobello in 1908, 'the first permanent funfair of its type in Scotland'.[24] This privatisation of show grounds entailed a greater degree of pre-planning and communication, made possible by the trade journals, an efficient postal system and bank transfers by telegraph. It also encouraged the construction of more ambitious structures like switchback railways and theatres, and allowed for longer stays at profitable locations, thus establishing 'the long-running seasonal "shows" that were a feature of many working-class neighbourhoods'.[25]

Christmas shows also started to become more important for fairground showpeople, and key points in the introduction of moving pictures to Scottish audiences. In the winter of 1896, George Green had bought a projector from R. W. Paul in London for use in the circus building at the Carnival.[26] In Edinburgh, the Christmas and New Year carnival at Waverley Market, controlled by H. E. Moss and managed by a travelling showman, John Wilmot, was a highlight of the Hogmanay celebrations.[27] By 1902, the *Showman's Year Book* listed Christmas carnivals at Aberdeen, Dunfermline, Dundee, Edinburgh, Forfar, Fraserburgh, Galashiels, Glasgow, Govan, Greenock, Kelso, Kilmarnock, Kirkcaldy, Leith, Motherwell, Paisley, Renfrew and Stirling. These semi-permanent carnivals responded to a steadier demand for entertainment, as a result of increased leisure time and disposable income amongst industrial populations, and a more structured, clock-driven regularity at work and at play.[28]

Another manifestation of this new way to arrange social reproduction was the seaside holiday. Pleasure trips had become common from the 1840s onwards with the expansion of affordable steam-boat services, which preceded the growth of the railway network. As Irene Maver argues, places like Dunoon and Aberdour became specialist resorts for West Coast and East Coast holiday-makers. Employers started sponsoring the company away-day to promote wholesome recreation amongst workers. Even though the steam-boats gained a reputation for their abundant provision of alcohol, these excursions were seen as more respectable than the fairs.[29] In the summer, then, films could be seen in the seaside pavilions used by Pierrot troupes and Punch and Judy shows. However, live variety remained a priority at the seaside, even after permanent cinemas had appeared to cater for the holiday trade. In Saltcoats on the West Coast, for instance, the Kemps, originally a fairground family, opened two successful cinemas, which switched to live variety in the busier summer months. When cinema had become an ordinary feature of urban life, holiday entertainment had to re-emphasise its difference, in a familiar two-step dance of regularisation and distinction.

From September to December, and then in the run-up to Easter, public entertainments sought shelter from the weather in various kinds of permanent buildings. In the cities, the theatrical season started in late August. By then, travelling troupes would have been busy throughout the summer months booking venues in small towns and rural districts. Public halls became the main site for all kinds of shows and gatherings, including the cinematograph as a sole attraction or as part of a variety programme. The civic histories of these places, and their flexible role as a gathering space, helped legitimate film as a part of community life.

Public halls had been built in hundreds of Scottish towns throughout the nineteenth century, and continued to be a priority after the turn of the century. Their financing, ownership and intended function varied greatly, as some were built by local clubs and societies, others were municipal property and a few were run for profit by private landlords. On the other hand, their architecture was rather uniform, providing a large flat hall that could be used for dancing or bazaars, or set up with a stage and wooden forms for shows and meetings. Larger buildings could have several spaces and might be attached to a library or reading room, and the frontage could be more or less ornate; in most cases the hall was a free-standing building, but there were also halls tucked away behind tenements or on top of pubs. Despite these differences, as an auditorium space for cinema entertainment, public halls offered appropriate conditions.

To give a sense of the widespread availability of such spaces, the Canmore database lists 647 drill halls, 136 Masonic halls, over a dozen temperance halls and over a hundred buildings described as public or village halls.[30] Drill halls were primarily intended for the use of the Volunteer Corps or, later, the Territorial Army established in 1907; Masonic halls were obviously used for lodge meetings; and organisations like the Good Templars, the Ancient Shepherds and the Salvation Army had raised subscriptions to build their local bases, which they used for their own promotional and fundraising entertainments as well as meetings. When they were not being used for their primary purpose, however, these spaces were available for hire. In rural areas, the halls were governed by committee instead of being managed by a single entrepreneur or lessee.

This collective control makes these halls akin to the kind of small-town American opera houses described by Robert Allen.[31]

The cinematograph reached these venues as part of an existing supply of travelling entertainment connected with a highly developed visual culture. Since the times of the Camera Obscura, Scotland had been a leading centre for optical technology. Photographers like George Washington Wilson in Aberdeen, James Ross in Edinburgh and James Valentine in Dundee were renowned innovators. In the second half of the nineteenth century, magic lantern operators had been offering their services to local organisations for educational and fundraising events. The addition of the cinematograph to the magic lantern show was a straightforward continuation of this model for tailored, on-demand shows, and benefited from the already established legitimacy of screen-based public entertainment. The programmes and their promotional rhetoric cultivated this association, offering, like Lizars of Aberdeen, 'High-class exhibitions, suitable for Drawing Rooms, At Homes, Social Gatherings, etc., etc., given in Town or Country . . . Programme as submitted at BALMORAL, 25th Oct., 1898, BY COMMAND OF THE QUEEN'.[32]

While Lizars continued to foreground their bespoke services, the more entrepreneurial lantern lecturers became promoters of their own concert parties. These were relatively stable troupes (often family groups) combining various forms of performance to produce a variety programme that would visit hired halls for one or two nights. A typical show included vocal and instrumental music, artistic dancing and one or two humorists. In addition, before cinematography, lantern slides were used at the start of the show.[33] When the cinematograph was added to the magic lantern, the screen entertainment aspect of the show gained prominence. It is in this context that some of the Scottish cinema pioneers made their names as travelling entertainers. The photographers and opticians Lizars not only sold cinematograph equipment but also added moving pictures to their existing lantern service, which was frequently engaged for semi-private entertainments.[34] Peter Feathers, from his Dundee base, toured widely in Angus, Perthshire and Fife, showing some of his own films. By December 1896, rival Aberdeen lanternists, Robert Calder and William Walker, were promoting their services as providers of moving pictures and 'floral tableaux vivants', with prestigious musical accompaniment.[35]

Calder's show was particularly impressive in its geographical reach. Calder's importance as an image maker is discussed later in Chapter 8. His touring profile, meanwhile, is a well-documented example of a prestigious but flexible operator. Calder started out as a limelight lantern operator based in Aberdeen, available to hire for 'magic lantern exhibitions, carefully conducted in town or country' in the 1890s.[36] By the middle of the decade, Calder was working on his own account and visiting small towns around Aberdeenshire with a complete show that included music and recitations. After acquiring a cinematograph in December 1896, Calder's operation became much more ambitious. Over the following years, his outfit, often including prestigious musicians and performers, paid regular visits to towns and villages in Shetland, Caithness and Argyll, while also running shows around Fife and central Scotland. At most of these towns, Calder's show appeared at a public hall of some description: Lerwick Town Hall, Falkirk Town Hall, Blairgowrie Public Hall, the Victoria Hall in Braemar and Campbeltown, the Inglis Memorial Hall in Edzell, the Adam Smith Hall in Kirkcaldy and so on. These venues were very different in capacity and splendour, but they tended to be the best available. In the main cities, Calder's show appeared almost exclusively at the most prestigious places: The Music Hall in Aberdeen, St Andrew's Halls in Glasgow and Gilfillan Hall in Dundee.

Often, and particularly in large towns with powerful councils, the first approach to these large-scale public halls was through the municipal initiative of Saturday evening concerts. As Trevor Griffiths has written, since the second half of the nineteenth century 'moral reformers had promoted Saturday as a point in the week when leisure might be encouraged' – non-alcoholic leisure, that is.[37] By the turn of the century, the range of attractions available to Glasgow residents on a Saturday was extensive. Since its acquisition of St Andrew's Halls in 1890, the Glasgow Corporation had stepped up its efforts to reach a wider public and increase the revenue from its entertainment programme. Much had to do with one man, Walter Freer (1846–1930), who had recently been installed as a curator of the Corporation's halls. The son of a Chartist weaver, Freer was a very enthusiastic supporter of the temperance cause, and had started his career in venue management at the Wellington Palace, owned by the Good Templars.[38] The St Andrew's Halls had struggled to build an audience when they were in private hands, so Freer decided to boost their popularity by running Saturday afternoon concerts at a cost of one penny or threepence.[39] These proved very popular, extending to seven other halls controlled by the Corporation over the following years.

The Glasgow Corporation concerts are interesting for two reasons: first, they incorporated films as part of a variety programme into a type of event that was arguably on the borderline between commercial and non-commercial entertainment; secondly, the St Andrew's Halls were also hired by some of the first travelling exhibitors and they presented film-only programmes, commercially, for several weeks of the year.

Corporation halls blurred the boundaries between the public and the private, the civic and the commercial, and the discourses of temperance and of 'rational recreation', forms of recreation for the working classes which had been promoted by social reformers throughout the nineteenth century, were central to their unstable identity. Glasgow's Saturday Evening concerts lasted for over seventy years and, according to Elspeth King, 'attracted some of the best operatic singers in Europe and considerably raised the standard of musical entertainment in Glasgow'.[40] Paul Maloney has argued that this kind of event broadened the audience for variety entertainment in the city by setting it in 'a secure, publicly regulated environment' with 'the unmistakable imprimatur of respectability'.[41] This extended to the cinema, both through the valorisation of spectator entertainment in the discourse of self-improvement and through the medium's links to the traditions of lantern lecturing.

An interesting chapter in the history of cinema in Scotland, and one which is likely to be unique to this nation due to its feudal patterns of landownership, is that of film shows put on by estate owners for tenants and their children. In landed estates around Scotland, the end of the year was customarily marked with a gathering in the big house, where the workers and crofters living on the estate, and their families, were given some food and presents. Besides the small, usually utilitarian gifts, and oranges for the children, the guests were 'treated' to some kind of entertainment. It was not unusual that the laird's daughters would put on a play or display their musical training, and there might be dancing after dinner. The magic lantern and other optical toys had become a common addition to the entertainment by the turn of the century, when the cinematograph made an appearance. At the Christmas celebrations at Durris House in 1896, for instance, Walker's Cinematograph was part of a programme of entertainments lasting ten hours, which also included singing, sketches, a lottery, gifts for the children and dancing for the adults.[42]

The *Aberdeen Journal* lists countless examples of Christmas entertainments, up until the start of the First World War. At Gordon Castle, 'the wives and female friends of the servants and tradesmen' were treated to Walker's Cinematograph, with musical accompaniment by Lady Settrington, with the Duke watching from the corridor.[43] At Philorth estate, '[t]he pictures were displayed in the large hall of the mansion-house' and followed by dancing and 'substantial presents of beef'.[44] These shows were provided by lanternists like Walker, Calder and Lizars, who had already built a respectable reputation amongst the landed gentry and could claim royal patronage. Later on, less experienced operators seem to have taken over, possibly owing to the greater availability of projectors for those who could afford them. As late as 1912, the *Northern Chronicle* reported that a hundred employees of the Brahan estate enjoyed dinner 'prepared and served by the Castle staff', and then 'a cinematograph show manipulated by Mr Munro, Dingwall'. Similarly, in late 1913 Master William Duncan had shown comic films to the workers and families of Udny.[45] The particular history of Scottish land-ownership and the local New Year traditions thus shaped the context of exhibition and reception of early cinema in distinctive ways. Chapter 4 offers further insights on the particularities of rural and small-town exhibition.

The experience of moving pictures in a rural audience of neighbours, in a castle's dining hall, could not be further removed from the favoured format of the big cities: the music hall screen. While the once-a-year cinematograph treat for crofting communities was clearly an extraordinary event, in the cities film soon became a regular part of the music-hall programme. The 'bioscope turn' was a discrete segment of a music-hall programme, booked in the same way as the other acts. As Robert Allen has argued, the modular format, like that of American vaudeville, made it a particularly suitable context for the incorporation of the new medium of moving pictures into an existing entertainment practice.[46] On the other hand, that structure was as rigid as it was commercially successful, constraining exhibition practice so that, as Vanessa Toulmin argues, '[m]usic hall showings in the early 1900s in particular did not advance either the entertainment context or the film program itself'.[47] In Scotland, the convergence of music hall and films eventually led to cine-variety as an enduring format in permanent cinemas, but during the itinerant years the bioscope was subordinate to music-hall circuits and practices.

Within this model, however, there were as many variations as types of halls. At the turn of the century, as Paul Maloney has written, a top tier of the Scottish music-hall sector went from 'tawdry working-class form' to 'mainstream popular theatre genre', through a transformation of its venues, their industrial organisation and the tone of their programmes.[48] New, respectable Palaces of Varieties, built by large syndicates, hosted the very first public screenings in Scotland, as had been the case in Paris and London. Lumière's Cinematograph had its Scottish premiere at the Empire in Edinburgh, which had opened in 1892 as a flagship venue for H. E. Moss's expanding circuit of variety theatres.[49] With twenty halls in 1900 and thirty-six in 1906, Moss's Empires was a UK-wide operation that epitomised the commercialisation and concentration of music-hall ownership that had taken place in the late nineteenth century.[50] The circuits' 'national organising infrastructure', as Adrienne Scullion has argued, 'was at the root of the success of the theatre magnates of the music-hall era'.⁵¹ It introduced modern business methods to the provision of live entertainment, making it 'highly organised, formalised, nationally integrated and standardised'.⁵² This solid financial standing was appropriate for high-end, large-gauge film shows like the Biograph, contracted with the Moss, Stoll and Thornton circuit of music halls in April 1897.⁵³

The national infrastructure of variety syndicates allowed them to offer longer contracts, attracting the most prestigious forms of film exhibition. Meanwhile, independent music halls had to settle for lesser fare, and found it very hard to compete with the lavish buildings erected with joint-stock capital.⁵⁴ This lower end of the market was served by the 'standard gauge men' remembered by A.C. Bromhead, Gaumont's first British agent, in his memoirs of the early trade. These small-time operators showed films for an average fee of £3 a week, and sometimes as little as 30s.⁵⁵ Like the travelling exhibitors in rural areas, music-hall bioscope turns in the cities were billed as a 'complete service', and were paid a flat rate for arranging equipment, films and projectionist. In his discussion of 'small-time vaudeville' in the USA, Robert Allen has called this approach 'pre-industrial' as it did not require the division of labour within the cinema business.⁵⁶ Unable to get the long-term contracts and circuit engagements that seemed the holy grail of the theatrical profession, these bioscope operators offered their services through variety agents or classified ads just like any other music-hall act, placing their business cards in theatrical trade journals like *The Era* or *The Stage*. Each act or its agent negotiated its terms with each music-hall manager, and it could be 'retained' for additional weeks if the entertainment had proved successful. Compared to one-night-only public hall shows, then, music-hall exhibitors were less itinerant, but their position was particularly precarious.

Over time, some music hall managers started dispensing with these services, deciding to cut out the middleman and acquire their own cinematograph equipment, thus becoming the first clients of film renters. A good example of this in Scotland is the Britannia Panopticon, still standing to this day on Glasgow's Trongate. Opened as a music hall from 1857, the Britannia first showed films in August 1896 when the manager, William Kean, hired Arthur Hubner's bioscope turn as an attraction that showcased the new installation of electric light in the theatre.⁵⁷ Hubner had been the first to show moving pictures in Glasgow at the Skating Palace. He had his own cinematograph apparatus which he used at the Britannia but also in other Glasgow venues and in neighbouring towns. On Sundays, he went over to the Wellington Palace to screen films such as *The Life of Christ* (version unidentifiable) at Martinengo's sacred concerts.⁵⁸ His successor as manager of the Britannia Panopticon was A. E. Pickard, a larger-than-life character who ran the venue with great success as a popular cine-variety show, and went on to build a circuit of cinemas.[59] Under Pickard's management, the cinematograph became a more permanent fixture in the programme, alternating occasionally with new technologies like Gaumont's sound-on-disc system, the chronophone. Film distribution then came under the remit of the venue manager, breaking down the pre-industrial, integrated trade of the travelling bioscope operator.

The film exhibitors working in Scottish music halls often came from other forms of itinerant showmanship and retained links to those circuits. As detailed studies of particular individuals have indicated, early exhibitors inhabited different roles in a fluid manner, adapting their practice to different contexts.[60] One of the Britannia's performers provides a good example of this flexibility. J. F. Calverto had started his career as a ventriloquist and shadowgraphist, appearing at music halls throughout the UK as part of travelling troupes or hired as an individual act. In December 1890, for instance, he shared the Britannia's stage with 'Pat Bergin, the well-known one-legged dancer', 'Hina, the wonderful rope performer' and other singers, comedians and dancers.[61] By the middle of the decade, he had risen in the ranks and was acting as agent for Charles Coborn, the very successful singer of 'The Man who Broke the Bank at Monte Carlo', and for French comedian Max O'Rell. At this point he seems to have been confident enough in his managerial experience to return to Scotland and run his own touring concert parties.

In this new enterprise, Calverto was keen to include the new attraction of moving pictures. He was not the only ventriloquist to take an interest in films; 'Prince' Bendon would make that transition more successfully. At the end of 1896, Calverto advertised for a 'really good cinematograph and operator, immediately, for long tour'.[62] By the new year, this new outfit was put to use as part of a tour of about seventy towns with a large concert party, which included a singing and dancing trio, a 'Scotch' comedian, a soprano, a tenor, a violinist and a pianist, with Calverto's own ventriloquist act headlining, and the Vitagraph showing 'startling and realistic effects'. Calverto's 1897 tour with the cinematograph covered the country from north to south, starting at Lerwick and working its way down to Ayrshire. Calverto remarked that he had already visited most of the towns before with his own or other companies. He hoped, however, to 'remain in Glasgow for the concert season' and tour Scotland for three months a year at most.[63]

The tour was not entirely successful, and the cinematograph reappeared only at the end of 1899. By then, Calverto advertised as an entertainer agent, and his roster included Chalmers' Cinematograph with pictures of the Boer War.[64] A later venture, in which he supplied a projector and operator for a different concert party, came to an acrimonious end which has been documented in a court case from 1903.[65] Establishing his business as the Glasgow Entertainment Bureau, Calverto kept a catalogue of 'entertainers for all purposes', intended mainly for private promoters of local committees, bazaars and parties. In this guise, he organised benefit shows for causes like the March Riding Committee at Peebles, the Aberdeen Trades Council or the Haddo House gathering in Aberdeenshire – but the cinematograph was used only sporadically in these. Calverto's complicated, multi-tasking career never seemed to take off fully, but it serves to illustrate the problems of any watertight classification of travelling exhibitors. A different, more ambitious business model which also lost ground to the rise of permanent exhibition was that of the large, prestigious public hall shows by companies such as New Century Pictures and the Modern Marvel Company, which are discussed in the next chapter.

At the end of 1907, the editors of the *Stage Yearbook* remarked on the fact that, although the popularity of moving pictures was evident, and its presence in music-hall entertainments increasing, there were no permanent picture palaces of the kind found in Berlin, Paris or New York.[66] But change was afoot that year. While fairground bioscopes and private lantern shows continued to travel the length and breadth of the country, a more gradual conversion was taking place. Many travelling exhibitors took their usual places for the autumn season, stayed until the New Year, and then sought to extend their leases. In Aberdeen, Dove Paterson had set up residence at the Alhambra Winter Zoo. In Glasgow, Ralph Pringle had reopened the Queen's Theatre as Pringle's Picture Palace, followed weeks after by J. J. Bennell's extended lease of the Wellington Palace from the Good Templars. Lincolnshire showman Sydney Prince's Prince Edward Pictures visited Dundee, Aberdeen and Motherwell in 1906, and came back in 1908 to stay in Dundee throughout the winter.

The relationships that these exhibitors had nurtured over years of repeat visits to the same towns paid off, as local councils were more likely to negotiate a long lease with someone they knew. At Kirkcaldy, for instance, George W. Walker had been visiting the Corn Exchange with his 'Scots-Canadian Pictures', and contributing to charitable functions like the Old Folks' Festival. In October 1907, he obtained a three-month lease of the building, which he ran as a 'Pictorial Carnival'. When that lease came to an end, he applied for a five-year lease, during which he would put in new seating and electricity. While his bid was considerably lower than the competing one, he obtained the lease because 'He had been a good customer to the town in the past, and was likely to be a good customer in the future'.[67] The gradual introduction of moving pictures, supported by a careful strategy of civic positioning, had allowed exhibitors like G. W. Walker to gain the establishment's trust, which was indispensable for their public-facing business.

By the spring of 1908, it had become clear that film was here to stay. Less than two years later, the introduction of the Cinematograph Act triggered further consolidation, by disincentivising travelling exhibition. The Parliamentary Act, intended to establish safeguards against film fires and fire-related panics, was interpreted in Scotland as an addition to existing local regulations concerned with moral propriety and the conduct of public entertainments. The issue of temporary exhibition spaces was contentious. During the discussion of the Bill, it had been proposed to exempt small weekly shows, like those run by some churches and temperance groups, from licensing conditions. As passed, the Act exempted venues that were used for cinema up to six times a year, while any more regular venues needed to install fireproof projection booths, fire exits and other safety measures. The exemption would have protected most of the rural and small-town touring shows in Scotland. However, the Act included a clause giving powers to the Scottish Secretary to create further regulations, which were stricter in terms of fire shutters and enclosures. On the basis of the Act and its Scottish regulation, local magistrates had to compose their own licence forms, which created another layer of administrative interference. In Edinburgh, for instance, the magistrates decided to apply the Scottish Secretary's regulations to all shows, even those exempted from licensing under the Act. According to Edinburgh exhibitors, for temporary venues the adaptations required to comply with the Act would have prohibitive costs, and hence the cancellation of about five hundred local shows given every year was predicted.[68] As the city magistrates recognised, 'there was little doubt that the regulations would put an end to the private or semi-private exhibitor in church halls, &c.'.[69]

Over the following year, most of the cases brought before the courts for contraventions to the Act referred to the use of unlicensed premises for one-night-only shows, or for failing to give the required notice to local authorities. In Aberdeenshire, Walter Mayne, a small-time showman who ran a travelling bioscope on his own, was fined twice in 1910 for occupying unlicensed halls; George Melvin, who ran the Arbroath Theatre, was fined for an unlicensed show in Stonehaven Town Hall.[70] Meanwhile, the bigger halls and most frequented towns made the required alterations and came a step closer to becoming permanent cinemas. Once a town had a permanent cinema, it ceased to be particularly profitable for touring companies. The case of Aberdeenshire can serve to illustrate the consequences of this process of stabilisation and centralisation on the provision of film shows to peripheral areas. By the end of 1910 there were at least five full-time cinemas in Aberdeen and one in Elgin, but a review of the 'District News' column of the *Aberdeen Journal*, where local events were reported, shows that by 1910 the number of cinematograph entertainments given outside the city had plummeted to below the levels at the end of the 1890s.

In most parts of Scotland there was a lull in cinematograph activity between 1908 and 1911. Growth was concentrated in the larger population centres, where travelling exhibitors had settled and taken long-term leases. Rural halls often reverted to musical entertainment. Not for long, however. As the following chapter will explore, the establishment of the Scottish cities as thriving centres for the film trade was accompanied by the expansion of permanent cinema venues in hundreds of smaller towns. Although the commercial practices were to undergo momentous transformations in the transition to fixed-site exhibition, the main structuring elements of the trade were already present in itinerant shows. These included the reliance on repurposed venues, circulation patterns and personal skills; the interdependence between urban and rural exhibition; and the fluidity of the exhibitor's role and social position.

Notes

1. Advertisement, *Fife Free Press and Kirkcaldy Guardian*, 14 July 1900. Available at <http://www.britishnewspaperarchive.co.uk/viewer/bl/0001062/19000714/177/0008> (last accessed 30 September 2016).
2. 'An Enterprising "Langtonian"', *Fife Free Press and Kirkcaldy Guardian*, 30 January 1897. Available at <http://www.britishnewspaperarchive.co.uk/viewer/bl/0001062/18970130/128/0004> (last accessed 30 September 2016).
3. Gaudreault, *Film and Attraction*, 63–4; Burrows, *Legitimate Cinema*, 14.
4. Kember, *Marketing Modernity*, 44–83.
5. Gaudreault and Marion, 'A Medium Is Always Born Twice . . .'
6. Shail, 'Intermediality: Disciplinary Flux or Formalist Retrenchment?'.
7. Pryluck, 'The Itinerant Movie Show and the Development of the Film Industry', 49.
8. Toulmin, 'Telling the Tale. The Story of the Fairground Bioscope Shows and the Showmen Who Operated Them', 236.
9. Bakker, *Entertainment Industrialised: The Emergence of the International Film Industry, 1890–1940*.
10. Vélez-Serna, 'Showmanship Skills and the Changing Role of the Exhibitor in 1910s Scotland'.
11. Allen, 'Reimagining the History of the Experience of Cinema in a Post-Moviegoing Age', 51–2.
12. McNeill, *Kirkcaldy Links Market*.

13. Toulmin, 'Telling the Tale. The Story of the Fairground Bioscope Shows and the Showmen Who Operated Them', 226.
14. In 1896, the secretary of the Showmen and Van-Dwellers' Association reckoned that more than four thousand vans travelled weekly on the British railways. 'Showmen and Van-Dwellers', *The Era*, 1 February 1896. Available at <http://find.galegroup.com/bncn/> (last accessed 9 October 2016).
15. 'The Showman World', *The Era*, 29 April 1899. Available at <http://www.britishnewspaperarchive.co.uk/viewer/bl/0000053/18990429/073/0020> (last accessed 9 October 2016)
16. Brooker, 'The Polytechnic Ghost'; *The Ghost on the Fairground*.
17. Scrivens and Smith, *The Travelling Cinematograph Show*.
18. Toulmin, *Pleasurelands*, 62.
19. Feeing fairs for farm labourers had traditionally clustered around Martinmas (11 November) and Whitsun (15 May). Lammas Day, in August, was more festive; a large fair is still held in St Andrews. By the end of the nineteenth century, most small rural fairs were on the wane, due to the extension of permanent commerce through railways and cattle markets. Marwick, *List of Markets and Fairs Now and Formerly Held in Scotland*; Adair, 'Calendar Customs', 122.
20. 'The Showman World', *The Era*, 25 March 1899. Available at <http://find.galegroup.com/bncn/> (last accessed 2 September 2010).
21. Manuscript letter, Peter Swallow to George Green, dated at Kilmarnock, 3 March 1905. Glasgow, National Library of Scotland's Moving Image Archive, 5/8/28.
22. Toulmin, '"Within the Reach of All": Travelling Cinematograph Shows in British Fairgrounds 1896–1914', 31.
23. *Glasgow Weekly Programme* No. 28, 26 July 1897.
24. Bruce, *Showfolk*, 89.
25. Ibid., 40.
26. This anecdote is told in a letter kept at the National Library of Scotland's Moving Image Archive, and quoted in Toulmin, 'Telling the Tale: The Story of the Fairground Bioscope Shows and the Showmen Who Operated Them', 221.
27. Swallow, *Roundabout Scotland*, 52.
28. Griffiths, 'Work, Leisure and Time in the Nineteenth Century'; Bakker, *Entertainment Industrialised: The Emergence of the International Film Industry, 1890–1940*, 72–85.
29. Maver, 'Leisure Time in Scotland during the Nineteenth and Twentieth Centuries', 178–9.
30. Royal Commission of the Ancient and Historical Monuments of Scotland, *Canmore* database. Available at <https://canmore.org.uk/> (last accessed 1 October 2016).
31. Allen, 'Relocating American Film History: The "Problem" of the Empirical', 68–9; Waller, 'Introducing the "Marvellous Invention" to the Provinces: Film Exhibition in Lexington, Kentucky, 1896–1897', 223–34.

32. Advertisement, *Aberdeen Journal*, Friday 25 November 1898. Available at <http://www.britishnewspaperarchive.co.uk/viewer/bl/0000575/18981125/005/0001> (last accessed 30 September 2016).
33. 'It was the custom to open the show with a short pictorial entertainment, consisting of a few "still" lantern slides, generally of an educative character': Skinner, *My Life and Adventures*, 53–4.
34. Griffiths, *The Cinema and Cinema-going in Scotland, 1896–1950*, 18–19.
35. Advertisement, *Aberdeen People's Journal*, 19 December 1896. Available at <http://www.britishnewspaperarchive.co.uk/viewer/bl/0000773/18961219/019/0001> (last accessed 30 September 2016).
36. Advertisement, *Aberdeen Evening Express*, 11 January 1893. Available at <http://www.britishnewspaperarchive.co.uk/viewer/bl/0000444/18930111/111/0003> (last accessed 30 September 2016).
37. Griffiths, 'Work, Leisure and Time in the Nineteenth Century', 186.
38. 'Death of a former Glasgow official', *Glasgow Herald*, 22 September 1930.
39. Freer, *My Life and Memories*, 89.
40. King, *Scotland Sober and Free*, 12.
41. Maloney, *Scotland and the Music Hall 1850–1914*, 192.
42. 'Gala day at Durris House', *Aberdeen Journal*, 23 December 1896. Available at <http://find.galegroup.com/bncn/> (last accessed 29 June 2012).
43. 'The Cinematograph at Gordon Castle', *Aberdeen Journal*, 28 October 1896. Available at <http://www.britishnewspaperarchive.co.uk/viewer/bl/0000032/18961028/061/0006> (last accessed 30 September 2016).
44. 'Christmas entertainment at Philorth', *Aberdeen Journal*, 31 December 1898. Available at <http://www.britishnewspaperarchive.co.uk/viewer/bl/0000575/18981231/142/0008> (last accessed 30 September 2016).
45. 'Udny', *Aberdeen Journal*, 27 December 1913. Available at <http://www.britishnewspaperarchive.co.uk/viewer/bl/0000576/19131227/099/0007> (last accessed 9 October 2016)
46. Allen, *Vaudeville and Film, 1895–1915: A Study in Media Interaction*, 65.
47. Toulmin, 'Cuckoo in the Nest: Edwardian Itinerant Exhibition Practices and the Transition to Cinema in the United Kingdom from 1901 to 1906', 57.
48. Maloney, *Scotland and the Music Hall 1850–1914*, 57.
49. Scullion, 'Geggies, Empires, Cinemas: The Scottish Experience of Early Film', 14.
50. Bakker, *Entertainment Industrialised: The Emergence of the International Film Industry, 1890–1940*, 35.
51. Scullion, '"The Cinematograph Still Reigns Supreme at the Skating Palace": The First Decades of Film in Scotland', 82.
52. Bakker, *Entertainment Industrialised: The Emergence of the International Film Industry, 1890–1940*, 14.
53. Brown and Barry, *A Victorian Film Enterprise: The History of the British Mutoscope and Biograph Company*, 14.
54. Chanan, *The Dream That Kicks*, 158–60.

55. Bromhead, 'Reminiscences of the British Film Trade', 9.
56. Allen, 'Vitascope/Cinématographe: Initial Patterns of American Film Industrial Practice', 192.
57. Bowers, *Glasgow's Lost Theatre*, 80–3.
58. *The Glasgow Programme*, 18 October 1897.
59. The Pickard's Papers project website has more information on Pickard, and a digitised collection of scrapbooks and correspondence. Available at <http://pickardspapers.gla.ac.uk> (last accessed 1 September 2016).
60. Walsh, 'Standards of Practice in Transition: The Showmanship of Jasper Redfern as It Emerged'; Rossell, 'A Slippery Job: Travelling Exhibitors in Early Cinema'; Cook, 'Albany Ward and the Development of Cinema Exhibition in England'.
61. 'Amusements in Glasgow', *The Era*, 20 December 1890. Available at <http://www.britishnewspaperarchive.co.uk/viewer/bl/0000053/18901220/099/0018> (last accessed 9 October 2016).
62. Classified ads, *The Era*, 21 November 1896. Available at <http://www.britishnewspaperarchive.co.uk/viewer/bl/0000053/18961121/060/0027> (last accessed 9 October 2016).
63. 'A Chat with Calverto', *Shetland Times*, 24 July 1897. Available at <http://www.britishnewspaperarchive.co.uk/viewer/bl/0000666/18970724/099/0007> (last accessed 9 October 2016).
64. Classified advertisements, *The Era*, 17 February 1900. Available at <http://www.britishnewspaperarchive.co.uk/viewer/bl/0000053/19000217/109/0028> (last accessed 9 October 2016).
65. Calverto's bioscope turn was to appear as part of Alexander Mathieson's three-week tour of medium-sized towns in central Scotland. On the first night, a technical problem ruined the performance, and Mathieson abandoned the tour, prosecuting Calverto for lost revenue. Griffiths, *The Cinema and Cinema-going in Scotland, 1896–1950*, 23. The papers for the case, including promotional material, correspondence with venues, and lists of hire costs, are in the National Records of Scotland, and a copy is available at the National Library of Scotland's Moving Image Archive.
66. 'The Triumph of the Animated Picture', 48.
67. 'Kirkcaldy Town Council', *Fife Free Press and Kirkcaldy Guardian*, Saturday 15 February 1908. Available at <http://www.britishnewspaperarchive.co.uk/viewer/bl/0001062/19080215/037/0002> (last accessed 9 October 2016).
68. 'Wake up, Scotland! Drastic Action by the Authorities: 500 Edinburgh Entertainments Spoiled', *Bioscope*, 17 February 1910, pp. 39–41.
69. 'Edinburgh Magistrates and Cinematograph Exhibitions', *The Scotsman*, 10 February 1910. Available at *ProQuest Historical Newspapers* <http://search.proquest.com/docview/483838308> (last accessed 9 October 2016).
70. 'Contravention of the Act at Aberdeen', *Bioscope*, 10 March 1910, p. 43. 'Away up North', *Bioscope*, 6 October 1910, p. 21; *Bioscope*, 9 March 1911, p. 53.

CHAPTER 3

Fixed-site Cinemas and the First Film Renters

María A. Vélez-Serna

In the space of a few years after 1907 the film trade in the UK and in Scotland was transformed completely. By this point, travelling exhibitors had reached all corners of the country with their bioscope projectors, showing films in fairgrounds, halls and private houses. The most successful amongst these had started to consolidate their trade by leasing sites for longer periods, but these were still temporary shows, based on an artisanal business model. By the start of the First World War, moving picture exhibition had turned into an industry that employed thousands of people in over four hundred venues. The growth was gradual, but, once the first cinemas proved their viability, the expansion accelerated. This period of rapid change has been thought of as 'second birth' or 'distinguishing birth', as the moment in which cinema emerged as a distinct cultural form rather than as a component within the mixed programme in music hall, fairground or parlour entertainment.[1] The establishment of moving pictures as a fixed-site, permanent show transformed their relationship with audiences, rewarded new styles of showmanship and required a complete overhaul of the distribution system. In Scotland, this process was fast-paced but organic, retaining a connection to earlier practices. At the same time, it required the development of new structures and, in particular, the emergence of a regional film distribution sector.

As explained in Chapter 2, the first permanent cinemas opened in halls that had been in use by travelling showmen for seasonal shows, and many fairground entertainers made the transition to permanent cinema owners. Across the UK, Vanessa Toulmin estimates that over ten per cent of fairground cinema operators ended up opening permanent cinemas.[2] Most of the better-known Scottish fairground exhibitors did so, sometimes with remarkable success. Amongst the other types of film exhibitors the transition had already started with the growing duration of seasonal shows. By 1911 William Walker had opened the Coliseum cinema in Aberdeen, Peter Feathers was running the Stobswell in Dundee and Robert Calder was about to take a job managing a Fraserburgh venue. In the space of six years up to the start of the First World War, however, permanent cinema venues opened at an average rate of almost two a week across Scotland. The travelling exhibitors' pioneering role was thus quickly superseded by a new wave of cinema entrepreneurs coming into the business from a variety of backgrounds, as Trevor Griffiths explains in Chapter 5 below.

Owing to the unstable nature of an emerging business and the abundance of short-lived venues, the numbers we have for this expansion are not precise. In a widely cited article, published just before the outbreak of war, Frank W. Ogden Smith estimated that Britain had seven thousand film theatres, with a combined capital of around £13 million.[3] However, only about half as many venues are listed in the 1915 edition of the *Bioscope Annual*, including four hundred in Scotland, while the *Kinematograph Year Book* offers 553 Scottish venues for the same year, including many that only showed films at most once a week. So any number between four and five hundred can be taken as a reference point, while remembering that it is not comprehensive. In his article about London 'penny gaffs', Jon Burrows has shown how the licensing and trade figures underestimated or deliberately played down the number of these humble shop-front venues in the capital, leading to the historiographical myth that Britain somehow skipped the nickelodeon phase.[4] But even if penny cinemas were not a feature in Scotland, the nickelodeon or shop-front show was not the only precedent or a necessary step towards fixed-site cinemas – particularly not outside the main cities.

The expansion of permanent film exhibition in Scotland must be understood in the context of a very uneven geographical distribution of the population, which was concentrated along the central belt (on the axis connecting Glasgow and Edinburgh), the west coast south of the river Clyde, and the east coast from Fife to Inverness. As Chapter 4 will show, an important feature of Scottish demographics was the abundance of smaller towns, with settlements of two to ten thousand people accounting for twenty-one per cent of the population in 1911. The four main cities of Glasgow, Dundee, Edinburgh and Aberdeen were home to twenty-seven per cent of Scots, making Scotland more urban than the United States, but less than England. The tenfold growth of Glasgow between 1801 and 1901 had transformed it into an industrial metropolis, and a likely setting for an enthusiasm for cinema that became a common reference in the city's lore.

The rapid expansion of permanent, dedicated places of film exhibition in the UK around 1910–11 has been called the 'cinema boom', but this risks making it sound more sudden than it was. In the Scottish cities, permanent exhibition developed quickly but organically, as a change in the patterns of use of existing places of entertainment, before it moved into new and purpose-built spaces. As discussed in Chapter 2, the first stage of the process was simply a slower itinerancy, as travelling companies extended their leases of large public halls that had proved successful. In Edinburgh, the Modern Marvel company held increasingly long engagements at the Queen's Hall, as had the B.B. Pictures at Glasgow's Wellington Palace. In several venues throughout the country, the winter season of 1907–8 did not draw to a close, and regular cinema shows ran through the year for the first time. By the end of the summer, there were five film-only shows operating in Glasgow, three in public halls and two in music halls.[5] Only four years later, Glasgow had more than seventy dedicated cinema venues, including the first purpose-built cinema which opened in 1910. The expansion of cinema exhibition was fast, but it was also tentative and incremental. Cautious businesspeople committed to full-time film shows only once they were certain that public demand would support them. This situation is at a remove from the high-risk, 'get-rich-quick' image that emerged later in relation to cinema investment.

In an influential article, Nicholas Hiley's analysis of company registrations in the UK between 1909 and 1914 arrived at the conclusion that the building of cinemas during those years was fuelled by speculative capital rather than by increased demand.[6] This narrative has been contested by Jon Burrows and Richard Brown, who argue that the over-capitalised, risky ventures described by Hiley were exceptional. Instead, they show that the cinema boom was driven by 'small-time businesspersons' who were relatively risk-averse.[7] Board of Trade records show a large number of small private companies or unincorporated partnerships which conducted the bulk of the trade, especially outside major cities. This description seems to fit the Scottish situation better, according to the annual company registration figures published in *The Scotsman*. In Scotland, the number of joint-stock companies registered during a year with the purpose of either building or 'carrying on' a permanent film show peaked in 1913 at fifty-two, and the median capital of these private companies was around £3,000, which was roughly the cost of erecting a purpose-built cinema. Trevor Griffiths's more systematic analysis of shareholders' lists for forty-six cinema companies established in Scotland from 1909 to 1914 reveals that most investors and board members were not previously connected with the entertainment business. The lists were, according to Griffiths, 'dominated by a professional and commercial middle class attuned to the emergence of new investment opportunities'.[8] In an economy subject to marked cyclical fluctuations in activity, with a depressed housing market, investment in cinema ventures was a sound option. The piecemeal nature of the move to purpose-built venues is evidence of a cautious approach which at first tried to minimise sunk costs, that is, costs that cannot be recovered, by adapting existing venues, drawing on the proven success of temporary exhibition in the same spaces, and maintaining facilities for live entertainment – stages and dressing rooms – in case cinema proved to be a passing fad. While there was investment in new buildings, many companies were constituted to lease or take over existing venues such as skating rinks and public halls, most often places where a show was already being run. In fact, the largest of the early Scottish companies, the B.B. Pictures Ltd, registered in 1910, produced a brochure with photographs of the halls it controlled, stating:

> It will be seen that the policy of the management has been to secure the use of existing halls – test them, if successful, retain them, if not, abandon them.
> This policy is intended to continue, as it is believed to be more prudent than to erect buildings, which, if unsuccessful, might become a permanent loss of revenue.[9]

The first hall taken over by the B.B. Pictures' director, James Joseph Bennell, had been the Wellington Palace in Glasgow. This was a music hall dating from 1874, located on a side street in the Gorbals, a densely populated working-class area just south of the city centre. The large hall, seating two thousand, was across from a biscuit factory and not far from two schools and had lately been used by the Good Templars, a temperance organisation that put on Saturday concerts as an alternative to the pub. In the East End of the city, George Green, who managed the Vinegarhill fairground site, had been showing films in another old music hall, the Whitevale Theatre. Just down the road, George Urie Scott refurbished the Annfield Halls, located in the back court behind a row of shops. Not too far from there, the Bridgeton Town Hall, with accommodation for a thousand patrons, had been taken over by Margaret and George Laird and renamed the Star Palace. All these venues charged similarly low prices – generally 2d for adults, 1d for children and in some cases 4d for better seats. However, they were not akin to New York nickelodeons; not only were they larger venues but they were also running two longer shows a night rather than a continuous rotation of a short programme, as, unlike the nickelodeons, they depended less on audience turnover than on volume. Furthermore, these were places with a history in the neighbourhood, either as entertainment or civic venues, where election speeches were given and temperance meetings were held. Their reconfiguration as permanent sites of moving picture entertainment could sustain some of these associations.

As cinema took over existing venues like drill halls and public halls, it displaced the multiple functions of a community venue to make way for a commercial but permanent entertainment offer, or replaced another commercial entertainment use such as a skating rink or a music hall. The displacement effect was stronger in the East End than in other parts of the city, suggesting that the expansion of cinema did not always necessarily bring a widening of local entertainment options for working-class neighbourhoods. It is also coherent with observations made by J. A. Lindstrom in Chicago, who argued that nickelodeons were located not simply in immigrant or working-class neighbourhoods but especially in 'zones in transition', either areas with mixed land use, where immigrant housing was combined with commercial and industrial use, or newly developed areas where 'satellite loops' (local retail centres) were appearing.[10] In Glasgow, this seems to be the case in Maryhill, in the north of the city, and in Cathcart in the south, for instance: picture theatres appeared in seemingly more 'well-heeled' districts as their working-class audiences moved up the social ladder.

In contrast with the situation in other parts of Britain, in Scotland purpose-built cinemas were only a fraction of exhibition venues before the war. It was unusual for the first cinema in a medium-sized town to be purpose-built. The infrastructure left behind by a half-century of temperance campaigning, by an abundance of drill halls, and by the realignment of the Scottish Presbyterian churches which created a superfluity of church buildings, provided the first homes for moving pictures. In addition to this, the decline in popular interest in roller skating also left a scattering of large, adaptable buildings already associated with commercialised leisure. Companies needed a much smaller capital to install some lights on the façade of the local hall, pavilion or skating rink and rename it an Electric Theatre. In Scotland, then, the first wave of expansion of fixed-site exhibition, from 1909 to 1912, was characterised by the permanent lease of premises already used for entertainment, and thus favoured larger spaces rather than the cramped conditions associated with the nickelodeon model. Between one-quarter and one-third of the permanent exhibition venues operating by 1912 were existing halls, with an average capacity of over eight hundred seats. Only around one in every six venues was purpose-built, although substantial alterations might have been carried out. Purpose-built venues tended to be slightly larger than halls, but converted skating rinks surpassed both with average capacities of over a thousand seats each. Theatres, variety theatres and music halls, which could switch

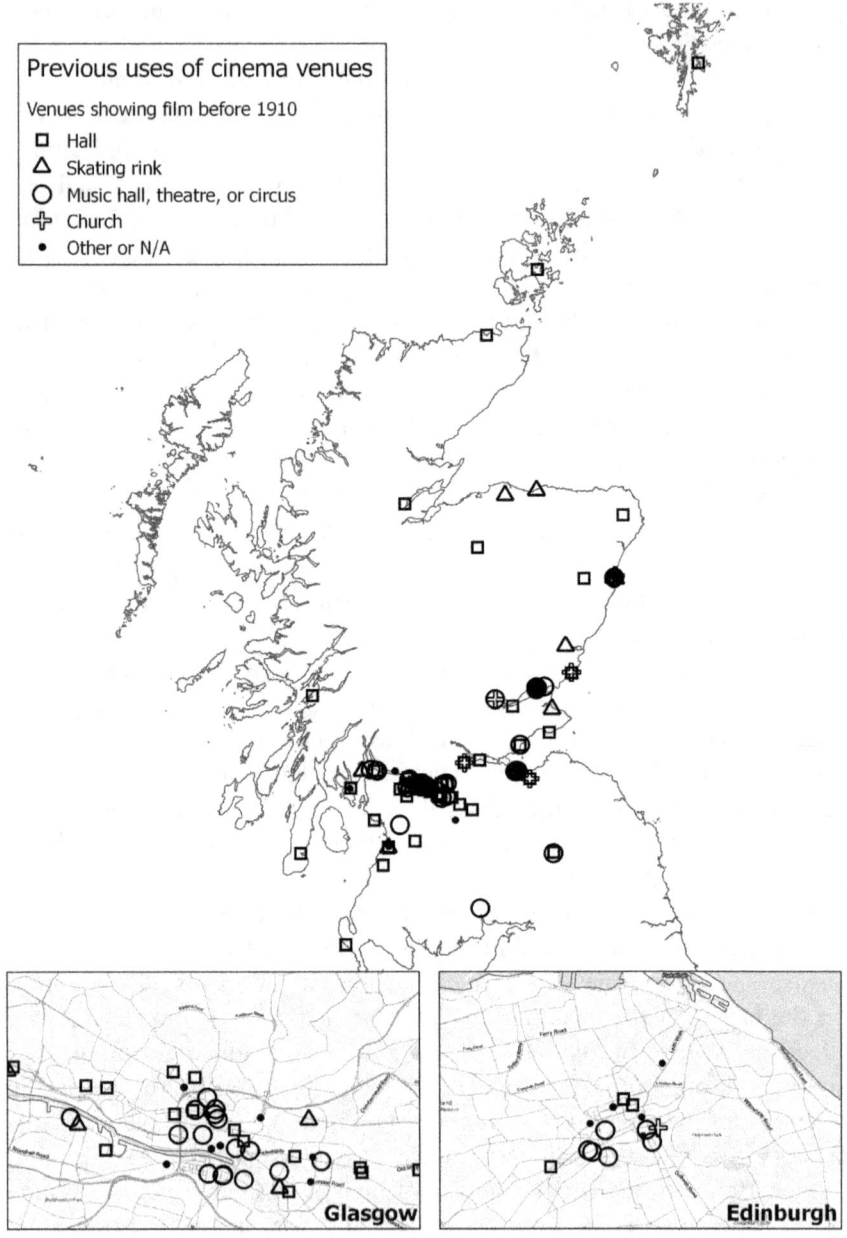

Figure 3.1 Previous uses of cinema venues operating before 1910.

FIXED-SITE CINEMAS AND THE FIRST FILM RENTERS

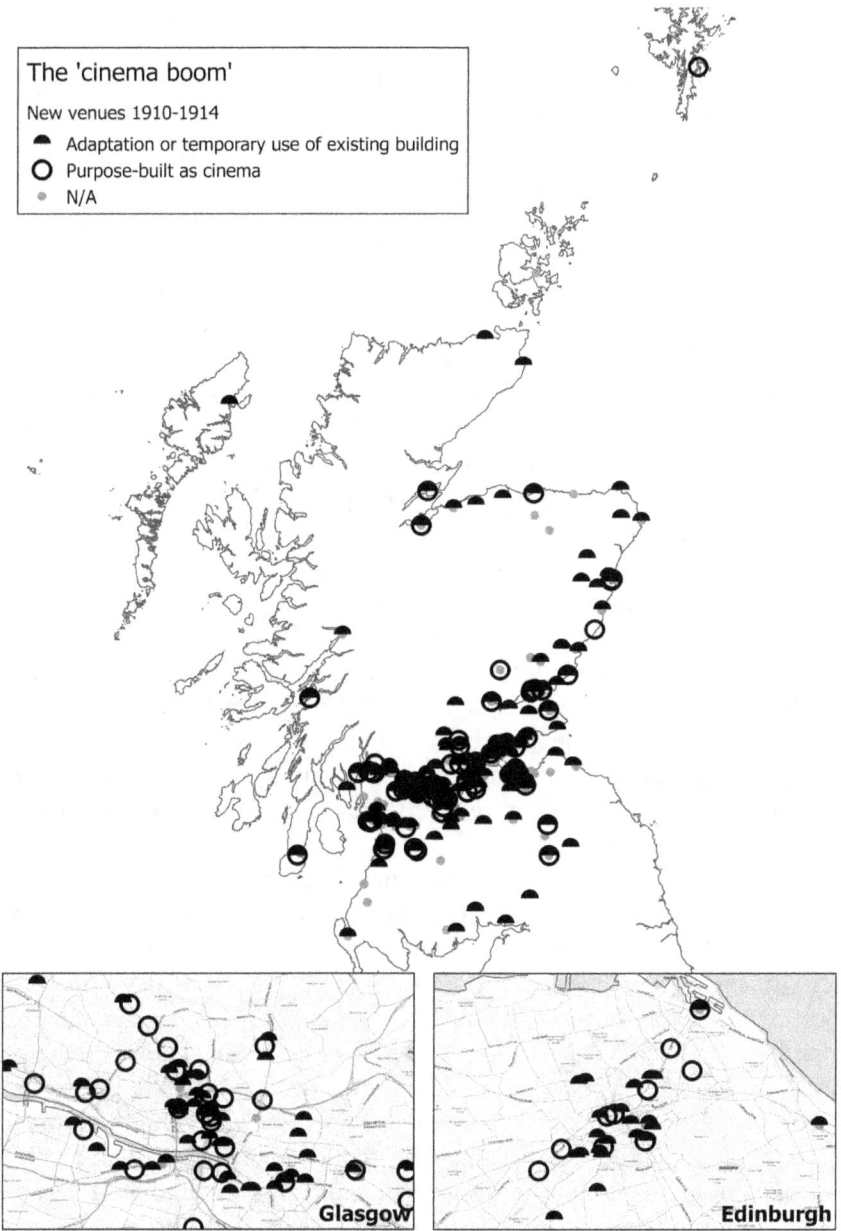

Figure 3.2 Adapted venues and new cinema construction, 1910–14.

back and forth between different types of entertainment following popular demand, were substantially larger, but fewer in number.

Like rural audiences, suburban working-class patrons were likely to encounter films in a neighbourhood hall reinvented as a picture palace from as early as 1908, while more affluent spectators had to wait longer for full-time, film-only venues. While there were many opportunities to see films in large city-centre venues like Hengler's Circus and the St Andrew's Halls, or music halls like the Britannia Panopticon, the cautious nature of investment in cinema development delayed the entrance of dedicated cinema venues into Glasgow's main commercial thoroughfares. J. J. Bennell might have been expressing a common cautious opinion when he recognised that he 'had pinned [his] faith to the working classes and the twice nightly house' because he 'had only a limited faith in pictures'.[11] On the other hand, new entrepreneurs were entering the field, and bringing with them new ideas about potential audiences. The West of Scotland Electric Theatres company was floated at the end of 1909 and opened its first venue, Glasgow's first purpose-built cinema, the Charing Cross Electric Theatre on Sauchiehall Street, in May 1910. Moving even closer to the entertainment centre of the city, the London-based national chain Provincial Cinematograph Theatres opened the Picture House further along Sauchiehall Street at the end of the year. Both venues ran a continuous programme and charged 6d for admission. After this point, many other purpose-built venues, with ever-more sumptuous lobbies and tea rooms, opened in the centre of Glasgow to cater for a more selective public.

Although the year with the most cinema openings before the war was 1912, fewer than a fifth of the 112 venues opening that year were in new buildings. The following year, with no more sites to repurpose, building activity picked up. More than forty purpose-built cinemas opened in Scotland in 1913. This was the tail end of the 1910–12 construction peak identified by Nicholas Hiley for the whole of Britain.[12] The new cinemas of 1913 included very few hall or skating rink conversions, but the average capacity did not increase significantly, because it was already relatively high. Scottish venues, as documented, tended to be larger than the UK average found by Hiley. A significant contribution to that difference came from the regular use of larger town halls (such as those in Bo'ness, Greenock, Kirkintilloch and Paisley), and the inclusion of some variety theatres licensed for cinema.

Coming from the respectable trade press, these figures could be hiding the existence of smaller, fly-by-night venues. However, in the absence of evidence to the contrary, it is reasonable to argue that the expansion

Table 3.1. Cinema capacity in 1914 (Scottish venues in database: 601: venues with capacity data: 407)

	UK cinemas by size in 1914, from Hiley 1999		Scottish cinemas up to 1914/15	
Seating capacity	%		*Count*	%
1–500	28		72	17.7
501–800	35		140	34.4
801–1000	16		83	20.4
1001–2000	18		100	24.6
2000+	3		12	2.9
Total	100		407	100.0

Sources: Nicholas Hiley, '"Let's Go to the Pictures": The British Cinema Audience in the 1920s and 1930s', *Journal of Popular British Cinema* 2 (1999): 39–53 (p. 41); *Early Cinema in Scotland* database, from various sources including *Bioscope Annual* 1915; http://earlycinema.gla.ac.uk/, data retrieved 12 April 2016

of cinema in Scotland took place in larger venues, with existing civic architecture playing a key role. There was still a huge amount of variation between these venues. Just before the First World War, on any ordinary day in Glasgow it was possible to see animated pictures in a church, a wooden hut or an ornate concrete shell; for 1d or 1s; with or without a lecturer, an orchestra or a variety turn; in peripheral working-class neighbourhoods or in the more fashionable corners of the city centre. Throughout the country, metal sheds, drill halls, manses, markets, baths and billiard rooms were pressed into service. In the hands of entrepreneurial showpeople, these sheds became Picture Palaces, Electric Theatres and Picturedromes. By 1914, there were cinemas in more than 130 towns, including Fife mining villages and market towns in Aberdeenshire and the Borders, as well as the industrial central belt, and from Annan to Lerwick. The patterns and particularities of this development are examined in Chapter 4.

While the popularity of cinema amongst the industrial populations of Glasgow and Dundee has been widely recognised, the business models that allowed urban exhibition to thrive depended on a connection to local and broader circuits. Travelling exhibitors had used the routes of fairground and touring concerts, showing the same material to different audiences; fixed-site operators needed to offer a regular change of programme in order to ensure repeat custom. The fixed-site cinema is thus a different type of node in the emerging networks of film distribution, which were gradually crystallising as a separate business sector. Fixed-site venues required the development of the distribution trade, and of a regional network that was able to supply films to a very diverse exhibition sector. In this system of relationships and infrastructure, small towns, suburban, and city-centre venues were interdependent, and connected through trade hubs at Glasgow and Edinburgh. The emergence of film distribution as a distinct trade created a new arena for Scottish entrepreneurs in the 1910s and 1920s.

For the 'first generation' of cinema managers (those who came into the business before 1915 or so), obtaining good films to show was a challenge. Transformations in all sectors of the industry were casting a new role for exhibitors, one that was more clearly delineated and involved less multi-tasking. As Brown has explained:

> The adjustment [to fixed-site cinemas] involved the abandonment of a highly personalised transactional model characterised by bespoke service, low replacement rates and long periods of time, with a much more dynamic but impersonal method, more appropriate for high replacement rates and short periods of use.[13]

At the core of this reconfiguration was the emergence of film renting. The 'low replacement rates' of the pre-boom era reflected the fact that exhibitors had invested significant amounts to buy the films directly from producers, and could not afford to replace them until they had extracted an equivalent value from a long tail of showings. Under the rental system, the ownership of film prints passed to the renter, and thus the weekly price paid by the exhibitor was lowered. This lower cost of film hire had a double effect: it made extended rural tours as a means of recovering costs unnecessary; and it reduced the entry barriers, enabling many more exhibitors to set up shop. This, in turn, exacerbated competition in urban areas. In 1913, Glasgow had eighty-five licensed venues, of which about fifty were full-time cinemas.[14] Aberdeen and Dundee had at least twenty venues each, and Edinburgh more than forty.[15] The pressures of competition between urban exhibitors set the conditions in which many of the future developments of the film trade took shape. Although the wide network of small-town cinemas was the ballast that stabilised the industry, the interests of those exhibitors were increasingly marginalised.

Competition between urban cinemas was fought on three battlefields: prices, amenities and up-to-dateness. Newly built venues could offer grander buildings, more comfortable seating and ancillary attractions such as tea rooms and fountains. But, as audiences became more selective and informed, being able to show the newest films soon became crucial. Exhibitors thought that if they did not have the latest film, and the opposition did, they would lose business. The 'fallacy of first runs', as *The Bioscope* put it in 1910, was the reigning factor in the stratification of exhibition following the runs system. Given that a limited number of prints of any given film were available, these prints had to be leased to cinemas in a particular order. This ordering of venues as part of a distribution chain focused on the film's release date. Since most cinemas in the UK changed their programme twice a week, each half-week was one step in the distribution cascade. The 'first run' meant the first three days after release, when the film was showcased at the more prestigious venues; second-run were the venues that would get it after that, and so on. The price of hire was reduced for each subsequent run. The formalisation of this system translated geographic and socio-economic distance into a time lag: the smaller the town, and the cheaper the cinema, the older its films would be.

Plotting the release dates of the films in a sample of cinema programmes from January 1913, against the populations of the burghs where the same films were being exhibited, illustrates the nature of this lag. Figure 3.3 shows one dot for each film, with its release date as given in the trade press on the x axis and the population of the burgh where it was being shown on the y axis. Population is plotted on a logarithmic scale in order to emphasise the difference between small and medium towns, while the films shown in the four largest cities in the sample form the rows towards the top half of the graph. Although there is considerable spread, an elbow-shaped pattern is visible: the oldest films (towards the left-hand extreme of the graph) are mostly being shown in towns of under 25,000 inhabitants. In the towns with a population of under ten thousand, no film was mentioned that was less than two and a half months old by January 1913. On the contrary, in Glasgow, Edinburgh, Aberdeen and some of the satellite burghs (Hamilton, Paisley), the oldest films date only from October. Of the forty-four urban cinemas in the sample, at least a dozen included brand-new releases in their programmes, although none seems to offer an all-new bill.[16]

Breaking these figures down into more detail reveals that provincial venues with access to newer films tended to be part of regional cinema chains. The traditional account of the development of the trade in Britain highlights the importance of large horizontally-integrated exhibition companies operating as cinema circuits, following the model of the music-hall circuit. In this narrative, a few English companies established during the early years of the cinema boom became the financial bedrock of the British film trade, and gave rise to various attempts at vertical integration.[17] Some of those UK-wide circuits had Scottish venues: Provincial Cinematograph Theatres Ltd (PCT) had Picture Houses on Edinburgh's Princes Street

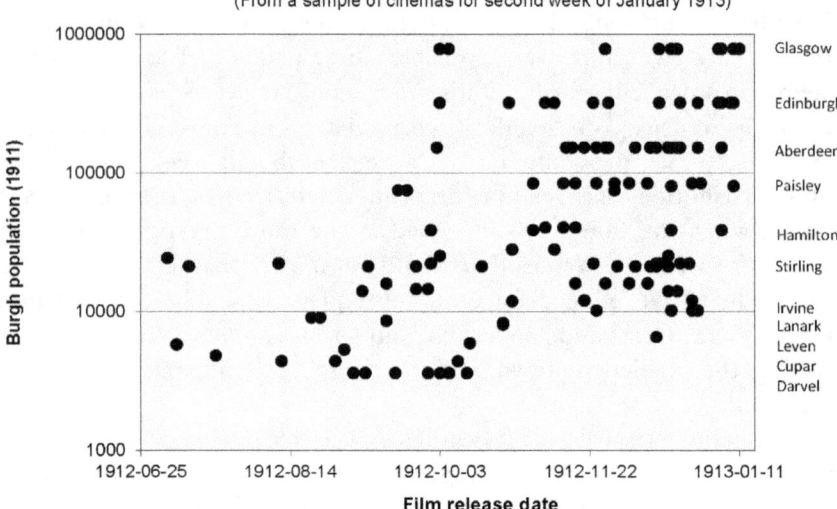

Figure 3.3 Release patterns for a sample of programmes showing in Scottish cinemas during the second week of January 1913.

and in Glasgow on Sauchiehall Street. These were large, well-appointed city-centre venues with first-run programmes that charged a minimum admission price of 6d. In contrast, Pringle's Picture Palaces, a company established in the North of England by Ralph Pringle, a travelling exhibitor, located its Glasgow and Edinburgh venues in working-class areas on the edges of the city centre. Converted from music halls and skating rinks, these venues charged 2d for admission and showed films that were a couple of weeks old. These two chains had been amongst the pioneers of fixed-site exhibition in Scotland: opening in 1907, Pringle's Queen's Theatre was one of the first permanent cinemas in Glasgow, and PCT's Picture House offered continuous shows and new standards of luxury on a major city-centre street from 1910. However, their presence in Scotland remained limited, never reaching beyond the main cities; the Scottish venues were on the periphery of their circuits, and their film booking arrangements were co-ordinated centrally.

Burrows and Brown's article on the financial aspects of the cinema boom challenges the preponderance of the big circuits in the expansion of permanent exhibition, pointing out that, after a brief flourishing of highly capitalised company formation in 1908–9, the trade was dominated by smaller, private companies.[18] The Scottish exhibition trade did not undergo such a dramatic spike in investment, as the largest circuits tended to expand only gradually and on the back of already thriving concerns. By the start of the war, there were five Scottish companies that controlled six or more venues: B.B. Pictures, Green's, G.U. Scott, R.C. Buchanan and Bostock's. Between them, they controlled more than fifty cinemas, mostly in the central belt. In contrast, at least a hundred venues were owned by a company controlling only one cinema, while almost half of all venues in Scotland were coupled or part of a small local circuit.

Coupled venues, splitting hire costs and shuttling reels back and forth during the screenings, can be considered as the most basic case of horizontal integration in exhibition. There were many such cases around Scotland, such as Aberdeen Picture Palaces, a relatively small company that will make an appearance in later chapters, or R. V. Singleton's circuit based in Lanarkshire mining villages. Such modest arrangements depended on close geographical proximity, not only for change-overs but also because they often shared a manager. The exhibition trade north of the border was thus dominated by local companies from an early point. Rural circuits not centred upon a first-run metropolitan venue included companies like the Elite Entertainments Syndicate in Aberdeenshire (Huntly, Nairn, Keith and Buckie) and T. J. Scott's East Lothian circuit (Peebles, Dunbar, North Berwick, Linlithgow and Haddington). More powerful urban circuits capitalised on their connection to earlier forms of entertainment. R. C. Buchanan, for instance, was an actor and theatre owner who took over music halls and theatres in Edinburgh, Dundee, Motherwell and Coatbridge. E. H. Bostock was a very successful menagerie and circus showman from Buckinghamshire, who had started showing film as part of the variety entertainment at the Hamilton Hippodrome.[19] By 1914, he controlled at least eight venues, mostly in old music halls or circuses, all within ten miles of Glasgow.

Control of eight venues marked the point at which it started to be more profitable for a circuit proprietor to buy films outright rather than hiring them from a renter. Once an exhibitor had made this shift, the logical next step was to recoup the cost of films further by hiring them out to other exhibitors. This was then a key moment in the emergence of local and regional film hiring practices that retained some autonomy for as long as films could be bought on the open market (that is, acquired as straightforward commodities, rather than as intellectual property where exploitation rights remained with the manufacturer). Controlling eight or more venues not only allowed exhibitors to counterbalance their expenditure on film, and to develop a lucrative renting side to their business, but it also increased their bargaining power in negotiating hire prices with the renters, and allowed them to present fairly new films even in suburban, low-priced venues. Once the link between exhibition and distribution was established, the dominance of the companies that were large enough to capitalise on it was secure. This interdependence was the foundation for the temporary success of Scotland's pioneer cinema distributors, Green's Film Service and the B.B. Pictures.

Considered side by side, the cases of Green's Film Service and the B.B. Pictures encapsulate the forces and processes that shaped the development of local companies before the war. Although UK-wide chains had a dominant presence in the main cities, Green's and the B.B. Pictures were more prominent in certain towns and neighbourhoods, and their prominent branding means they figure highly in oral history accounts of cinema-going, especially in Glasgow. Much less known is their role as distributors, which started between 1910 and 1912 and was an indispensable factor in the Scottish cinema boom.[20] James Joseph Bennell of the B.B. Pictures, as mentioned above, had rented the Wellington Palace, in the south side of Glasgow, from the Good Templars in 1907. With a background in temperance lecturing in the North of England, he had toured with a hired bioscope and then with the Bradford-based company New Century Pictures. Working for that company, he visited Glasgow twice a year for public-hall engagements that grew steadily longer. When Bennell, with his 'limited faith in pictures', decided to expand his operations, he took leases on large halls in working-class areas in Glasgow, Dundee and other towns in the central belt of Scotland. (Interestingly, the two venues first leased in Edinburgh were not successful.) This low-cost strategy was a condition for the rapid expansion of the B.B. circuit (the initials were popularly understood to stand for 'Bright and Beautiful', though they may have started as the initials of Bennell's wife), which by 1910 controlled fourteen halls, eight of which were permanent. Shortly after starting the permanent operation of the Wellington Palace, Bennell's film supplier offered him for purchase a few films, which he used 'at shows [he] organized at [the Glasgow districts of] Govan, Kinning Park, Springburn, Kingston, Langside, Dixon, and Pollokshaws Public Halls'. After using the films for his own shows, he then obtained some further profit by hiring them on to other pioneer exhibitors, such as Bob Stewart and Thomas Haddon, who ran travelling shows.[21]

After this experiment, Bennell continued renting his films from the London company, Jury's, until 1909, under an agreement that allowed him to sub-let them. By then, Bennell's circuit had expanded sufficiently so that he decided to start buying the films outright.[22] In order to secure a good selection of films, Bennell travelled to the London showrooms every other week, and opened an office in the capital in 1911. The business had been floated in 1910 as the B.B. Pictures Ltd. The prospectus for the flotation valued the film library at almost £8000, and claimed the firm had over a hundred customers. The B.B. Pictures' rental side was indeed so successful that, in the first half of 1910, it was already generating more profit than the eight exhibition venues combined. Months later, the company had opened a branch office in Manchester, 'to secure some late bookings, which really were the only profitable ones – all the earlier income being absorbed to pay for the films'.[23] This suggests that a dependent relationship had been created between the circuit of cinemas and the renting business. Box office from the cinemas covered the costs of the film prints, but the profit was made in renting them. A clientele that included cinemas in Manchester, Wolverhampton, Sutton Coldfield and South Wales was unwittingly helping to subsidise the first-run films enjoyed by Scottish audiences in B.B. cinemas.[24] The economies of scale also worked to keep prices relatively low for other exhibitors renting from B.B., at prices from 10s to £5 per 1,000 feet of film for a week.[25]

The B.B. Pictures' distribution business depended on an open-market model where films could be purchased outright, and made to pay over long stretches of time. It also depended on having privileged access to the manufacturers in London, mediating between them and individual Scottish cinema managers. These two conditions were eroded throughout the war years by the growth of exclusive dealing and the development of vertical integration, especially of American firms. Many manufacturers stopped selling films to independent renters, so their supply chain collapsed. The B.B. company held on, still offering 'cheap subjects to suit the smallest hall',[26] until 1917 when all the stock was sold to Argosy Films.

A comparable story is that of George Green and Green's Film Service. The Greens had arrived in Glasgow from Lancashire at the end of the nineteenth century as travelling showpeople, and since 1896 had been showing films in fairgrounds, at their carnival grounds in Glasgow's East End, and in a growing circuit of working-class venues.[27] As with B.B. Pictures, by the time the company controlled eight cinemas they calculated that it would be cheaper to buy films outright, and so Green's Film Service was launched in February 1912. By May 1915, when the Film Service moved to new premises in central Glasgow, *The Bioscope* claimed that the firm had 'over a hundred customers having complete programmes' and three motor cars to deliver the films to them.[28]

The bulk of Green's trade was in open-market programmes. Through an office in London, they bought up to four prints of the most popular titles. While the industry moved towards longer films, Green's continued to supply cinemas that demanded shorter (two-reel) features, in particular so that they could be interspersed with live variety.[29] Green's own cinemas, which tended to be in direct rivalry with the B.B. Pictures, had the first run of new film acquisitions. Over the years, Green's became well known as distributors of serials, and later on became booking agents for Nordisk and Triangle.[30] Towards the end of 1917 they acquired the rights for the sought-after new Mutual films, also known as the 'million dollar Chaplins'.[31] Despite these hits, by 1919 the Film Service was faltering as changes in trade methods prevented regional renters from owning film prints for exploitation. Meanwhile, exhibition continued to thrive, and in 1927 Green's Playhouse opened in Glasgow as the largest cinema in Europe and proof of the strength of Scottish exhibition.[32]

Apart from these firmly established renter-exhibitors, the trade was dominated by branches of London-based renters, and, later on, agents for the American producers. The first company to establish a branch in Scotland was Gaumont, which had offices at Glasgow's Trongate in 1908. Pathé, Jury's, Ideal and Barker were amongst the other companies with local representatives. Films were also marketed in Scotland by independent regional renters that were not cinema owners. These smaller concerns tended to concentrate on cheaper programmes of older films, arguing that newer films did not mean better films and that it might be better for a show to exploit tried-and-tested films that had been selected with a certain kind of audience in mind. The pioneer was William 'Prince' Bendon, who had started dealing films from his house in the south side of Glasgow in 1900, and established the Bendon Trading Company which mostly supplied music halls and theatres. United Films Ltd, established in December 1910 by ex-Bendon employee James Bowie, made a point in their advertisement: 'we are not showmen but are the best servants of showmen'.[33] Their attempt at vertical integration looked at production instead, and the story of their 1911 film *Rob Roy* is told later in this volume. Another spirited entrepreneur active around 1915 was Jack Carlton Baker, a maverick renter and local sales agent for the *Kinematograph Weekly*, who proclaimed his independence from the Renters' Association with the slogan: 'I mind my own business and give best value for money'.[34]

All these companies created a very complex patchwork of film supply, a fully fledged regional trade that succeeded in maintaining a regular supply system catering for the diversity of Scottish venues and audiences. They accommodated Scottish particularities such as the wider prevalence of cine-variety, even as live performance was being abandoned by the trade as it moved towards further industrialisation. At a time when the intermixing of live variety with short films had been almost completely abandoned in London, the 1915 *Bioscope Annual* described thirty-six per cent of

Scottish cinemas as presenting 'pictures and varieties'. Glasgow, Dundee, Ayr and the mining towns of North Lanarkshire and Linlithgowshire had a much higher proportion, with almost half of Glasgow's venues incorporating live turns. A less flexible, more centralised system of film supply would have struggled to support the relative autonomy of local cinema managers to run their show competitively.[35]

By 1915, the various backgrounds and trajectories of Scottish exhibitors and renters had produced a tangle of diverse and interconnected practices, and sustained all sorts of cinema spaces. You could find small and large venues, with fountains and palms in the foyer or hard wooden benches, charging 1d or 2s for the latest, glossiest Italian epic films accompanied by an orchestra, or an assemblage of Wild West shorts and slapstick comedies mixed with local entertainers and a singalong. If you lived in Glasgow, you could have that choice without even leaving the neighbourhood, as venues clustered together and competed with one another. Even as more top-down distribution models started to dominate, with the Hollywood majors promoting longer, more expensive films and mobilising people's growing affection for particular 'stars', a large part of the cinema experience was determined locally.

In Scotland, like elsewhere, moving pictures were initially presented in spaces that were already associated with existing cultural practices, from the fairground to the church hall and from the music hall to the legitimate theatre. As the number of new and repurposed venues ballooned, choice (of venue, but increasingly of film) became a central promise of urban exhibition, allowing audiences to exercise distinction and aspiration through their cinema-going practice. This competition in the cities funded the development of a strong regional distribution sector, connected to London but creating autonomous networks. While distribution methods responded to the overabundance of cinemas in Glasgow and Edinburgh, and to changes in the global film trade, they were in part dependent on the 'long tail' of small-town exhibition, where the more socially inclusive and often multi-functional nature of exhibition venues provided a different context for cinema.

Notes

1. Gaudreault and Marion, 'A Medium Is Always Born Twice . . .'
2. Toulmin, '"Within the Reach of All": Travelling Cinematograph Shows in British Fairgrounds 1896–1914', 31.
3. Frank W. Ogden Smith, 'Picture Theatre Finance', *Bioscope*, 4 June 1914, pp. 1008–9.

4. Burrows, 'Penny Pleasures: Film Exhibition in London during the Nickelodeon Era, 1906–1914'.
5. 'Round the Provinces', *Bioscope*, 2 October 1908. 'Round the Provinces' (p. 6) gives films shown at the Panopticon only. The reference to the number of shows is under 'Items of Interest' on p. 15.
6. Hiley, '"Nothing more than a 'craze'": Cinema Building in Britain from 1909 to 1914', 124.
7. Burrows and Brown, 'Financing the Edwardian Cinema Boom, 1909–1914', 17.
8. Griffiths, *The Cinema and Cinema-going in Scotland, 1896–1950*, 41.
9. 'The Story of the B.B. Pictures', printed pamphlet. Glasgow, National Library of Scotland's Moving Image Archive, 5/7/135. With thanks to Dr Peter Walsh for providing me with a scanned copy.
10. Lindstrom, 'Where Development Has Just Begun: Nickelodeon Location, Moving Picture Audiences, and Neighborhood Development in Chicago'.
11. J. J. Bennell, 'The Cult of the Cinema', *Bioscope*, 20 September 1917, p. xxii.
12. Hiley, '"Nothing more than a 'craze'": Cinema Building in Britain from 1909 to 1914', 119–21.
13. Brown, 'The Missing Link: Film Renters in Manchester, 1910–1920', 58.
14. Office of Public Works, 'List of premises licensed under the Cinematograph Act, 1909, and the Accommodation therein' (12 July 1913). Glasgow, Mitchell Library, Glasgow City Archives, D-OPW 61/5. This number was up from fifty-seven venues licensed in 1911 according to Oakley, *Fifty Years at the Pictures*, 7.
15. Low, *The History of the British Film 1906–1914*, 51.
16. This is consistent with the practices described by Burrows regarding cheap London cinemas, many of which obtained their programmes as a mixed package of very old and not so old films, from renters who, in turn, bought their stock in the second-hand market. Burrows, 'Penny Pleasures II: Indecency, Anarchy and Junk Film in London's "Nickelodeons", 1906–1914', 179.
17. Low, *The History of the British Film 1906–1914*, 20–2.
18. Burrows and Brown, 'Financing the Edwardian Cinema Boom, 1909–1914', 14.
19. 'E. H. Bostock', in *Who's Who in Glasgow in 1909*, Glasgow Digital Library. Available at <http://gdl.cdlr.strath.ac.uk/eyrwho/eyrwho0331.htm> (last accessed 2 April 2012).
20. Vélez-Serna, 'Preview Screenings and the Spaces of an Emerging Local Cinema Trade in Scotland'.
21. J. J. Bennell, 'The B.B. Film Service From Start to Finish', *Bioscope*, 20 September 1917, pp. xvi–xvii.
22. Ibid.
23. Ibid.
24. Kissell, 'Cinema in the By-ways', 26.

25. 'Away up North', *Bioscope*, 9 March 1911, p. 41.
26. Advertisement, *Bioscope*, 1 April 1915, p. 18.
27. By the late 1920s, Green's controlled twenty-four cinemas in Scotland. McBain, 'Green's of Glasgow: "We Want 'U' In"', 56.
28. 'Scottish Renter's Rapid Rise', *Bioscope*, 29 April 1915, p. 459.
29. Advertisement, *Bioscope* (Scottish section), 11 January 1917, p. 181; Advertisement, *Entertainer* 4, no. 177, 17 February 1917, p. 8.
30. *Bioscope*, 26 July 1917, p. 348.
31. *Bioscope*, 29 November 1917, p. 97.
32. McBain, 'Green's of Glasgow: "We Want 'U' In"', 56.
33. Advertisement, The United Films Ltd, *Bioscope*, 15 December 1910, p. 56.
34. 'Trade Jottings', *Entertainer* 3, no. 123, 5 February 1916, p. 9.
35. A more detailed discussion of the cinema manager's role can be found in Vélez-Serna, 'Showmanship Skills and the Changing Role of the Exhibitor in 1910s Scotland'.

CHAPTER 4

Cinema and Cinema-going in Small Towns

John Caughie

To begin with statistics. The census carried out on 2 April 1911 reported the total population of Scotland as 4,760,904. The four major cities of Glasgow, Edinburgh, Dundee and Aberdeen had populations of 784,496, 320,318, 165,004 and 163,891, respectively, constituting thirty per cent of the total population.[1] Predictably, there was a marked concentration of population around the industrial areas in the central belt of the country, with forty per cent of the population concentrated in the three industrial counties, Lanark, Renfrew and Dumbarton, an area which included Greater Glasgow, the heavy-industry areas which bordered it to the east, and the shipbuilding sections of the River Clyde to the west. It is these areas that created the legend of the popularity of cinema in the early part of the twentieth century, with Glasgow, as the hub of cinema-going, cinema-building and exhibition, claiming for itself the title of 'Cinema City'.

At the same time, the census reports that thirty-four per cent of the population lived in towns whose population was between two thousand and thirty thousand, and a further twenty-three per cent lived in mainland and island rural communities. That is to say, fifty-seven per cent of the total population lived in towns, villages or dispersed rural communities with populations up to thirty thousand. Scotland joins Ireland, Sweden and Norway with the lowest population densities in Europe; and the lowest densities in Scotland (around nine people per square kilometre) are in the dispersed communities of the Highlands and Islands, an area that constitutes almost fifty per cent of the land mass.

Turning to cinema exhibition, we have identified around eight hundred venues in which cinema, the cinematograph or animated pictures were shown with some regularity for some of the time between 1896, when the cinematograph was first exhibited in Scotland, and 1928, when cinemas began to consider moving to sound. This figure is by no means definitive, and it is cumulative rather than absolute, with many venues operating only for part of the time within the period. As well as the purpose-built cinemas which began to appear just before the outbreak of the First World War and the picture palaces which were built in the major cities before and after the war, the venues also include town halls, temperance halls, drill halls, church halls and a range of multi-purpose buildings. They do not, however, include the various temporary and mobile venues of the itinerant fairground trade.

Of this cumulative total, about a third of the venues were located in the four major cities – Glasgow, Edinburgh, Dundee and Aberdeen – all with populations over a hundred thousand. On our figures, Glasgow accounted for around 150 venues, while Edinburgh had fifty-two; Dundee had thirty-nine; and Aberdeen had twenty-six. While this concentration in major cities is significant, it is also significant that a little more than half the venues were located in towns with a population of less than thirty thousand. The figures are tentative, but the distribution of venues is suggestive.

If we are to understand early cinema and cinema-going as a national experience, it is important to understand its development and distinctiveness in small towns and rural communities. It is undoubtedly true that the concentration of cinemas in cities and major industrial areas engenders both competition and co-operation which encourages and facilitates dynamism, change and the evolution of the business of exhibition. Much of the history of early cinema is founded on the development of exhibition in major cities. At the same time, in Scotland, as elsewhere, around fifty-eight per cent of the audience were habitually attending around fifty-three per cent of the venues which were situated outside major cities and urban conglomerations. To understand the experience of cinema geographically as well as historically, this chapter is concerned with the distinctive experience of early cinema for more than half the population.

If there is a demographic imperative to account for the experience of early cinema for a significant section of the public, there is also in Scotland a suspicion that small towns have played a distinctive and particular part in cultural and social history. 'If modernism', says Robert Crawford,

> is often associated with urban centres – Paris, London, Dublin, New York – then Scottish modernism is strikingly eccentric. The Orkney and Shetland Islands and small coastal towns like Montrose were more important to its nurturing than Glasgow and Edinburgh.[2]

This eccentricity has a long history. The appeal of a decentralised, non-metropolitan and organically democratic community can be traced back at least to the 'godly band' of the Covenanters in the sixteenth century, and their insistence on the presbytery and the democratically elected kirk session as the arbiters not only of strict morality but also of education, poor relief, welfare and a kind of social justice within the community. It resurfaces in the nineteenth century with the 'Great Disruption' of 1843 when 450 ministers broke away from the established Church of Scotland over the issue of the Church's relationship to the State and of the definitive right of the local Presbytery to elect its ministers by popular assent, free from the patronage of wealthy landowners. As Tom Devine suggests, the parish became, at least in principle and in aspiration, a democratically elected 'Parish State' with responsibility for a kind of parochial 'public sphere'.[3] 'Eccentricity' – or decentralisation – seemed to be written into the democratic formation. Parishes and small towns carried a history of struggles and bloodshed for local autonomy and independence from bureaucratic or aristocratic determination which left traces in civic life, social institutions and regulation. Some traces of this history may account for the diversity and 'eccentricity' of the experience of cinema in small towns in Scotland, where local magistrates, rather than any centralised authority, were the arbiters of regulation. On this basis, my working assumption had been that it would be interesting to focus on small towns because they would be different from large towns, and would be a useful corrective to the standardisation of cinema history according to metropolitan norms. I had not expected small towns to be so different from each other.

My approach was selective rather than comprehensive. Rather than attempting to cover every small town in Scotland, I selected a handful of towns which seemed to be broadly representative of social and economic areas: Bo'ness, an industrial service town on the edge of the central belt; Hawick, a Borders textile town; Campbeltown, an agricultural and whisky town in the developing Clyde tourist area; Oban, a West Highland town within a crofting area and with a growing tourist trade; and Lerwick, geographically remote, but central to the North Atlantic fishing industry. In the 1911 census, the population of Lerwick was 4,664; Oban was 5,567; Campbeltown was 7,625; Bo'ness was 14,034; and Hawick was 16,877. Much of the study was conducted diachronically by a reading of local newspapers for each of these towns from 1896 to 1927. While local newspapers were a secondary source, often in the absence of any primary sources for cinema business, they provide an extremely useful route into mapping cinemas within the local culture: how they were regarded civically and how they were received by the popular audience. It is also important to recognise that, in the early years of the twentieth century, weekly local newspapers were a source not only of local news but of national and international news, with comments on the 'Imperial Parliament', letters from London, and, during the First World War, extensive coverage of diplomatic and military engagements. Inevitably and tragically, the wartime coverage included Rolls of Honour of the dead and missing, as testament to the immense impact that the war had on small communities. My account of early cinema in small towns is local, partial and indicative; but it is, at the same time, dynamic, inviting further work towards a more complete account.

The timetable and nature of first contact with the cinematograph in small towns and rural communities is instructive. The first recorded public screening of the cinematograph in the 'remote' Lerwick on 12 May 1897 was six months earlier than the first recorded screening in Bo'ness, thirty miles from Glasgow and twenty from Edinburgh, on 27 December 1897. The first screening in Lerwick formed part of the show of Robert Calder's Famous Cinematograph and Pictorial Concert Party, whose extensive tours are mentioned in Chapter 2 above. The first screening in Bo'ness, on the other hand, in the week between Christmas and New Year, was given in the Volunteer Hall by the Parish Church Bazaar Committee and chaired by the Reverend Robert Gardner BD.

In its first decade, the reach of the cinematograph and animated picture shows into rural communities was considerably more extensive than it was in later decades. It was welcomed by the Church and the landed gentry as evidence of 'rational entertainment', a scientific novelty which, as Charles Musser suggests, provided 'elevating experiences capable of winning citizens away from those rival amusements that were corrupting and base'.[4] The *Oban Times* in January 1898 records a cinematograph exhibition given in Inveraray by the Duchess of Argyll to an audience of around eight hundred, comprising three hundred children and her crofting tenants;[5] or, in December the same year, in Glendaruel in Argyllshire the cinematograph was included in 'Christmas Entertainments and Services organised by Mrs Walker-MacIntyre of the Manse for the schoolchildren, with a gathering in the evening presided over by the minister and well-attended by the gentry'.[6] Perhaps most surprisingly, in 1906, during a particularly intense period of internecine conflict in the Church after the contested union of the United Presbyterian Church and the Free Church in 1900, the *Oban Times* reports a cinematograph exhibition held in Strachur Parish Church which sought to bring together the two warring congregations in peace, reconciliation and moving pictures. The exhibition was held on Christmas Day.[7] In many rural districts the cinematograph appears not so much as an instrument of modernity but as an extension of the benevolent patronage of feudal landowners, or as an instrument of enlightenment and moderation in the Presbyterian Church.

In rural communities, north and south of the central belt, cinematograph exhibitions were typically 'treats', provided by gentry, schools or churches, usually through the agency of touring operators hired for the occasion. Lizars and Company, a Glasgow-based optical and photographic business which had specialised in lanterns and lantern slides, developed a business supplying cinematograph equipment and operators on demand across the country, and they were still operating in rural districts into the 1910s.

In small towns, on the other hand, as María Vélez-Serna has described in Chapter 2, early exhibition was more likely to depend on touring companies and concert parties who appeared in public halls. As well as the extensive concert party tours organised by individuals such as William Walker and Robert Calder, touring families were also common. The Ormonde family, led by Dr Ormonde, 'the marvellous Rosicrucian' and his wife, toured from Lerwick to Campbeltown as the 'Mahatmas of the West', bringing with them Edison's Animated Pictures. They were accompanied by their 'Sunflower Coterie'; Dr Ormonde and Mdlle Stella performed clairvoyancy, and their daughter, Lottie, played the violin.

The films these concert parties brought were mainly one-reelers – topicals, scenics, sketches and comic 'screamers' – which could easily be inserted into a mixed programme of variety and animated pictures. As well as providing entertainment, they broadened horizons through travel films – *A Trip to Samoa* (1905) or *Elephants Stacking Timber* (1903) – and functioned as a kind of newsreel, recording national events – *Scenes at Mr. Gladstone's Funeral* (1898) or *Great Railway Smash in England* (1906) – and international news – *Messina Earthquake* (1909). In October 1899 in Campbeltown, Calder advertises that he has '150 Pictures to Select From, 50 to 60 shown each night. With full concert party.'[8] This large catalogue of films came from a variety of sources. The titles he advertises include *The Dreyfus Trial – Scene at the Verdict*, one of the many dramatised versions of the Dreyfus affair produced that year. This may have been part of Méliès's version.[9] Other films listed included topical films of local interest, such as Warwick's *The Prince of Wales in Edinburgh* and the *Great Golf Match: Vardon v Park*, as well as military display titles *The Highland Brigade Camp at Lochaber*, and the *Fife and Forfar Light Horse*. Connections to world events were important, including a *Street Scene in Johannesburg* and *President Kruger in his Carriage* which were also probably Warwick Trading Company subjects from 1898. *Andrée at the North Pole* was an 1897 re-enactment of a doomed polar expedition, by the Lumière brothers.

Topicals and topical re-enactments of the proliferating 'small wars' that preceded the Great War – the Balkans, the Spanish–American, the Russo-Japanese and the Boxer Rebellion in China – were popular and, particularly during the Boer War, served to intensify patriotism. Touring companies also included local topicals in their programmes, and, again in Campbeltown in 1900, the Empire Kinematograph and Grand Concert Party advertises *The Kintyre Cattle Show* and *The Arrival of the Davaar at Campbeltown Pier* alongside *The Fight for the Flag in Transvaal* and *Lord Roberts and Our Troops*.[10] It is not difficult to see why small towns and rural areas welcomed the cinematograph as an instrument of enlightenment, up-to-date and modern, bringing a cosmopolitan perspective to the parochialism of non-metropolitan communities at the same time as it celebrated the daily life of the community.

This began to change with the movement towards fixed-site and purpose-built cinemas in small towns around 1912 and 1913, a little later than the movement in major cities. In 1912, the much-travelled Robert Calder gave up his concert party and went to manage a picture house in Fraserburgh, eventually returning to his original profession as a jobbing joiner. Many of his colleagues followed him, and touring companies began to disappear from small-town venues between 1912 and 1913. The reasons for this shift are discussed in Chapter 2 by María Vélez-Serna, but one significant factor is the arrival of the so-called 'super-film', the three- or four-reeler. An editorial in *The Bioscope* in 1911 remembers

> when a drama of 1,000 ft. was often grumbled at on account of its length, but it seems as if that day were past, and the demand for a picture play constituting the usual length of an entire programme has sprung up.[11]

The editorial regrets this shift and believes that it threatens the variety which is the defining characteristic of the cinematograph programme: a threat so serious, in fact, that it may kill the distinctive appeal of the cinema and its claim 'that it has come to stay'.

> Moving pictures are not merely of a dramatic or humorous type, but can give the public, in the short space of one, or maybe two, hours, a complete entertainment, diversified, full of variety, every picture depicting something totally distinct from the subject of another.[12]

The Bioscope, of course, misjudged the appeal of extended narrative, but it correctly identified a shift away from the short, enlightening, 'rational entertainment' which was broadly approved, towards the entertainment values of the narrative 'feature' film which dominated the programme and introduced modes of behaviour, romantic and sometimes criminal, which could no longer be universally approved as 'models' for young people and the unenlightened masses. Increasingly, in the 1910s and 1920s the reach of the cinematograph is retracted from dispersed rural communities and multi-purpose sites and is concentrated in fixed-site venues and purpose-built cinemas. From my sample, the Hippodrome in Bo'ness opened in March 1912, and in 1913 the Picture House in Campbeltown opened in May; the Picture House in Oban in July; the North Star in Lerwick in September; and the Pavilion in Hawick in November.

From the outbreak of the First World War onwards there was clearly a historical undercurrent of rationalisation in distribution, a globalisation of production through the increased efficiency of Hollywood, and a standardisation of exhibition. Partly this may have been due to a fall in production in countries in the arena of battles where industry was concentrated on wartime supply, but partly also it was due to the streamlining and centralisation of the American industry in and around Hollywood. Initially the effects of this undercurrent were most visible in large metropolitan centres, and most evident in the movement away from mixed programmes of live variety acts or 'turns' and a movement towards programmes that were 'pictures only'. A further editorial in *The Bioscope* a few weeks later in 1911 notes the significant difference in the demands of the audience in London for 'pictures-only' programmes and the continuing demand in the North of England for mixed programmes

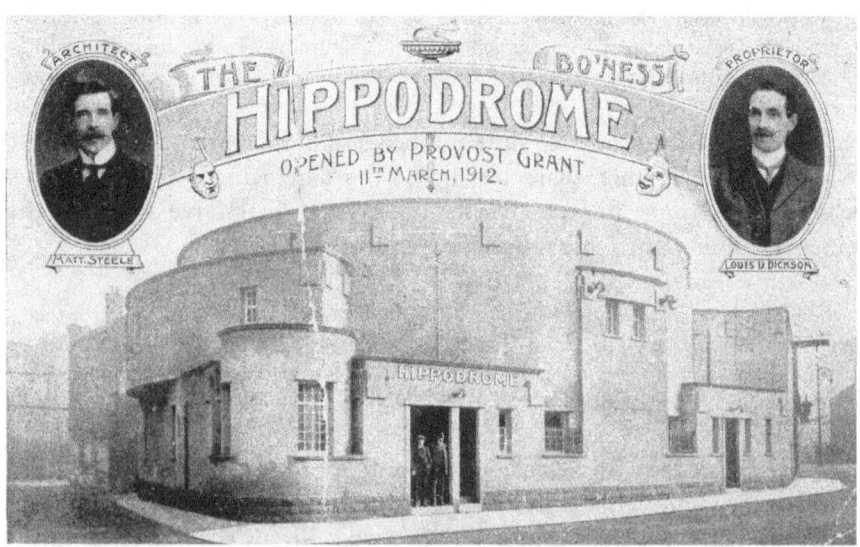

Figure 4.1 Copy postcard. Exterior of the Hippodrome Cinema, Bo'ness.

of pictures and variety 'turns'.[13] This distinction seems to be true also in Scotland, and seems to mark the distinctiveness of small town cinema. The history, however, is uneven.

Between 1897 and 1927, Bo'ness had six venues showing the cinematograph: the Drill Hall, the Town Hall, the Electric Cinema, the Hippodrome, the Pavilion and the Picture House (later known as the Star Cinema). At certain stages, there were four venues showing films in various mixes of variety and cinema to a Bo'ness and parish population of around 14,000 people. In 1914, all venues were showing a mix of cinema and variety; by 1927, two cinemas, the Hippodrome and the Picture House survived. In 1927, the Picture House was showing pictures only, while the Hippodrome was still mixing cinema with live acts.

What is striking in Bo'ness throughout the period is a curious pattern of venues attempting to give up variety turns, and then either reverting to a mixed programme or closing. The Pavilion, opened in 1919 by Louis Dickson, attempted, as a complement to the mixed programme which he showed at the Hippodrome, to show pictures only. After three years, it closed. In February 1913, the Electric Theatre announced that it was going to give up 'turns' and show pictures only. It introduced the 'novelty' of continuous performances in March – 'Come in when you like! Go out when you like!' – only to find, in April, that it had been taken over by new management, and variety 'turns' were reintroduced. It closed in 1915. Even the Picture House, converted from the old Episcopalian church and opening in January 1920, sought to establish itself as a cinema, showing pictures only. But in October 1921 it closed for refurbishment, reopening in December with a stage to allow for more variety turns. Touring variety, however, was becoming increasingly expensive, both in cost and in management time, and in 1922 the Picture House announced that, owing to 'trade depression', it was giving up variety and would continue as a pictures-only programme. At the same time, by 1927 the Hippodrome still persisted with a mix of live variety and film: at the very end of the period, it was still showing 'Mdlle Dalmere's TABLE CIRCUS, Performing cats, rats, monkeys, canaries, etc' or 'The Two Scotch Thistles' live on the stage alongside *The Thief of Bagdad* (1924) or *Nostromo* (1926) on the screen.

Of the three major venues in Hawick, the Hawick Pavilion, until at least 1928, was advertising itself as a 'Picture and Variety Theatre'; The Theatre on Croft Road was interrupting its picture-only programmes with visiting theatre companies from London; and the King's on a Saturday night became a Palais de Danse. Throughout the period, Hawick seems to have maintained the demand for a mixed programme of pictures and live acts, and all the major buildings were multi-purpose. This persistent mix of variety and pictures is an important feature of cinema in such small towns. It reminds us that for much of the population the experience of cinema-going was not yet a singular, silent or solitary experience of being lost in the movies, but was an active, participative and communal engagement in a 'good night out'. In such a mix of cinema and live performance, of 'absorption and theatricality', of watching and interacting with the performers, the audience was not yet quite disciplined, and people had not yet quite learned how to behave.[14] The cinematic experience was not yet finally defined.

At the same time, however, the persistence of variety is not universal. If we look at Lerwick, or Oban or Campbeltown, we find that the cinemas, from their introduction in 1913, were advertised as picture houses, and their advertised programmes seemed mainly to be pictures-only. In Lerwick at the opening of the North Star the audience is assured by the management 'that the pictures shown will be of a highly instructive and educative character with occasional comicalities thrown in' and that they 'intend running it as a picture house only without the aid of any extra "turns"'.[15] At the same time, the North Star programme may at certain points have incorporated live turns. The letter book of Arthur Mann, the manager of the North Star cinema in Lerwick, which survives for a few months in 1915, shows that, although they are not advertised in the local press, he is booking variety acts through an agent in Dundee. Already, however, he is complaining about the difficulty of securing the quality of touring acts that he wants:

> My dear Macnair
> Just a word – if you value your reputation as an agent don't for God's sake book The Three Nelsons for in sketches or want of real histrionic talent they Are The Limit.
> I have your wire stating you can't fix up an artist for next week and am not certain whether or not I will keep them. I really think it would pay me to let them go now – however you did your best. Many thanks for your efforts on my behalf.[16]

It seems probable that touring live acts booked through an agent disappeared from the programme soon after, to be replaced only occasionally by known local performers – local musicians, local comedy and local recitations – or with occasional special live events: a singing competition in the North Star in 1926, for example, open only to men working in the fishing industry. For the most part, however, programmes seem to have been pictures-only after 1918, and by the 1920s, unlike the programmes of Bo'ness or Hawick, the programme looked much like the programme of many a city-centre cinema in Glasgow or Edinburgh. The problems in Lerwick of geographical access and the unpredictability of North Sea weather made touring variety a particular problem and an expensive risk.

If we turn to Oban, however, we find that touring concert parties with their cinematograph exhibitions seem to disappear almost completely from about 1903, and that, when the Picture House opens in 1913, it opens as a picture-only cinema. As María Vélez-Serna indicates in Chapter 3, the building of cinemas was fuelled by a variety of factors, not simply by increased demand. The disappearance of concert parties, with or without animated pictures, however, is unusual. Oban had been connected to Glasgow and the south by the West Highland Railway since 1897, and, in that sense, is much more accessible than Lerwick. So remoteness is not, in itself, the answer. What seems distinctive is that Oban had a rich entertainment programme throughout the period, but it was a Gaelic programme, with Gaelic singers and Gaelic choirs, with the Gathering Hall and other public halls catering to Gaelic taste. In the 1911 census, more than fifty per cent of the population of the Oban area habitually spoke Gaelic, and the culture was still closely tied to the Jacobite heritage: the letters columns of the *Oban Times* are full of debates about the clans, the correct translation of Gaelic words, the 1745 Jacobite Rising and the precise role of Bonnie Prince Charlie. In 1914, just after the outbreak of war, a recruiting sergeant could still make an appeal in Ballachulish to 'the descendants of the old brave men of the "45"'.[17] Within that particular culture, Oban is as different from Lerwick or Bo'ness as it is from Glasgow or Edinburgh, and what determines the place and the functioning of cinema and of touring concert parties is not transport links but a distinctive and local cultural history.

However, within that distinctive and local cultural history and within the diversity of the experience of cinema, certain common currents in popular taste begin to emerge. Westerns were popular throughout the period and in all regions. The popularity of Charlie Chaplin began to emerge in 1915, though in Campbeltown, in May 1915, he was still sufficiently unfamiliar to be billed as Charles Chaplain. His growing popularity, particularly when he was contracted to Essanay, instituted a system of block booking where control of the main features of the programme passed increasingly away from the local exhibitor to the centralised distributor. The popularity of serials had a similar effect. Something of this can be seen in the few months of the North Star letter book which are preserved in the Shetland archive. On 16 August, Arthur Mann wrote to Green's Film Service from whom he booked his films to ask 'whether you will hire me the *Trey of Hearts* alone for exhibition at Lerwick on Monday and Tuesday of next week'. *Trey of Hearts* is the current serial of which he had already received two instalments. It is clear, however, that he was unhappy with the service he was receiving from Green's, and attempting to extricate himself from their service. On the programme of films which he had just received, he comments:

> Some of these films are substitutes for the one's [sic] listed and while – these unfortunately not being filled – I have nothing to say as regards the substitutes. What I do complain of is that most of the films in my programme for this week are quite 40 weeks old. I think I have intimated to you before that I absolutely refuse to pay 10/- for a 5/- service and I will be glad to know whether you mean to improve.[18]

In a letter to McNair, his agent for variety acts, Mann commented that Green's were 'living up to their bad reputation' and that he intended to stop doing business with them.[19] In the end, he threatened Green's with legal action and successfully acquired the remaining episodes of *Trey of Hearts*. At the same time he was approaching B.B. Pictures, the other large distributing company in Glasgow, with a view to establishing a contract with them. And in the meantime, he was discussing with his 'Governor', his managing director in Aberdeen, the possibility of setting up a circuit which would include Brechin, Laurencekirk, Stonehaven, Aberdeen, Lerwick, Kirkwall, Thurso, Forres and Banff. All of this is being done by letter, dependent on the mail boat between Aberdeen and Lerwick which ran daily in the summer season and less regularly and more dependent on weather in winter.

Lerwick may be an extreme case of accessibility and services – there are records of screenings being cancelled because the 'North boat' had failed to deliver oil for the generator or because companies had failed to make allowances for the long daylight on Shetland evenings – but it gives some sense of the difficulties of organising distribution and exhibition in remote communities. There are no similar archive records for most other small towns, but it is likely that similar patterns of business and local difficulties developed. And yet, the programmes did materialise, exhibition was driven by the same pressures towards rationalisation, centralisation and 'block-booking' as were experienced by cinemas much closer to the metropolis, and common threads of popularity and demand did emerge. By the 1920s, *Les Miserables*, *Quo Vadis*, *Bonnie Prince Charlie*, *The Idle Class* or *Peg o' My Heart* might be seen across Scotland, in city centres and small towns, and the beginnings of a common cinema culture – or a globalised industry – began to emerge.

In many small towns the cinema was seen as a civic asset, part of the heraldry of the town's modernity, an integral component of the town's cultural self-perception, a guarantee of being 'up-to-date'. In Bo'ness and Hawick, the new cinema buildings in 1912 and 1913 were opened by the provost of the town with a full civic ceremony that welcomed the potential of the cinema to 'educate and elevate the tastes of the people',[20] and there is frequent comment in the press on developments in the cinemas. In Lerwick, for example, where the local Council showed relatively little interest in the North Star Cinema, a letter from a retired schoolmaster in Burravoe and a Fellow of the Royal Geographical Society was published the *Shetland Times*:

> Sir, The floating of a picture palace company in Lerwick is a significant feature of the progress of that town, and wherever these houses have been established the social status of the people has advanced both in a diminution of drink consumption and in general purity.[21]

Throughout Scotland, cinema proprietors were part of a new entrepreneurial class and many of them took on roles in local councils, and, in a few cases, as Members of Parliament. The civic status of cinema, its sense of belonging to the community, may have been enhanced by the production of local topicals, as discussed in Chapter 8. In Bo'ness, Hawick and Campbeltown, for example, cinema proprietors, local cinematographists or commissioned agencies like Gaumont or Green's supplied the cinemas with short topical films which recorded the major events in the town's calendar – the Bo'ness Children's Festival or the Borders Ridings – or illustrated the daily lives of the inhabitants. While these topicals were commercially designed to bring spectators to the cinema, they also played a part in establishing the cinema as a reflection of civic and social life, depicting the community in its everyday activities and its special occasions.

It is also true, however, that in other small towns – from my sample, Oban – the cinematograph and the cinema seem ancillary. In Oban, for much of the period, the cinema programme was advertised only occasionally. Even in the 1920s, there could be months without any advertisement of the programme appearing in the press and they were dependent instead on handbills, distributed on the street. This meant that the cinema was barely noticed by the local press as a civic and cultural amenity, and so it seems more clearly defined as a commercial activity than a part of the local culture. Part of this may be attributed to a cultural predisposition, and part to the intervention of external investors. While Lerwick had its registered office in Aberdeen, much of the investment came from local merchants, and the company chairman lived locally in Hillswick. Oban, on the other hand, seems largely to have been instituted by investment from entrepreneurs in Glasgow and there is little evidence of local initiative. To resist any temptation to attribute the distinctive apathy towards cinema of the civic institutions in Oban to a West Highland or Island mentality, the Lewis Picture House, opening in strict Presbyterian Stornoway in 1915, was opened with a civic welcome by the Provost – with every confidence 'that the house would be so conducted that those who had misgivings about "the pictures" coming to Stornoway would find that their fears were groundless'.[22]

It is worth saying something about the distribution of cinemas in the West Highlands and Islands since it attracts a certain mythology. If one draws an almost straight line from Lerwick to Oban, with a slight bend to incorporate Thurso, and then continues the line to Campbeltown, only one purpose-built or fixed-site cinema exists to the west of that line: the Lewis Picture House in Stornoway. This is an extensive land mass with a population of around 350,000, but with a very low population density. Apart from Stornoway (with a population of 3,806), Portree is the only settlement to have a population larger than 1,000; the 1911 census records its population as 2,431. I have been able to find evidence in *The Bioscope* of only one screening in Portree, an illustrated talk on Canada in 1909 in the Gathering Hall with 1,500 feet of cinematograph films.[23] (Illustrated talks on Canada were common while Canada was eagerly recruiting immigrants from the crofting and rural communities.) The mythology which the absence of cinema has attracted is that it is due to the dominance of the strict Presbyterian Free Church of Scotland, popularly known as the 'Wee Frees'. There is undoubtedly evidence that the Presbyterian Church did not approve of certain forms of entertainment – there is a Skye slander case in 1912 when a Free Presbyterian minister was found guilty of slander for having called the parishioners who organised a concert in Borreraig Public School in Glendale, Skye, the 'scum and refuse' of the place – but there is very little evidence that the Church intervened directly in forbidding cinema, at least in the first few decades. The Picture House in Oban was built on land adjoining St Columba Church, and while church representatives attended the Dean of Guild's meeting at the planning stage it was to ensure that it did not infringe on their property. There is no evidence of objections in principle. For much of the period after the disputed Union of 1901, the Presbyterian Church was much more caught up in its own factional battles, and accounts of damage to and possessions of church property and psychological or physical damage to its ministers are much more common than any evidence of a particular concern with the cinema. On the basis of the available evidence, one has to assume that the distribution of venues for cinema exhibition in rural districts in the West Highlands was due to population density and transport access rather than to the moral objections of the Church. Thurso and Wick had populations of more than 3,000 and had been accessible by the Highland Railway since 1871. Oban and Campbeltown had populations over 4,000 and were accessible by rail or by sea. An additional factor may have been that, in many Highland and Island towns where cinema appeared, there were significant seasonal population boosts either through tourism or through the itinerant North Atlantic fishing industry which followed the herring around the West and North Coasts. While the Free Church may have been significant in establishing a local culture that was not immediately predisposed towards cinematographic entertainment, the evidence of Stornoway and Oban suggests that, at least in the early years, this predisposition was not absolute and the role of religion was prescriptive rather than proscriptive.

In fact, the town from my sample in which the Church seems to have played the most vociferous part was Hawick. The role of cinema was much discussed in Hawick. In a Town Council debate in 1910 on whether it would be appropriate to have cinematograph screenings in the Town Hall on a Sunday, one Councillor urged that it was 'better to go to cinematograph shows than to fried fish shops'.[24] In its report on the Cinema Commission in 1917, the *Hawick News* is more sympathetic to the view taken by Chief Constable Ross in Edinburgh, who provided evidence that there was little evidence of a link between cinema and juvenile crime, than it is to the contrary view of Chief Constable Thom of Hawick, who believed that boys were stealing money in order to go to the cinema, and urged local 'censure' for children's matinees [25] Taking a more extreme view in 1918, in the week in which the Town Hall was showing *The Birth of a Nation*, the Reverend Mr Robertson of the Baptist Church spoke of the problem of childhood and the 'abominable immorality that was rampant in the country'. 'There were contributing causes to the awful problem of youth today' he said,

> slackening of parental control, the widening of the gates of indulgence, the slackening of moral restraint, and one of the greatest contributing agencies to the demoralisation of the young of the country, to his mind, was the CINEMA AND PICTURE HOUSE... [T]he cinema, in the presentation of its suggestive pictures to the mind, was one of the devil's most blatant instruments for the destruction of all that was pure and holy.[26]

In 1919, the Reverend John Anderson of the United Free Church, lecturing on the virtues of Alexander Peden, one of the leading Covenanters of the seventeenth century who anticipated a new godly race, denounced cinematographic entertainment as a major obstacle to the dawning of that new race.[27] On each occasion, however, on which the *Hawick News* reported the hostility of the Church or, indeed, of the police, to the popularity of cinema, the editor stepped in to modify the views, and, while there was clearly an ongoing debate between the Church, the police, the Council and the press on the opportunities, threats and popular appeal of the cinema, it does not seem to have dented the enthusiasm of Hawick audiences, and the vigour of the debate may, in fact, be a symptom of its particular civic significance. The Church in Hawick seems to have been exceptionally vocal rather than unusually effective, and what is striking is how long a shadow cultural history throws – the Jacobites in Oban and the Covenanters in Hawick – and how much cinema is situated within a geography of local memories and cultures.

This study of cinema in small towns and rural communities is by no means comprehensive or universal. Further particularities, divergences and local anomalies will no doubt emerge as one moves through North-East market towns and farming communities, East Coast fishing towns and the agricultural townships of the South-West. While one can trace in the years after the First World War the undertones of globalisation and standardisation, the study of cinema in small towns and remote locations reminds us how contingent that process was, and the extent to which the history of cinema was not yet quite determined by the metropolitan experience. Precisely the excitement of this period of cinema history is that it has not yet been quite institutionalised or 'house-trained'. 'The cultural turn', says Miri Rubin, 'asks not only "How it really was" but rather "How was it for him, or her, or them?"'[28] And that question, and cinema's place within it, raises questions not only of cultural history but of the geography of that history, and the distinctiveness of local cultures and local experiences.

Notes

1. Population statistics are drawn from census reports in *A Vision of Britain Through Time*, available at <http://www.visionofbritain.org.uk> (last accessed 13 September 2016).
2. Crawford, 'Country Lear'.
3. Chapter 5, 'The Parish State', in Devine, *The Scottish Nation, 1700–2000*, 84–102.

4. Musser, *The Emergence of Cinema: The American Screen to 1907*, 56.
5. *Oban Times*, 15 January 1898.
6. *Oban Times*, 31 December 1898.
7. *Oban Times*, 6 January 1906.
8. *Campbeltown Courier*, 14 October 1899.
9. Luke McKernan offers a complete annotated filmography of Dreyfus films here: McKernan, 'Lives in Film, no. 1'.
10. *Campbeltown Courier*, 13 October 1900.
11. *Bioscope*, 7 September 1911, p. 471.
12. Ibid.
13. *Bioscope*, 21 September 1911, p. 591.
14. See Fried, *Absorption and Theatricality*. And for cinema, see Rushton, 'Early, Classical and Modern Cinema'.
15. *Shetland Times*, 13 September 1913.
16. Shetland Archive. Wet Copy Letter Book. North Star, Lerwick. Letter from Arthur Mann to A. B. Mcnair (agent) Dundee, 5 August 1915. With kind permission of Shetland Archive.
17. *Oban Times*, 19 September 1914.
18. Shetland Archive. Wet Copy Letter Book. North Star. Lerwick. Letter from Arthur Mann to Green's Film Service, 16 August 1915. With kind permission of Shetland Archive.
19. Letter from Arthur Mann to A. B. Mcnair (agent) Dundee, 30 August 1915. Wet copy letter book. North Star. Lerwick. With kind permission of Shetland Archive.
20. *Bo'ness Journal*, 15 March 1912.
21. *Shetland Times*, 17 May 1913.
22. *Bioscope*, 25 March 1915, p. 1151.
23. *Bioscope*, 13 May 1909, p. 7.
24. *Hawick* News, 21 October 1910.
25. *Hawick News*, 26 October 1917.
26. *Hawick News*, 4 January 1918.
27. *Hawick News*, 7 February 1919.
28. Rubin, 'What Is Cultural History Now?', 80.

CHAPTER 5

Making a Living at the Cinema: Scottish Cinema Staff in the Silent Era

Trevor Griffiths

Explanations for cinema's appeal more often than not begin, and in some cases end, with the films and the stars who populated them. From early in the First World War, exploitation made much of the presence on celluloid of figures, whose familiarity was such that only first names need be employed. In November 1915 the Grand Theatre, Glasgow, mounted a 'Charlie [Chaplin] and Mabel [Normand]' competition, in which members of the audience were invited to act out a scene between the two Keystone performers.[1] Yet the appeal of cinema-going as an embedded recreational form rested on more than stars alone. For exhibitors, including major circuits such as Green's, variable support for films rendered them an unreliable source of income, producing weeks in which, at the box office, famine followed feast. More consistent returns were to be generated by encouraging repeat visits by patrons and these would be maximised by making the cinema-going experience as pleasing as possible. Key to this was the in-house staff who engaged in face-to-face contact with picture-goers. In 1926, Green's produced a booklet for staff on *Cinema Service*, which among other things recommended greeting audience members with a smile, while warning against being 'perky-pungent or fresh'.[2] If such advice was reserved for front-of-house staff, the quality of the cinema-going experience more generally rested on the broad range of cinema employees, from the manager who, especially in the early days, booked the programme and then endeavoured to sell it to potential customers; the musicians who in the silent era did much through their accompaniment to realise the film for audiences; to the operators (projectionists) whose ability to run films at the correct speeds and without undue flicker made watching a comfortable experience; to the attendants responsible for managing the audience within the auditorium and ensuring their safety, particularly the safety of cinema's many young patrons; and to the cleaners charged with the removal of the detritus of previous screenings, which could range from tobacco ash, chewing gum and spectacles, to, in one case, half a dozen bottles of hair restorer.³ Surveys of cinema-goers from the mature silent era, such as the questionnaires issued by Sidney Bernstein of the Granada theatre chain, confirmed that, while pictures and stars remained the principal attractions, members of the audience, both male and female, attached importance to the quality of the orchestra, while, for both, 'Courtesy and Service of Staff' figured above price in their calculation of whether or not to attend.⁴

For all the importance of such employees for the everyday functioning of cinema, the history of this labour force, seen in terms of its conditions of employment, its levels of pay, the degree to which it attempted to organise collectively and its gender balance, remains substantially unwritten, with only the musicians subject to extended discussion.⁵ This chapter seeks to extend coverage to the generality of employees, but proceeds with certain limitations in mind. First, for reasons which will become apparent, it is a workforce which it is impossible accurately to quantify in overall terms. What we have instead are occasional snapshots, indicating the staffing of individual halls, comprising a small and not necessarily representative sample of the six hundred or so venues active across Scotland at any one time. So, the Cinema House, on Glasgow's Renfield Street, a city-centre hall with a capacity of seven hundred when it opened in 1911, employed a staff of nineteen, comprising a manager, an assistant manager who also doubled as chief operator, an assistant operator, a spool winder, a booking 'clerkess', four ushers, two check takers, a front doorman, a head cleaner, a cleaner and an orchestra of five.⁶ As a point of comparison, the Hippodrome in Bo'ness which opened a year later and was licensed to hold 1,000 ran with two operators, two money takers, five checkers and an orchestra of six, along with an unspecified number of cleaners.⁷ Secondly, available documentation does not allow equal billing to be accorded to all grades of employee, with star status reserved for a favoured few. Within the limits enforced by this selective approach, several broad themes are pursued: the experience of working in the cinema is considered with regard to overall career patterns and the degree to which mobility between grades was either possible or facilitated. This has implications for the temper of relations within the industry. On a tour of cinemas in the United States, the Scottish correspondent of *The Bioscope*, James McBride, encountered a generally harmonious relationship between employers and their staffs, so that capital and labour could be viewed as operating in partnership.⁸ How far that could apply within a Britain marked by industrial confrontation and political radicalism in the very years in which silent cinema reached maturity provides part of the matter of this chapter: to what extent did the class antagonism characteristic of Red Clydeside colour the industrial politics of the Scottish cinema trade and what features of the industry functioned either to emphasise or diminish its impact?

Alongside income and status hierarchies, differences of gender also pervaded this labour force. Women were extensively employed within the industry, making up just over half of the Cinema House's initial complement of nineteen. Yet their role was substantially confined to providing the music (two pianists and a cellist at Renfield Street), and performing various ancillary tasks as ushers and cleaners. Their weekly wage rarely exceeded £1, while among male employees only the apprentice and therefore teenage spool winder fell below that figure.[9] Engagement in more responsible posts remained rare, so that in 1919 the trade paper *The Entertainer* could remark that, while the adult cinema audience was over seventy per cent female, no woman fulfilled the role of booking manager to ensure that films matched the preferences of an increasingly feminised generation of picture-goers.[10] This observation was all the more significant, coming as it did immediately after a period during which the demands of war and attendant problems of labour shortage in non-essential industries had created opportunities for young women in particular to move into areas of work from which they had previously been excluded. The degree to which the cinema came to offer a 'new and democratic space' or provided a setting in which established gender differences continued to be played out is considered towards the end of this chapter.[11] To begin with, however, a brief overview of roles and relationships across the various grades is offered.

For most of those employed in picture houses across Scotland, the industry was not their principal means of support throughout the year. Of the 390 venues listed in the 1921 edition of the *Kinematograph Year Book*, reflecting the industry at its postwar peak, and for which full details on the frequency of screenings are available, about one-third ran fewer than two shows a night across six nights of the week, often opening only on selected days through the week.[12] Here, hours worked were not such as to make the cinema a sole or perhaps even primary source of employment. Even when shows were more frequent, the presence of staff employed on a part-time or flexible basis was notable. Some were required only when shows were due to start or between screenings, so that the standard industrial working week (from 1919) of forty-eight hours was experienced by few. So, while operators were paid on the basis of a forty-nine-hour week, for musicians the standard that applied just after the First World War was twenty-four, with rehearsals and matinees additional to that.[13] Even then, most orchestras, rather than being engaged across the year, were hired for the period of peak business from autumn to spring, missing out the slacker summer months, when takings could be depressed by a combination of potentially better weather and less attractive programmes. The Cinema House (from 1925 the Regent Cinema) was not untypical in reducing its orchestra between the end of April and the beginning of September.[14] Frustration at this repeated pattern of employment may have informed the view of the Amalgamated Musicians' Union in September 1920 that its members could not 'be put away in a cupboard when not wanted for months at a time, and then brought out and dusted and put back into the orchestra when required'.[15] Even operating boxes, where safety considerations and the need to maintain oversight of the operation of complex machinery demanded more sustained attendance and continued diligence, were often staffed by part-timers. At Pringle's Picture Palace in Edinburgh during the opening months of the First World War, the operator Hugh Simmers was employed during the evenings only, his days being spent working as an electrical salesman.[16] Such cases informed debate in wider labour circles. At a meeting of the Aberdeen Trades Council in December 1920, the delegate from the National Union of Railwaymen called, in language redolent of conventional gender priorities, for 'one man one job', pointing up in the process the complications created by those who secured second jobs in local picture houses.[17] The methods usually employed to assign individuals to certain occupations and so begin to reconstruct their experiences and their outlook fall down in the face of such complexity. For example, attempts at quantification from census returns become redundant, and even isolated observations such as that by the Ministry of Labour which estimated the number affected by the wage agreement concluded between the Exhibitors' Association and the Musicians' Union across Scotland (with the exception of Aberdeen) at five hundred must be treated with due caution.[18]

The challenges posed for the trade by this pattern of work were not only statistical. Negotiations over wages were often complicated. In response to demands in 1916 for a 5s a week increase in pay to compensate for the rise in the cost of living during the early stages of the war, some proprietors, such as those at the Empire and the Pavilion in Motherwell, urged that, as they only offered 'spare-time employment', the burden should be borne by those who were the workers' principal employers.[19] For unions within the entertainment industry, the basic task of securing high and stable levels of organisation was rendered more complex. In 1928, the Scottish Trades Union Congress heard complaints from the National Association of Theatrical Employees and the Musicians' Union of blacklegging by those, who when working as, among other things, miners, railwaymen or shop assistants were diligent in paying their union dues, but who were less so when engaged in second jobs at local cinemas.[20]

The predominance of part-time employment sustained the view that the functioning of picture houses depended overwhelmingly on a small number of staff, whose contribution could be deemed essential. Such was the opinion of Louis Dickson of the Hippodrome, Bo'ness, in making the case in May 1916 for exemption from military service for the cinema's Music Director, Robert Miller. Dickson sought to distinguish between Miller and most other members of staff, arguing that only three of the Hippodrome's complement of thirteen (plus cleaners) were key to the house's everyday operations, rendering them irreplaceable: namely, the manager, the operator and Miller himself.[21] Such observations serve to justify the focus on these grades in the discussion that follows, but in the process light is thrown on relations across the workforce as a whole.

In shaping the fortunes of the business, the role of the manager was central.[22] As James McBride observed, unlike the position in the USA, directors of cinema companies across Britain rarely had direct experience of the trade, their interests being overwhelmingly commercial, driven by the desire to maximise returns.[23] By contrast, managers had, with few

Figure 5.1 Workers from the Hillfoot Picture House, Alva, on a staff outing, no date. Photo courtesy of the National Library of Scotland's Moving Image Archive.

Figure 5.2 Staff of the Gaiety Theatre, Clydebank, later the Bank Cinema, c.1910. Photo courtesy of the National Library of Scotland's Moving Image Archive.

exceptions, spent most of their working lives in the exhibition sector or a related part of the entertainment business. Such at least is suggested by individual profiles offered by the trade press. So, J. W. J. ('Billy') Marsh of Glasgow's Cinema House worked for a time as an electrical engineer before becoming an electrician in a London music hall. His cinematic career began in the operating box at the Southall Electric Theatre followed by the Cinema House, where he was appointed second operator on its opening in 1911. After six months, he was promoted to the post of chief operator, later becoming assistant manager.[24] Other managers brought with them a solid grounding in the practice of showmanship. In the mid-1920s, the running of the La Scala at Saltcoats was in the hands of a former violinist on the variety stage, who had himself managed touring theatrical companies.[25] Armed with such experience, managers were charged with securing programmes likely to appeal to house patrons, overseeing the maintenance of the physical fabric of the building, ensuring order, particularly at crowded Saturday evening shows, and thereby securing the house's reputation within the local community. In pursuing their business, managers found themselves answerable to a variety of publics: directors and shareholders, anxious as to the profitability of the concern, audience members seeking attractive entertainment with which to occupy their free time and a workforce occasionally vociferous in defence of its status reflected both in wages and working conditions. For *The Bioscope*, this often seemed a thankless task:

> A manager works the longest hours, receives less ha'pence relatively, and more kicks actually, and has to put up with more interference than any other member of the staff. He is called 'manager' because, in spite of this, he sometimes manages to hold down his job.[26]

In so doing, they would often experience considerable change, both collectively and individually. Over time, their role in booking films and constructing programmes progressively diminished with the growth of theatre circuits and the actions of surviving independents who increasingly moved to pool their booking arrangements in order to bolster their ability to secure the most attractive subjects on the best (lowest) terms. So, by 1927, it was estimated that around one-third of exhibitors across Scotland were part of circuits for booking purposes.[27] This left managers to apply the knowledge and experience of showmanship garnered within the cinema trade or some other branch of the entertainment business in order to maximise the appeal of programmes. A leader in the *Scottish Kinema Record* in September 1922 emphasised the importance of their efforts, identifying 'exploitation' as a key contributor to maintaining profitability in a difficult trading environment.[28] Energies were employed selectively and were more often designed to enhance further the appeal of subjects which promised to be popular than to bolster outwardly unattractive programmes. In November 1928, the manager of the Rialto, Kirkcaldy, in anticipation of the impending screening of MGM's version of *Annie Laurie* contributed pieces to the local press, had the theatre bedecked with heather and required all (presumably female) ushers and check-takers to wear tartan skirts, white jumpers and plaids. Shows were preceded by a prologue involving the performance of the song accompanied by a Highland reel.[29] Appropriate product placement further acted to enhance brand awareness: at the Kinnaird Picture House in Dundee in September 1927, displays were mounted to boost the Herbert Wilcox production of *Nell Gwynn*, utilising candles bearing the lead character's name and *Our Nell* soap. Less predictably, 'trench' (in reality, dog) biscuits were employed that same year to push the film adaptation of Bruce Bairnsfather's *The Better 'Ole* at Poole's Synod Hall in Edinburgh, providing justification of sorts for the accompanying tag line: 'Poole's Programmes *always* take the Biscuit and so will Syd Chaplin in "The Better 'Ole" at the Synod 'Ole' (emphasis in original).[30] Payment structures provided a clear incentive for the systematic pursuit of exploitation. At both the King's Cinema in Aberdeen and the Regent in Glasgow, managers received, in addition to their basic salaries, a bonus equivalent to five per cent of net profits.[31]

Unsurprisingly given this level of reward, managerial posts proved attractive, so that some four hundred were reported to have applied for the vacancy at the La Scala in Paisley in 1928, the position going to a man who had previously worked as assistant manager with the British National Opera and Carl Rosa Opera Companies.[32] Successful managers were much in demand and could experience considerable geographical mobility, sometimes voluntary but occasionally enforced by circuits anxious to place them in houses where their impact would be maximised. For example, the directors of Caledon Pictures Ltd opted in 1927 to transfer the manager of the Elder Picture House in Glasgow to the nearby Lyceum in Govan. Long-distance moves were not uncommon, so that the same year the manager of the Picture House in Glasgow, part of the Provincial Cinematograph Theatres Ltd chain, found himself transferred to the circuit's house in Sheffield.[33] Faced with such a change, managers would have to respond to meet the tastes of their new customers. Yet in doing so they drew on the broad principles of showmanship that applied regardless of setting. A common approach to boosting business was promoted and managers within circuits were often encouraged to share ideas. From late in the First World War, managers of Green's houses met on a monthly basis to discuss approaches likely to maximise business.[34]

Gatherings in the interests of commercial efficiency were one thing; organisation to promote a sense of collective purpose among managerial personnel quite another. It took until the final full year of the silent era for a Kinema Managers' Association to be formed in Glasgow and district, with an attendance of forty-two at the inaugural meeting. From that point, the Association appears to have largely fulfilled a social function, with a billiards competition held the following September.[35] As a force in industrial politics, by contrast, it appeared mute, a function of the rivalry for custom which precluded the kind of collusion evident in other areas of the economy.[36] Managers' loyalties continued to be directed more to boards of directors and shareholders rather than to their peers, an outlook reinforced by linking wages to profitability. Showmanship remained the most crucial of managerial functions, a practice which extended beyond the films themselves to advancing the general interests of the firm.

In pursuing the latter, managers drew on business models long-established within the entertainment sector, based on acts of generosity designed to secure loyalty within the workforce and support across the wider community.[37] Cinemas thus regularly staged performances for the benefit of the immediate locality, acts of beneficence given due publicity in the trade and mainstream press. Opening nights provided an early opportunity to establish the house's importance within the community. So, in March 1921, the proceeds of the inaugural performance at the Queen's Picture House, Kilmarnock, were presented to the town's infirmary.[38] Local or national emergencies served to stimulate charitable efforts. As the First World War progressed, entertainments were mounted to fund the provision of comforts for the troops or served to amuse their children or their wounded comrades. In January 1917, the staff of B.B. Pictures organised a Social and Whist Drive for the Limbless Soldiers' and Sailors' Fund.[39] Ongoing problems occasioned by high casualty rates sustained such provision beyond the war's end. In July 1919, the Thursday performance at the Kilbirnie Cinema House went to support the Fallen Heroes' Fund.[40] In mining districts, the hardship resulting from prolonged industrial disputes in 1921 and 1926 galvanised acts of support, so that halls in Coatbridge, Bannockburn, Kirkcaldy and Whifflet assisted in the funding of local soup kitchens in 1921, while the later more extended struggle generated comparable responses in Burntisland, Broxburn and Shotts, among other places.[41] On occasion, support extended beyond the financial, as when in August 1919 the manager of the Picture House, Denny, organised an outing for his patrons, and the Picture House, Kilmaurs, supplemented the questionable attraction of an onion-eating contest by distributing clothing to needy members of the audience.[42] Beyond charitable acts, cinemas also supported other community endeavours, the Picture Pavilion in Largs raising funds to provide jerseys for the local Largs Thistle Football Club.[43] As the trade press occasionally felt bound to acknowledge, there was more to this than mere altruism, the good standing of houses being thought to encourage a more loyal clientele.[44]

A commitment to the business was also to be nurtured among the workforce. In the winter months, indoor gatherings provided occasions at which trading success could be celebrated and the contribution of staff acknowledged. The annual social for employees of the Arcadia Picture House, Bridgeton, held at Bellgrove Hall in March 1926 included an address by the company chairman, while the following year the dance organised for the staff of the King's Cinema, Perth, was overseen by the manager and the chief operator.[45] During the summer, not even Scotland's capricious climate could discourage firms from organising outings for their employees. Late in May 1927, the staff of the Lyceum, Govan, were treated to a motor tour around the Three Lochs before proceeding to high tea at the Queen's Hotel, Helensburgh. The previous year, employees of the Picture House, Falkirk, had been taken to Aberfoyle, moving on to a programme of sports at Stronachlachar on Loch Katrine, competing for prizes provided by the house's manager.[46] Outings were usually scheduled for Sundays, never a day of regular business in this period, and served to bring staff together in a manner which the usual work routine seldom if ever did. Nevertheless, the emphasis regularly given to the generosity of employers and managers in facilitating such gatherings also served to underline the hierarchies informing the work relationship. The point was taken up by McBride, who noted that the British industry had largely failed to follow the American practice of enabling workers to partake in profits by encouraging them to take up shares in the business.[47] Instead, reward structures emphasised a reliance on discretionary benevolence, as firms opted either at Christmas or the end of the financial year to distribute bonuses among their staffs. This also enabled distinctions within the workforce to be acknowledged, so that in 1927 the Regent Picture House agreed payment of a £100 bonus to the manager, with future income linked in part to profits, while the following year a 'satisfactory' trading performance was seen to justify payment of the usual bonus to remaining staff, which was not to exceed £20 in all.[48] In the Scottish case, then, profit-sharing assumed a form that accentuated rather than moderated existing power relationships.

Within workplace hierarchies, operators occupied an ambiguous position. Their responsibility for overseeing technically complex machinery and high-tension electrical equipment made them key to the successful and safe projection of film. Yet as *The Bioscope* lamented in a series of articles late in 1926, this importance was not reflected in pay levels.[49] At the Grand Central Picture House, Aberdeen, run by James F. Donald (Cinemas) Ltd, the operator's wage lagged well behind those of the manager and the orchestra conductor, and even fell below the pay of most of the house's musicians.[50] For some, this low standing occasioned little surprise. The words of the presiding Sheriff at a sitting of the Dumfries and Galloway Military Appeal Tribunal in September 1916 may have captured a wider perception: 'It may be only my ignorance, but I thought that all an operator had to do was to turn a handle'. Opinion within the trade was, however, clear that, as the Agent's response had it, 'He has a good deal more to do than that', so that *The Bioscope* pressed that action be taken to enhance the post's standing.[51] The solution was seen to lie in regulating entry to the trade through a formalised system of training, an approach that had been discussed in Edinburgh in 1920 at a meeting between the Edinburgh and East of Scotland branch of the Cinematograph Exhibitors' Association (CEA) and the Electrical Trades Union (ETU), which aspired to represent the interests of local operators. That had resulted in proposals that entrants to the operating box serve a five-year apprenticeship, with wages beginning at £1 a week at sixteen years of age, rising to £2 10s in their final year.[52] Even this did little to transform pay levels and worked, if anything, to confirm the discrepancy between the job's outwardly skilled status and attendant levels of reward.

This outcome could be traced in part to the absence of a single body to press the operators' concerns. The problem appeared to have been addressed in the later years of the First World War, as losses due to voluntary recruitment and then conscription worked to deprive cinemas of men of military age. By 1917, a shortage of operators was noted across Scotland, resulting, it was claimed, in the closure of many rural halls.[53] In urban centres, managers noted the problems of retaining staff, with operators in particular being lured elsewhere by the promise of higher rewards.[54] With their scarcity value thus signalled, operators moved to organise in their own defence. In the east, from Edinburgh to Aberdeen, the Electricians took up the operators' cause. Around Glasgow, by contrast, the lead was taken by the National Association of Theatrical Employees (NATE), so that by 1919 it was claimed that some three-quarters of operators across the city were members.[55] Yet by 1925, NATE was seeking the support of the Musicians' Union in pressing for recognition by the CEA; its membership in local cinemas was described as almost non-existent.[56] While volatility in enrolments owed much to a change in the economic environment, the effect was compounded by continued ease of access to the operating box. Across the 1920s, both NATE and the ETU pressed for a minimum age to be established for entrants to this branch of the trade. The call by the Clyde branch of the ETU in 1930 to fix sixteen years as the minimum was, like previous such demands, posed in terms of safety.[57] The Glen Cinema tragedy in Paisley at Hogmanay the previous year, in which seventy children died, had occurred in a hall in which the assistant operator, responsible for rewinding the reel, was a fifteen-year-old boy.[58] For the unions, however, concern also centred on the supply of labour, the influx of the war years having resumed during a decade of heightened unemployment when the cinema appeared to offer a source of regular and sustained work. This may help to explain the appeal of the fraudulent scheme run in the early 1920s by Peter Robert Mackenzie of Edinburgh, offering training as an operator on payment of a deposit of up to £50.[59]

If the absence of controls on entry complicated attempts at organisation, the problem was compounded by a tendency to regard the operating box as a stepping-stone towards the manager's office. Alexander Roberts, manager of the Picture House, Dalkeith, in 1917, was not unusual in having previously worked as an operator, in this case at the Hippodrome in Bo'ness.[60] It was a progression frequently charted in the trade press, as in 1920 when the chief operator at the Wishaw Picture House succeeded to the manager's position.[61] The importance attaching to individual upward mobility served to weaken a sense of collective purpose among operators and continued to frustrate attempts to enhance their job status.

No such ambiguity marked the standing of cinema Music Directors. Their importance to the health of the business had long been recognised, to the extent that publicity even before 1914 made much of the quality of musical provision and the person primarily responsible for that. In outlining its appeal to patrons, the Cinema House in Edinburgh made reference in 1912 to the comfort of its seats, the 'Perfect Courtesy from the Well-Trained Staff of Attendants' and the 'Perfect Ventilation', but also stressed the presence of a 'Perfect Bijou Orchestra of Skilled Musicians'.[62] The following year, the centrally located Princes Cinema and the Silver Kinema in Nicolson Square underlined the quality of the musical accompaniment by reference to their respective Music Directors: Herr Ernest Kosting and K. Deablitz, the latter described as 'a Principal of the Scottish Orchestra'.[63] Further west, the presence of a German musician, Herr Iff, was presented as proof of the quality of music accompanying the films at Glasgow's Hillhead Picture Salon.[64] Into the 1920s, halls continued to give prominence to orchestral provision when setting out the range of amenities on offer. At Synod Hall in August 1928, attractions for patrons included new cinematograph equipment and lighting effects, alongside a New Orchestra under a Music Director recruited from the Plaza in London.[65] The importance which audiences attached to such provision must, in most cases, be inferred from such publicity. More direct insights are occasionally afforded us, however. Late in 1919, picture-goers at Montrose's Municipal Cinema were reported as complaining at the programmes mounted, on the unlikely grounds that they provided too much for the money paid, being considered too long and comprising too many films, so that intervals of 'good music' were considered preferable. Perhaps reflective of this view, the local press took to publishing details of the music planned for each performance.[66] In some cases, managers went further, inviting patrons to determine the accompaniment to programmes. A Musical Committee was established at the La Scala, Aberdeen, in 1918.[67]

Such moves, which might be thought to pre-empt the role of Music Directors were, in practice, rare and selections of music were for the most part entrusted to the professionals, who aimed to ensure, as was observed of the showing of D. W. Griffith's *Way Down East* at the New Picture

House, Edinburgh, in November 1922, that the accompaniment 'assisted materially in imparting a realistic touch to the film'.[68] This was thought to be best achieved by the appropriate matching of sound and image. Where practice fell short of that ideal, criticism invariably followed. In July 1915, *The Entertainer* remarked with disapproval about a performance in which a deathbed scene had been accompanied by the *Merry Widow Waltz*.[69] The problem survived the war, so that, as late as 1927, an unnamed correspondent to the *Cheltenham Echo* gave voice to a commonly held perception in noting the manner in which

> the haunting strains of the exquisite 'Chant Hindou' was pressed into service to give special point to a sand storm, a rough-and-tumble fight, and, above all things, a close-up of the very low comedian consuming a banana.[70]

To ensure against such lapses, Music Directors had charge of cinema music libraries. As a result, a change in personnel would often entail an overhaul of both the available repertoire and the orchestra itself, justifying the emphasis placed in house publicity on the presence of particular personalities. In the great majority of houses, the recruitment and pay of musicians rested with the Music Director, rather than the manager and the directors. The latter would seek to set an overall budget for the orchestra. At the Regent in Glasgow in 1928, for example, a maximum charge for the provision of music was fixed at £88, but the Music Director was encouraged to keep costs down to nearer £80.[71]

In effect, then, musicians at most of Scotland's cinemas were employees of the Music Director, and not of the company itself. Rather than this encouraging recurrent conflict within orchestral ranks, a shared outlook between conductor and rank-and-file musicians was more often evident. J.S. Ratcliffe, Organiser of the Scottish and North-East District of the AMU, noted that Music Directors were broadly supportive of the union's attempts to extend membership across local picture houses.[72] Individual points of controversy provided practical instances of a shared perspective. In the summer of 1914, management at the Alhambra in Stirling dismissed the house's pianist without reference to the Music Director. The latter thereupon resigned, leading the AMU to call out the whole orchestra in support. Within two days, both the pianist and the Music Director had been reinstated and those musicians still outside the union had agreed to observe officially sanctioned rates of pay.[73] The constructive relationship thus demonstrated was cemented further in June 1916 by the formation of a Music Directors' section of the AMU for Scotland as a whole.[74] Subsequent wage agreements between the musicians' organisation and the CEA also came to include minimum rates for Music Directors.[75]

A unity of purpose was increasingly apparent, informed by a shared desire to uphold the reputation of the house orchestra by ensuring that qualified and so fully competent players were recruited. Career dynamics also promoted a sense of solidarity. The conductor's podium was a less likely route to the manager's office than was the operating box. A survey of the trade press across the 1920s reveals only one instance in which a Music Director was appointed to the manager's position, at the Capitol in Glasgow in 1927.[76] More often, tensions between conductor and manager emerged, most frequently around the notice given for impending programmes. Here, lack of time would prevent effective rehearsal, detracting from both the quality of performance and the broader standing of the Music Director.[77]

This then was a workforce characterised by significant income and status differentials and subject to considerable variations in working conditions. The obstacles to effective organisation on more than a sectional basis and a consequent disinclination to mobilise in defence of collective interests appeared marked. As a result, this was never an industry subject to major set-piece confrontations. Yet broader trends in industrial politics continued to impinge, in particular a move towards more elaborate systems of collective bargaining and a growing readiness to flex collective muscle. Here, as in other sectors, the years around the First World War were crucial. In 1914, the AMU's Scottish organiser was of the view that 'the Glasgow managers and proprietors are all very decent' and that they broadly accepted attempts to boost union membership and establish agreed rates of pay across the city.[78] Ten years later, the mood was altogether different, exhibitors being seen to lack a 'spark of humanity', as concern for profit overrode consideration for their workers.[79] The intervening decade had witnessed significant developments in collective organisation among both employers and staff. The relentless competition for business had long discouraged a common outlook among firms in the exhibition sector, but this was overcome in the face of a series of external challenges, from growing moral surveillance, to the readiness of legislators to see the trade as a useful source of tax revenue, and a labour force pressing for wage increases in the face of an escalating cost of living.[80] In 1916, the AMU, as well as attempting to enforce observation of agreed wage schedules for musicians across all local cinemas, moved to secure a 5s a week War Bonus for its members. The response was fragmentary, some companies declaring a readiness to meet the increase while others claimed an inability to fund further payments during a period of depressed trade.[81] An approach to the CEA to negotiate collectively over pay was rebuffed, the employers stating that such subjects did not fall within their remit.[82]

By the final year of the war, however, such constitutional niceties were set aside as exhibitors sought to grapple with the threat of escalating wage costs occasioned by a combination of price inflation and a growing shortage of key grades of labour. Collective bargaining procedures were further consolidated immediately after the Armistice, with the formation of a Conciliation Board for the industry across Scotland covering most cinema staff, among whom a sense of collective purpose was nurtured by boom conditions across the trade.[83] In quick succession, joint agreements were concluded covering rates of pay for musicians, operators and, through the efforts of NATE, cash-takers, ushers, attendants, cleaners and programme- and chocolate-sellers.[84]

The formation in early 1920 of an Industrial Council for all employed across the entertainment industry more generally marked the high point in the postwar acceptance of collective bargaining procedures.[85] That year, the Conciliation Board provided the mechanism by which a dispute involving the MU and Green's, who had responded to a call for a £5 weekly minimum for musicians by dismissing all bar their houses' pianists, was settled.[86] Even then, the limits of conciliation in reconciling differences over wage bargaining were apparent. Proposals for increases in rates advanced by both the Conciliation Board and the Industrial Council failed to secure support from either the CEA or the MU in 1919 and 1920 and a sense gained ground that processes worked to delay wage adjustments in a period of rapid change in the wider market.[87] When the Conciliation Board failed to secure agreement on a reduction in pay early in 1921, exhibitors, faced with a marked downturn in business, declined to take the matter to the Joint Industrial Council unless any decision by that body were considered binding. Although agreement was finally reached by means of the Conciliation Board, the experience justified a growing readiness on the part of employers to look beyond collective bargaining machinery, culminating in three months' notice being served in June 1923 for termination of the Board.[88] By the middle years of the decade, as an upturn in trade encouraged unions to seek a restoration of earlier wage reductions, exhibitors continued to seek alternatives to formal conciliation mechanisms, first through resort to arbitration under the Ministry of Labour for houses in and around Glasgow in 1925, while, in the following year, Edinburgh exhibitors threatened a wholesale lockout rather than concede an advance in rates.[89] An agreement between the CEA and the ETU over operators' pay in July 1926 brought to an end a decade of unusual collective tensions within the trade.[90] For what remained of the silent era, negotiations would once more focus on conditions within individual houses. In many respects then, the economic instability of the period during and immediately after the Great War brought an intensity to the industrial politics of the cinema trade that challenged without ever wholly undermining expectations of broadly co-operative relations between managers and workers.

It was a period of significance also for the industry's gender politics. Women were prominent in the provision of entertainment, a few managing the concert troupes which offered some Scots early exposure to the cinematograph while others supplied instrumental accompaniment to or vocal interludes within the cinema programme. Staffing arrangements more generally worked to confirm the domestic realities shaping most women's lives. To them was assigned responsibility for cleaning the auditorium and attending to the needs of an increasingly young audience, an extension of the caring, nurturing role practised within the home. In 1926, a female attendant was charged with finding seats for a girl aged twelve attending the Arcadia Picture House in Glasgow to protect her against the close and it appeared improper attentions of an adult male patron. Yet even here the limitations imposed by conventional ideas of femininity were apparent, as a male attendant and the assistant manager were eventually tasked with ejecting this persistent and unwelcome picture-goer.[91] With attendants occasionally subject to assault by audience members brandishing among other things razors and, in one extreme case, a hatchet, the desirability of a male presence in the theatre seemed obvious.[92] So, women were rarely encountered in positions of authority in which they were able to exert an influence over the programme's content. They could be found in the orchestra pit, but rarely wielded the conductor's baton. Similarly, the operating box was, before 1914, substantially a male preserve. While figures for Scotland are not available, some indication of the prevailing gender balance is offered by the observation that in the early months of the Great War only two cinemas in the area overseen by the London County Council employed women as operators and one of those worked as an assistant.[93] The subsequent enlistment of large numbers of employees created new opportunities for women and the extent to which female roles were amended as a result has much to tell us about contemporary perceptions both of the nature of the work and of assumed gender attributes.

By mid-1916, the prospect of greater numbers of female orchestral players led the AMU through its house journal to offer warnings of the physical toll taken by a punishing schedule that comprised rehearsals in the morning, an afternoon matinee and two shows in the evening: 'many robust men have been killed off with the strain'.[94] Where women had replaced men, it was claimed, while the playing was ladylike, it often lacked vigour and signs of fatigue were evident towards the end of the performance. Such arguments were not allowed to pass without comment. 'A Lady Instrumentalist' noted that problems emerged more from 'a perfect deluge of incompetent amateur musicians of both sexes' than from a greater female presence in orchestras.[95] Whatever the truth, the scope for greater female recruitment appeared real, so that even positions of authority were deemed suitable. Such was the view of the Local Tribunal which adjudicated on Louis Dickson's appeal on behalf of the Music Director of the Hippodrome in Bo'ness, which rejected his case arguing that 'a woman could easily be got to fill his place'.[96] If the trade press is an accurate guide, however, instances of such substitutions were few and were mostly confined to family members. One of the few women to become an orchestra leader, at the Palace in Aberdeen in 1915, was the daughter of the Music Director, then absent on military service.[97] The approach of the musicians' unions remained to secure agreed rates of pay for all, regardless of gender, ensuring that women were not taken on as cheap substitute labour. Despite this outwardly 'open' policy, by the mid-1920s women made up only fifteen to seventeen per cent of the ordinary membership of the union's Glasgow branch.[98] This may suggest that the bulk of female instrumentalists remained outside the union and continued to see performing in local picture houses more as a supplementary, part-time activity than as a potential career. References to female conductors and Music Directors remain sparse beyond 1918, underlining the limited change wrought by the war.

A similar observation applies to the operating box. In the first year of the war, the potential for extending the female presence was raised by Miss Emily Clements of Stratford East in London, in a letter to the Home Office, which advanced the suggestion 'that a woman could act as a bioscope operator at a picture palace as well as a man'.[99] The discussion that followed found no fundamental objection to women working in the nature of the job, doubts centring rather on safety concerns surrounding their dress, which should be 'an overall of serge or other woollen and uninflammable material', rather than 'cotton and flannelette'.[100] A covering Home Office minute raised a further point of concern in the operators' responsibility for safety. This involved the kind of prompt action felt to be beyond the capacity of most females: 'Women are more apt to lose their heads than men'.[101] A more significant obstacle was posed by the lack of experience in overseeing the operation of complex machinery, with the result that Military Appeal Tribunals, while rejecting the view that operators should be exempt from call-up, were equally clear that this was not work where female labour could readily be substituted. In the case of Hugh Simmers, the view was that the post could be filled by men over military age or those unfit for service.[102] Although training was offered potential female applicants by agencies such as the Edinburgh College of Cine Operators, the trade's own Employment Bureau gave preference to wounded ex-servicemen, an act of patriotism cementing cinema's part in the national effort late in the war. The appointment of a recipient of the Victoria Cross to the operating box at Glasgow's Annfield Halls was consequently trumpeted by the trade press.[103] At the same time, State bodies also pressed the employment of those no longer able to fight.[104] The gender balance within the cinema remained substantially unchanged, despite the stresses of war. Although in the 1920s women were found in both managerial and proprietorial positions, their scarcity served to underscore the absence of change elsewhere.

Cinema staffs of the silent era were varied in character, marked by significant and enduring differences in income, status and gender. They constituted a substantially part-time and unorganised labour force. Many sought work in the cinema but few anticipated a career from it. For the historian, as for picture-goers of the time, most employees remain out of view, meriting attention only in extraordinary circumstances, as when two female attendants at a Methil cinema suffered serious injury when, having washed their hands in petrol to remove paint and then run them under water, they proceeded to dry them by means of a gas jet.[105] This chapter has largely focused on a group of key workers, but has used them to point up relations between the various jobs and grades. In the process, it reveals a workforce subject to a managerial regime which stressed the discretionary power of employers and the importance of acts of generosity, from outings to wage bonuses. For some, the end to which a cinematic career was directed was the manager's office, muting any tendency to see relations within the workplace in antagonistic terms. The cinema was never a plausible arena for the playing out of class confrontations. Neither, however, was it wholly free of conflict, especially in the years during and immediately after the Great War, as recurrent bargaining over wages generated high levels of labour organisation and repeated threats of strike action. The retreat from confrontation, marked by the abandonment of collective-bargaining mechanisms, was rapid and profound, and created space for an older, paternalistic form of industrial leadership to reassert itself. Cinema workers were not class warriors. Their collective efforts, however, did much to shape the cinema-going experience for growing numbers of patrons across the silent era. They may have lacked the prominence given to stars of the silver screen, but their contribution to the growth of cinema as a medium of mass entertainment merits recognition.

Notes

1. *Entertainer*, 16 October 1915, p. 4, announcing the competition to be held the week beginning 8 November.
2. *Bioscope*, 14 October, p. 66; 21 October 1926, p. xv.
3. *Entertainer and Scottish Kinema Record*, 13 September 1919, p. 5; for an entertaining, and enlightening, list of audience remnants left behind at the Panopticon cinema on Glasgow's Trongate, see Bowers, *Stan Laurel and Other Stars of the Panopticon*, 166–7.
4. *Bioscope*, 4 August 1927, p. 20, for male patrons the orchestra ranked equally with the star.
5. Ehrlich, *The Music Profession in Britain since the Eighteenth Century*, Chapter IX; Davison, 'Workers' Rights and Performing Rights'.
6. National Library of Scotland, Moving Image Archive (hereinafter NLS, MIA), 5/22/3, The Glasgow Picture House Ltd, Minute Book, Meetings of Directors, 27 November, 5 December 1911.
7. National Records of Scotland (hereinafter NRS), HH30/4/4/21/1, Military Service Appeal Tribunal records (Lothians and Peebles), Notice of Appeal.
8. *Bioscope*, 2 September 1926, p. 36.
9. NLS, MIA, 5/22/3, Meeting of Directors, 5 December 1911.
10. *Entertainer*, 4 January 1919, p. 10.
11. The first view is pursued in Porter, 'Women Musicians in British Silent Cinema Prior to 1930', 564.
12. *The Kinematograph Year Book, 1921*.
13. *Scottish Cinema* (hereinafter *SC*), 5 July 1920, p. 29, for the conditions for operators in Aberdeen; The National Archives (hereinafter TNA), LAB 83/3315, Cinematograph Exhibitors' Association (Scottish Branch), Notice of Conciliation Board Agreement with Amalgamated Musicians' Union, 3 December 1919.
14. NLS, MIA, 5/22/4, Glasgow Picture House Ltd, Minute Book, Meetings of Directors, 12 April 1926; 1 May 1928.
15. University of Stirling, Special Collections (hereinafter UoS, SC), MU/1/2/116, *The Musicians' Report and Journal*, September 1920, p. 2.
16. NRS, HH30/19/2/6/3, Military Service Appeal Tribunal Records (Lothians and Peebles), Application for Exemption.
17. *Scottish Kinema Record* (hereinafter *SKR*), 18 December 1920, p. 12.
18. TNA, LAB 83/3315, Notice of Conciliation Board Agreement, 3 December 1919.
19. UoS, SC, MU/4/2/1/1/3, Amalgamated Musicians' Union, Glasgow Branch, General Meetings Minute Book, 9 April 1916.
20. *Bioscope*, 26 April 1928, p. 57.
21. NRS, HH30/4/4/21/4, Reasons in Support of Application.

22. 'Kinema managers are the key men of the industry, and our prosperity and good-will entirely depend upon their ability, efficiency, tact and character': Hutchison, *The Complete Kinemanager, Etc.*, 1.
23. *Bioscope*, 2 September 1926, p. 36; on the backgrounds of directors of Scottish cinema companies, see Griffiths, *The Cinema and Cinema-going in Scotland, 1896–1950*, 38–42.
24. *SC*, 29 March 1920, p. 10.
25. *Bioscope*, 29 October 1925, p. 56.
26. *Bioscope*, 22 April 1926, p. 69.
27. *Bioscope*, 17 November 1927, p. 65; see also Griffiths, *The Cinema and Cinema-going in Scotland, 1896–1950*, 122–3; Vélez-Serna, 'Showmanship Skills and the Changing Role of the Exhibitor in 1910s Scotland'.
28. *SKR*, 30 September 1922, p. 1.
29. *Bioscope*, 21 November 1928, p. iv.
30. *Bioscope*, 29 September, p. iv (Kinnaird); 3 November 1927, p. vi (Synod Hall).
31. Cinema Museum, Lambeth (hereinafter CM), Aberdeen Picture Palaces Ltd, Minute Book, Meeting of Directors, 26 March 1919; NLS, MIA, 5/22/4, Meeting of Directors, 11 July 1927.
32. *Bioscope*, 3 October 1928, p. 42.
33. *Bioscope*, 9 June, p. 44 (Caledon); 8 December 1927, p. 63 (PCT).
34. *Entertainer*, 18 August, p. 16; 27 October 1917, p. 7.
35. *Bioscope*, 19 May, p. 64; 12 September 1928, p. 49.
36. Bowden and Higgins, 'Short-Time Working and Price Maintenance', 319–43.
37. Bailey, 'A Community of Friends: Business and Good Fellowship in London Music Hall Management, c.1860–1885'.
38. *SKR*, 26 March 1921, p. 8.
39. *Entertainer*, 27 January 1917, p. 11; see also 30 December 1916, p. 11, and 13 January 1917, p. 10, for further examples.
40. *Entertainer and Scottish Kinema Record*, 26 July 1919, p. 3.
41. *SKR*, 28 May, p. 10; 4 June, p. 9; 25 June 1921, p. 5; *Bioscope*, 3 June, p. 41; 1 July, p. 33; 30 September 1926, p. 50.
42. *Entertainer and SKR*, 23 August 1919, p. 8; *SKR*, 10 December 1921, p. 1.
43. *SKR*, 4 February 1922, p. 7.
44. *Bioscope*, 28 October 1926, p. 83.
45. *Bioscope*, 18 March 1926, p. 60; 10 March 1927, p. 64.
46. *Bioscope*, 26 May 1927, p. 52; 2 September 1926, p. 58.
47. *Bioscope*, 9 September 1926, p. 21.
48. NLS, MIA, 5/22/4, Meetings of Directors, 11 July 1927; 27 December 1928; CM, The Queen's Rooms Cinema Syndicate Ltd, Minute Book, 15 September 1927.
49. *Bioscope*, 28 October, p. vii; 4 November, p. vi; 18 November, p. vi; 2 December 1926, p. vi.

50. CM, James F. Donald (Cinemas) Ltd, Grand Central Picture House, Return re Employees, 14 February 1927.
51. *Scotsman*, 12 September 1916, p. 3, for the contrasting views on operators' work.
52. *SC*, 8 March, p. 27; 22 March 1920, p. 24; NLS, MIA, 5/11/7, Cinematograph Exhibitors' Association, Edinburgh and East of Scotland Section, Minute Book, Section Meeting, 21 June 1921.
53. *Entertainer*, 17 February 1917, p. 13.
54. *Entertainer*, 19 May 1917, p. 8; 25 May 1918, p. 9.
55. *Entertainer and SKR*, 14 June, p. 9; 23 November 1919, p. 7.
56. UoS, SC, MU/4/2/1/3/2, Musicians' Union, Glasgow Branch, General Meetings Minutes, General Meeting, 12 April 1925; see also *Bioscope*, 18 March 1926, p. 56. By 1935, it was acknowledged that the combined membership of NATE and the ETU in London 'would not fill a respectable charabanc': Lloyd, *Light & Liberty*, 212.
57. TNA, HO 45/20876, Entertainments, Cinema Operators, Age and Qualifications, W.M. Biswell, District Sec., ETU to Rt Hon. William Adamson, Secretary of State for Scotland, 29 April 1930.
58. TNA, HO 45/20876, ETU to Town Clerk of City of Glasgow, 5 March 1930; NRS, HH1/1981, Scottish Home Dept, Cinemas, Extended Notes of Proceedings in Paisley Cinema Disaster, Trial of Charles Dorward, Evidence of James McVay, p. 114.
59. *Bioscope*, 8 October 1925, pp. 71–2.
60. NRS, HH30/17/2/25/6, Military Service Appeal Tribunal Records (Lothian and Peebles), Appeal for Exemption.
61. *SC*, 21 June 1920, p. 25; see also *Bioscope*, 15 December 1927, p. 53; 26 January, p. 54; 18 July 1928, p. 56, for similar career moves.
62. *Scotsman*, 30 September 1912, p. 1.
63. *Scotsman*, 3 May, p. 2; 24 September 1913, p. 1.
64. *Entertainer*, 4 October 1913, p. 14.
65. *Scotsman*, 25 August 1928, p. 1.
66. *Entertainer and SKR*, 29 November 1919, p. 1; *SKR*, 3 July 1920, p. 1.
67. *Entertainer*, 2 March 1918, p. 18.
68. *Scotsman*, 7 November 1922, p. 10.
69. *Entertainer*, 24 July 1915, p. 5.
70. *Bioscope*, 10 November 1927, p. xiii.
71. NLS, MIA, 5/22/4, Meeting of Directors, 8 August 1928; see also 5/22/3, Meeting of Directors, 28 December 1911, for details of the contract concluded with the house's first Music Director.
72. UoS, SC, MU/1/2/7b, *Musician's Report and Journal*, October 1913, p. 9.
73. UoS, SC, MU/1/2/8b, *Musicians' Report and Journal*, July 1914, p. 15.
74. UoS, SC, MU/1/2/9a, *Musicians' Report and Journal*, June 1916, p. 8.
75. TNA, LAB 83/3315, Terms of Agreement between CEA (Scottish Branch) and AMU (Scottish Branch), 13 May 1921.

76. *Bioscope*, 21 July 1927, p. 50.
77. *Bioscope*, 12 May 1927, p. xii.
78. UoS, SC, MU/1/2/8b, January 1914, p. 9; see also MU/1/2/7b, September 1913, p. 6, 'Picture show proprietors seem to be a very fair set of men to deal with on the whole'.
79. UoS, SC, no cat., *Musicians' Journal*, July 1924, p. 5.
80. Griffiths, *The Cinema and Cinema-going in Scotland, 1896–1950*, pp. 103–9; the revival of CEA organisation in the east of Scotland is noted in *Scotsman*, 24 July 1918, p. 4.
81. UoS, SC, MU/1/2/9a, April 1916, p. 5; MU/4/2/1/1/3, AMU Glasgow Branch, General Meetings Minute Book, General Meeting, 9 April 1916.
82. UoS, SC, MU/4/2/1/1/3, General Meeting, 14 May 1916.
83. UoS, SC, MU/1/2/10b, *Musicians' Report and Journal*, January 1919, p. 5.
84. *Entertainer*, 22 January 1919, p. 7; *SKR*, 6 March, 1920, p. 15; *SC*, 3 May 1920, p. 30.
85. UoS, SC, MU/1/2/11b, *Musicians' Report and Journal*, April 1920, p. 1.
86. Ibid., September 1920, pp. 2–3; MU/4/2/1/1/4, Musicians' Union, Glasgow Branch, General Meetings Minute Book, Special General Summoned Meeting, 8 August; General Meeting, 12 September 1920.
87. UoS, SC, MU/1/2/10b, November 1919, p. 4; MU/4/2/1/1/4, Glasgow Branch, Special General Summoned Meeting, 26 September; General Meeting, 10 October 1920.
88. UoS, SC, MU/4/2/1/1/4, Special Summoned General Meeting, 10 April 1921; MU/4/2/1/3/1, MU, Glasgow Branch, General Meeting Minutes, Special Summoned General Meetings, 22 May 1921; 30 April 1922; General Meeting, 8 June 1923.
89. UoS, SC, MU/4/2/1/3/2. MU, Glasgow Branch, General Meetings, General Meeting, 9 August 1925; TNA, LAB 83/3315, Terms and Conditions of Employment for Musicians employed in Cinemas in the Glasgow and West of Scotland Area, 21 November 1925; *Scotsman*, 17 March, p. 7; 20 April 1926, p. 6.
90. *Bioscope*, 1 July 1926, p. 33.
91. *Bioscope*, 25 March, pp. 48–9; 25 November 1926, p. 56; NRS, CS46/1926/12/60, Court of Session, Second Division, 1 April 1926. Reclaiming Note for Pursuer in Causa William McIlwain against The Arcadia Picture House (Glasgow) Ltd.
92. *Bioscope*, 11 November 1926, p. 66; 11 August, p. 46; 25 August 1927, p. 54.
93. TNA, HO 45/20876, James Bird, Clerk to London County Council to Under Secretary of State, Home Office, 10 May 1915.
94. UoS, SC, MU/1/2/9a, *Musicians' Report and Journal*, June 1916, p. 1.
95. Ibid., August 1916, pp. 1–2.
96. NRS, HH30/4/4/21/2, Local Tribunal, 3 June 1916. It might be noted, with a due sense of irony, that Dickson would himself be replaced by his

daughter on joining up later in the war. (I am grateful to John Caughie for this information.)

97. UoS, SC, MU/1/2/8b, *Musicians' Report and Journal*, February 1915, p. 8.
98. UoS, SC, MU/1/2/10b, *Musicians' Report and Journal*, August 1918, p. 2, reporting the increase in wages secured for a female pianist at Greenock; MU/4/2/1/3/2, Glasgow Branch, General Meetings Minutes, General Meetings, 8 February 1925; 14 February 1926; MU/4/2/1/3/3, General Meeting, 13 February 1927.
99. TNA, HO 45/20876, Miss Emily Clements to Home Office, 12 March 1915.
100. TNA, HO 45/20876, anon. to Clerk to London County Council, 1 June 1915; Bird to Under Secretary of State, 10 May 1915.
101. TNA, HO 45/20876, minute dated 12 May 1915.
102. NRS, HH30/19/2/6/2, Local Tribunal, 18 September 1917.
103. *Scotsman*, 28 April, p. 1; 8 July, p. 11; 16 September 1916, p. 3, for the Edinburgh College and offers of tuition; *Entertainer*, 2 December 1916, p. 18; 3 February 1917, p. 8.
104. *Entertainer*, 10 November 1917, p. 17, for the attitude of the Pensions Committee in Aberdeen.
105. *Bioscope*, 8 December 1917, p. 63.

CHAPTER 6

Early Municipal Cinema

Julia Bohlmann

In *Forgotten Futures*, the late film scholar and historian of visual culture Elizabeth Lebas defined municipal cinema as 'an alternative cinema', arguing that the films made by Glasgow Corporation and Bermondsey Borough Council between 1920 and 1980 represented a counterpoint to popular and commercial cinema.[1] Sponsored by the municipality and mainly conceived as informative texts about local events, culture and practices, municipal films addressed spectators as citizens rather than consumers. The present chapter draws on Lebas's definition of 'an alternative cinema', and seeks to expand it to include film exhibition. It suggests that the town council's engagement with cinema and its development of what came to be known as municipal cinema did not necessarily manifest itself in the making of films, but was reflected more broadly in the organisation of exhibition, in the spaces used, in the choice of which films it was appropriate to show, in how the cinema was financed and promoted, and in its relationship with the audience.

In Scotland, municipal cinema made its first appearance during the 1910s. Organised under the auspices of individual municipalities and run by local councillors, this form of film exhibition typically took place in town halls, aiming to create a civically and educationally responsible cinema as an alternative to commercialised entertainment culture. Municipal cinema can, therefore, be regarded as a constructive strategy to regulate and shape cinema's social role in Scotland. This chapter will discuss how it was implemented locally, focusing on the case of Kirkintilloch, a small town to the north-east of Glasgow.

The period after the First World War witnessed the attempt to establish several municipal cinema projects across Scotland. None, however, functioned as long or as consistently as the municipal pictures in Kirkintilloch, which hosted regular moving picture shows between 1914 and 1922. The Kirkintilloch case is particularly interesting also because of its links to the Independent Labour Party (ILP). Thomas Johnston, who, as Labour MP and Scottish Secretary, co-ordinated major civic projects in later years, was, as a young councillor in Kirkintilloch, an enthusiastic promoter of municipal socialism and the main supporter of the municipal cinema there.

Scotland was not the only country to municipalise some of its cinemas during the early period. Norway municipalised most of its cinemas during the 1910s as a result of a tightening of regulation. In 1913, the Norwegian government passed the Film Theatres' Act, demanding that local councils should 'license all public showings of films within the area of their jurisdiction'.[2] An indirect consequence of this Act was that Norwegian municipalities began to buy local cinemas on a large scale leading to the establishment of a public cinema monopoly, the National Association of Municipal Cinemas, in 1917. Apart from the motivation to regulate film exhibition, local authorities were drawn towards municipalisation due to the promise of earning a profit which might be used to pay for other public services. Municipalisation was supported especially by the Social Democrats and the Norwegian Left, suggesting that parallels can be drawn with the Scottish situation where the municipalisation of local services was an ILP policy. Municipal cinemas remained an exception in Scotland, however. The power of local authorities as cinema regulators was more limited than in Norway and political and legal structures in general were more supportive of private rather than public trading.

Attempts to municipalise entertainment in Britain were associated, as in Norway, with a desire to regulate it. Originating in the temperance and moral reform movements of the late nineteenth century, civic entertainments were intended to 'elevate to some degree the recreational taste of local citizens'.[3] Glasgow Corporation had been running municipal entertainments with such intentions since the 1870s. Staged regularly on Saturday afternoons, these entertainments – often taking the form of concerts – started to include moving pictures at the beginning of the new century, and by the end of the 1910s they faced increasing competition from cheap picture houses. In response, Walter Freer, curator of Glasgow Corporation Halls and driving force behind the Saturday concerts, announced Glasgow's plans to furnish all public halls with a cinematograph to run municipal picture shows.[4] Glasgow was not the only authority considering such a move at that time. Similar proposals came especially from a number of smaller towns such as Clydebank, Kirkcaldy, Montrose, Johnstone, Dunoon and Renfrew. The surge in postwar municipal cinemas even reached Stornoway on the Isle of Lewis, where it was hoped that a public cinema 'would be less likely to offend Free Church sensibilities'.[5]

Local authorities were not only motivated by moral arguments but considered municipal pictures for economic reasons. Their profitability was proved by the success of commercial cinemas and, thus, cinema was regarded as a potential source of income to fund other municipal activities. Trevor Griffiths maintains that this was particularly relevant during the early decades of the twentieth century when the increasing influence of a range of local authority activity brought about the expansion of public services in many Scottish town councils without a matching growth in revenue. By generating income through municipal cinema, revenues could increase without the town council having to raise the rates. Enthusiasm for municipal cinema schemes was particularly high during the immediate postwar years when property values were being reassessed and the likelihood of increased rates was great.[6]

Apprehensive about any type of public interference, the cinema trade lobbied against the spread of municipal cinemas. At a conference of the cinema trade in Glasgow in September 1918, the need to stop municipal competition was urgently brought to the attention of delegates. First and foremost, the cinema trade was anxious about the favourable position from which municipal cinemas might operate:

> Municipal trading in all except the absolute necessities of life – water, gas, and the like – is without doubt the most pernicious form of competition which the man of commerce has to face.[7]

Under the protected auspices of the local authority, municipal cinemas were thought to have unlimited access to public finances and were perceived to be in a better position to evade the sanctions of the 1909 Cinematograph Act with regard to safety requirements:

> No public hall can come near to complying with the restrictions which apply to all cinemas in the way of exits, fixed seats, etc., and it is far from right that with such obvious advantages they should be allowed to compete with halls which have to spend thousands of pounds . . . to satisfy the [Cinematograph] Act.[8]

Commercial exhibitors were concerned that municipal picture shows would appeal to the same patrons while having lower running costs. In 1919, when Glasgow was planning a municipal cinema scheme so comprehensive that it would 'embrace all the Halls under the Corporation' accommodating '300,000 patrons', an editorial in *The Bioscope* accused the Corporation of trying to eradicate commercial cinemas all together. At the same time the Corporation banned the building of new cinemas owing to a shortage of housing stock, a policy the editors claimed was connected to its municipalisation agenda:

> In effect it works out thus: We [Glasgow Corporation] want municipal cinemas. If we allow private enterprise to build cinemas, we shall not be able to run our municipal cinemas – therefore, we will stop building by private enterprise on the plea of houses first, and we will thus eliminate any further competition.[9]

Faced with a strong and civically well-connected trade lobby, and obstructed by legal and pragmatic considerations, Glasgow Corporation never realised its supposed agenda. The city was already well provided with more than eighty commercial cinemas and the local branch of the Cinematograph Exhibitors' Association had close links with the Corporation. For the trade more widely, however, what was at issue was the principle and precedent of any municipality establishing publically, socially and politically controlled cinemas that could lead to a Norwegian scenario:

> A far greater danger lies in the possibility that the practice once started will be followed, and the havoc wrought may be multiplied a hundredfold. From the municipality to the State is but a short step. Is the next step to be the State controlled cinema?[10]

Consequently, the journal encouraged exhibitors to take active steps against municipalisation. The principal strategy was to question the legitimacy of local authorities entering into commercial business with ratepayers' money:

> The Acts of Parliament under which our municipalities are constituted never for one instant contemplated that these municipalities should be permitted to embark upon commercial enterprises.[11]

In Scotland this led to two court cases, starting with a legal challenge against Dunoon Town Council in July 1921. In January, the Dunoon Council had decided to take over the Pavilion Cinema on Argyle Street to offer summer entertainments that included cinematograph shows, a move that was contested in the Court of Session by the proprietor of the Picture House, also situated on Argyle Street. The judge sided with the private owner, arguing that while the council was allowed 'to erect places of public entertainment' and 'to provide music by bands, concerts, or otherwise' this provision did not include cinematograph shows.[12] In Montrose on the east coast, on the other hand, ex-Bailie Davidson had started to run a municipal cinema in the Burgh Hall in 1919. According to *The Bioscope*, the pictures made close to £1,000 in profit, a success that prompted the owners of the Empire Picture House to 'commence a legal action' against Davidson in December 1921. The action, however, was not upheld.[13] Whereas legal intervention prevented municipal cinema in Dunoon, in Montrose the municipal cinema enjoyed a number of prosperous seasons before faltering in September 1923.[14]

As an alternative to commercial cinema, then, municipally controlled cinemas were resisted and challenged in the courts by the cinema trade. A significant part of public opinion was quite content with cinema as a private enterprise rather than as a public service. The case of Kirkintilloch, however, represents an alternative view of public service and of municipal responsibility.

As an emerging party, the Independent Labour Party, or ILP, had been formed in 1893, and from 1906 until 1932 it was affiliated to the Labour Party. Somewhat to the left of the Fabian Society, chaired by the Scottish socialist, Keir Hardie, and attracting such socialist luminaries as George Bernard Shaw and Edward Aveling, Marx's son-in-law, it accepted at its opening conference that its object was 'to secure the collective and communal ownership of the means of production, distribution and exchange'. Particularly strong in Scotland, its initial strategy was to create policies that focused on the municipal level, strengthening the role of town and burgh councils as providers of public services. In 1910, Keir Hardie published a pamphlet, *The Common Good: An Essay in Municipal Government*, which encouraged town councils to use the Common Good fund – a specific Scottish provision enabling municipalities to raise money through selling public services without seeking permission from central government – as a resource to improve living standards by delivering other public services, like housing, clean water and gas. 'The Common Good', Hardie wrote, 'would be invaluable as an aid in the development of municipal trading' from the basic supply of gas and electricity to the additional provision of affordable bread, coal and milk.[15] The specific institution of the Common Good fund created a practical basis for municipal enterprise in Scottish towns.

Tom Johnston was an enthusiastic promoter of municipal socialism along the lines proposed by Hardie. As Johnston's biographer Graham Walker points out, he 'came to embody much of [Hardie's] spirit of integrity and drive for social justice'. Johnston was born into a conservative and Presbyterian household in Kirkintilloch in 1881. When he left school to work as a clerk, he became interested in Fabian socialism and the politics of the ILP which he represented from the age of twenty-two. In 1906,

Johnston founded *Forward*, 'a paper for the respectable, self-improving working class' that quickly rose to become Scotland's leading socialist newspaper of the day.[16] Serving as a local councillor from 1913 to 1922, Johnston entered national politics when he was elected as Labour MP for West Stirlingshire in 1922, for Dundee in 1924, returning to West Stirlingshire till 1945. Most prominently, he was under-secretary in the Scottish Office between 1929 and 1931 and Scottish Secretary in Winston Churchill's national government from 1941 to 1945. If any central idea can be drawn from Johnston's political activities, it is his support of the collective and the Common Good through empowering municipalities and increasing state provision.

The municipal cinema in Kirkintilloch was a local manifestation of the idea of the empowered collective and its most immediate democratic representative, the Town Council. During his time as local councillor, Johnston fronted a number of municipal experiments, including 'a municipal piggery, a municipal goat herd, municipal kitchen, municipal jam making, municipal restaurant, municipal slipper baths and a municipal bank'.[17] Kirkintilloch's municipal cinema had, thus, a small share in the bigger idea of municipal socialism and advanced the notion that cinema could function as an accessible public service. Under the auspices of the municipality, the cinema, like the restaurant or the bank, was to provide an affordable public service, its profits enjoyed by the community. In a *Forward* article from Spring 1914, Johnston stressed that 'there is money in the Municipal Cinema [and] splendid propaganda in the agitation for the Municipal Cinema', and referred to its acceptance among Kirkintilloch town councillors as 'an avowed step in Socialism'.[18] A number of other Scottish town councils were praised by *Forward* for setting up municipal pictures in such small towns as Kirkcudbright, Coatbridge, Greenock, Govan and Alloa. Some of these ventures were short-lived. Alloa Town Council, for instance, 'retired from the business when fresh private enterprise shows were introduced ... surrender[ing] a valuable source of income to its Common Good funds', and Govan stopped its municipal cinema when it was annexed to Glasgow.[19] Municipal cinema in Kirkintilloch, however, survived for eight years.

Kirkintilloch had a population of 11,932 in the 1911 census, growing to about 13,000 inhabitants by 1925. Scotland's Forth and Clyde Canal, dividing the north from the south of the town, made the small town a place of industrial significance up to the middle of the twentieth century. The nearby coal mines, iron foundries, calico print works and chemical industries used its canal site at Southbank to ship raw materials and goods, and small vessels were built in Kirkintilloch until 1945. This meant that a large part of the area's population was working-class and fertile ground for Johnston's ideas of social planning.

Kirkintilloch Town Hall, a classical sandstone building positioned at the eastern end of Union Street to the north of the Clyde and Forth Canal, was opened in 1906 at a cost of £11,000 raised by public subscription. Apart from serving civic purposes, the hall was rented to touring private companies staging concerts, theatre performances and cinematograph shows. One such company was OK Pictures, a travelling film exhibition company headed by Jim Clark who 'established himself as favourite entertainment caterer in Kirkintilloch'.[20] But Clark and other travelling showmen were soon confronted with the competing attraction of a purpose-built local cinema, and bookings at the town hall decreased.

The Pavilion Picture House, located in close proximity to the town hall on the corner of Kerr and Oxford Street, opened in 1912 with a seating capacity for a thousand spectators. Initially, it was the only permanent cinema in Kirkintilloch, and was managed by Mr Simmons. Thomas Ormiston – a leading figure of the Scottish cinema trade whose circuit grew to twenty-two cinemas in the 1920s, and who, like Johnston, went on to become an MP for the constituency of Motherwell, though, unlike Johnston, as a Unionist – was recorded as the Pavilion's secretary in 1916

Figure 6.1 Kirkintilloch Town Hall, c.1937. Valentine Collection, licensor www.scran.ac.uk.

and 1921. The Pavilion opened six days of the week, offering one house at 7 p.m. from Monday to Friday and on Saturday a children's matinee at 3 p.m. as well as two evening performances.

Lamenting the 'considerable loss' the popularity of the Pavilion caused for the provision of entertainment in the town hall, and the consequent loss of income, Thomas Johnston and Bailie Gibson made a case for the installation of a cinematograph in the hall. The fully equipped hall, however, was not to be leased to a private cinema exhibitor as was common practice in town halls throughout Scotland. Film shows were to run under the auspices of the Town Council. At first sight, the co-conveners' motivations seem solely economic: 'running a cinematograph show . . . two nights a week, and a matinee on Saturday . . . would . . . make a profit of something like £151 17/8 a year'.[21] The educational function of a municipal cinema was, however, also emphasised:

> The form of entertainment most appreciated . . . was the picture house. The picture house exhibition had come to stay, and when that was the case most of them [the Hall and Park Committee] were of opinion that it should be in its very best, its very highest, and most useful form. They believed if they could give the public first-class entertainment that would be helpful and instructive at the same time it would be exceedingly valuable.[22]

The installation of a cinematograph apparatus was swiftly agreed, but the question whether the Council was in a legal position to use ratepayers' money for the running of municipal picture shows was unclear and caused 'several months' hard fighting' among Councillors. The main point of contention was that it was illegal for the Town Council to 'charge losses on cinema shows running, against any of the local rates'.[23] A solution was found by setting up a non-statutory sub-committee led by Johnston, Bailie Gibson and Messenger Fletcher, who agreed to

> run the entertainments on their own responsibility, giving an obligation to be personally responsible for any loss, and handing over any profit to the burgh's Common Good Fund.[24]

Moreover, profits were to be 'earmarked, so that . . . losses [would] be taken from the profit fund'.[25] On the afternoon of 14 November 1914, the municipal cinema opened to a civic reception. Introducing the municipal pictures to a hall crowded with children and adults, Bailie Gibson underlined once more its economic benefit to the community:

> It was for the public to patronise the pictures, as all the profits went to the public funds. No private individual took away any of the profits of these entertainments.[26]

The afternoon matinee opened with the Western *Bunco Bill's Visit* (Essanay Film Manufacturing Company, c.1914), a comedy starring John Bunny, and, 'in keeping with the announcement' that 'the programme contained an educational strain', the show finished with the colour film *Some Garden Flowers* (Pathécolor, c.1914). The feature film for the evening was *The Curse of War* (*Maudite soit la guerre*), directed by Alfred Machin for Belge-Cinéma Film in 1914, a tragic tale of two friends who have to fight each other in a senseless war. The bill also featured a shorter war picture showing 'French troops in manoeuvres' as well as another Western, *Red Saunder's Sacrifice* (Lubin Manufacturing Company, 1912), and a burlesque show. Despite the temporary lack of a full cinematograph lens which rendered 'the pictures . . . smaller than intended' on this first night, the *Kirkintilloch Herald* praised 'their remarkable steadiness', stating that the audience was sent home 'favourably impressed with what they had seen'.[27]

The Saturday matinee and the two houses on Saturday evening were the most popular shows of the municipal cinema. In addition, it opened on Monday nights (and subsequently on Fridays too), for which it offered more elevated programmes: an adaptation, for example, of 'a play from Sir Walter Scott's novels' during its first season.[28] The intention to offer a cheap but uplifting alternative to the commercial picture house was particularly visible at the beginning of the project. During the first few months, the slogan 'Humorous, Topical, Educational' was adopted alongside a competitive price policy. A reference to the public purpose of the cinema appeared in the weekly advertisements in the *Kirkintilloch Herald* immediately below the billing for 'The Municipal Pictures': 'The Public is particularly asked to note that any profits from these Entertainments go to the Public Funds'.

The municipal cinema committee soon had to compromise on some of its aspirations, in part due to competition from the Pavilion. The latter featured live variety on Saturday nights, so, while the municipal cinema initially only offered films, live acts came to figure prominently from about a month after its opening. Comedy would become an important ingredient in both cinemas' programmes, particularly during the war years.

Both cinemas incorporated local elements into their weekend schedules. The Pavilion screened a roll of honour showing 'kent faces' of local soldiers, 'received with applause' by the audience.[29] The municipal cinema established ties with the local community especially through its children's matinee on Saturday afternoons. Rather than showing the same films that would be shown in the evening, it offered special programmes for children. In early March 1915, for example, a cinematic adaptation of *Jack and the Beanstalk* was exhibited, and the following month the children were shown animal films. Packed matinee performances were

Figure 6.2 Advertisement Kirkintilloch Municipal Pictures. *Kirkintilloch Herald*, 18 November 1914. Image via British Newspaper Archive.

also achieved with the help of a scheme that rewarded children who went to the town hall regularly:

> The hall was crowded with weans in the afternoon, probably the chief draw being the near approach of the long-looked forward to gala and games, the reward of regular attendance at the matinees throughout the spring.[30]

The children's gala day, taking place in May or June each year, was filmed and shown at the last picture show before the summer break. The special appeal to children was maintained throughout the life of the municipal cinema. However, the educational aspirations of its organisers were tempered over time, and educational films, when they featured at all, were usually confined to Saturday afternoons and Monday nights.

During the first Christmas season the municipal cinema had to compete with another rival, the travelling cinema of OK Pictures. In the winter of 1914, the company that had previously used the town hall to screen its shows had to transfer to the Temperance Hall where a gas engine was installed 'for supply of electric light for the cinema machine'.[31] Whether it was for the expense of this installation, or the 'rather disappointing' entertainment it offered or owing to the general decline in travelling cinemas during that time, the company did not return to Kirkintilloch during the following winters.[32]

The flexibility of the Municipal Pictures Committee in engaging successfully in competition with the private cinema by adapting to audiences' taste meant it was instantly profitable, and secured a robust position in the entertainment culture of Kirkintilloch. When its first season drew to a close in June 1915, the Committee was able to hand over £100 of profits to the Town Council via the Common Good fund. Nevertheless, the legal position of the cinema, and its political position within the local Council, meant that scepticism continued in the press. The first successful season was received with mixed feelings by the editors of the *Herald*, who expressed their doubts in the form of a vernacular sketch entitled 'The Crack at the Brig'. In this weekly column commenting on local affairs, the two imaginary characters Tam and Rab criticised the public cinema as an unfair competitor to 'an or' nar company [an ordinary company]', arguing that it could avoid expenses that any private exhibitor had to face:

> The Municeepal Picters . . . had a baund of a' attendants warking for naething. They had nae manager tae pey. The ha'keeper's salary had been raised because o' the picters, but it wis the ratepeyers wha were peyin' it.[33]

In an angry letter to the paper's editor Tom Johnston accused the *Herald* of carrying on a 'steady campaign of hostility to the Municipal Pictures' and pointed out that the cinema's achieved profits were remarkable considering that the initial capital expenditure for installing electricity and a cinematograph into the town hall had been around £600. He then listed some of the cinema's permanent running costs:

> We paid . . . over £53 for printing and advertisements. Artists did not come for nothing, nor did the pianist, nor the violinist, nor the cash girls. We did not get police attendance, nor lithographed posters, nor the trolley display for nothing . . . We had a first-class manager, and we paid him first-class terms.[34]

The manager was T. D. Hutchison, who was well connected within the Scottish cinema trade. By 1917, a large part of the municipal cinema's feature programme was selected by Arthur Dent, who at the time was Scotland's sales representative for Famous Players-Lasky and Paramount. This shows that the municipal cinema committee delegated programming decisions to a skilled manager and a trustworthy distributor, who were committed to keeping up with current trends like serials. In January 1916, *The Exploits of Elaine* (Wharton, 1915) was shown at the Pavilion while the municipal cinema screened *The Broken Coin* (Universal, 1915). At the end of the war, both cinemas moved on to longer, five-reel dramas.

Each cinema attempted to construct and maintain its own identity by addressing a particular political constituency. Throughout the war, the Pavilion maintained a patriotic outlook and demonstrated this with a continuous commitment to exhibiting war dramas and films like *The British Troops at the Balkans* produced by Topical Budget, a newsreel company producing propaganda films for the Government's War Office in 1917. The municipal cinema seemed to offer a more ambivalent engagement with authority. On Friday evenings during the winter and spring season of 1917, audience members were invited to test their 'skills as Film Censors' as part of a competition.[35] While there is no information indicating exactly what taking part in this competition entailed, it reflected broader debates. The competition was conceived at a time when the nationwide discourse about cinema regulation and censorship was at an unprecedented height, resulting in the 1917 Cinema Commission.

The municipal cinema distinguished itself further from the private house in its pricing policy. With ticket prices ranging from 3d to 6d during spring 1916, the public cinema was slightly cheaper than the Pavilion, where tickets cost between 4d and 9d.[36] While this already separated those who could afford to visit the private cinema from others who could not, the differently priced tickets both cinemas offered represents a further social distinction within each cinema. The Pavilion, for example, used prices to divide the audience into patrons watching in the pits and those occupying the more comfortable stalls and the circle. From June 1916, an extra charge of 1d to 2d was added to each of these to cover the newly introduced entertainment tax. The following year, the Pavilion included the charge in the ticket price, selling tickets from 2½ d for a seat in the pits during the week and up to 11d for a seat in the circle on Saturday night.[37] By contrast, the municipal cinema opted to maintain existing prices at 4d and 6d, inclusive of tax, with the business bearing the cost of the duty.[38] This served both to undercut the Pavilion and to some degree to mitigate rising living costs for patrons. What is more, the municipal cinema's weekly advertisement increased significantly in size and by 1917 had become three times as big as the Pavilion's advert, effectively marginalising the competition on the pages of the *Kirkintilloch Herald*.

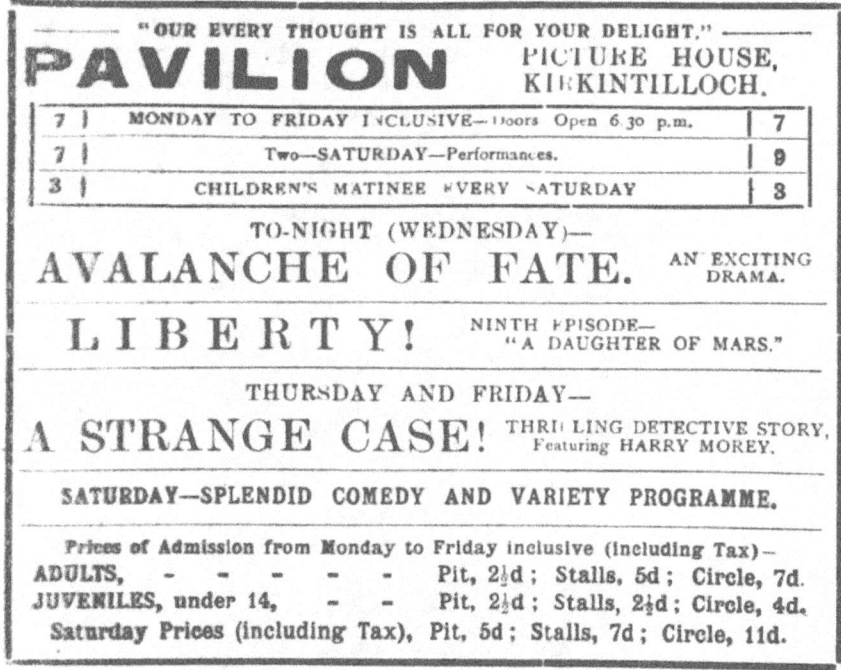

Figure 6.3 Advertisement Kirkintilloch Pavilion Picture House. *Kirkintilloch Herald*, 9 May 1917. Image via British Newspaper Archive.

In 1921, the first cracks started to appear. The new decade had brought an economic slump, and falling attendance figures made it harder to run a lucrative cinema. It was, nevertheless, the addition of a new cinema that had the most immediate impact on the fate of the municipal cinema. The Black Bull Cinema, which had been constructed on the site of a former public house, the Black Bull Inn, opened in the autumn of 1922. Ironically, the pub's conversion was a consequence of Kirkintilloch's municipal teetotalism, declared two years earlier and supported by Johnston.

The arrival of a second permanent commercial competitor altered the burgh's entertainment culture significantly, and the opening of the Black Bull as a cinema coincided with Johnston's departure from Kirkintilloch to take office as a Member of Parliament. This in turn changed the burgh's political landscape, leaving the municipal pictures committee with less determination and vigour. Coinciding with the recession, these factors served a blow to the municipal cinema from which it never recovered.

The manager of the Black Bull, James Lyle, knew how to fill a niche in Kirkintilloch almost instantly. His pricing policy challenged both existing

Figure 6.4 Advertisement Kirkintilloch Municipal Pictures. *Kirkintilloch Herald*, 9 May 1917. Image via British Newspaper Archive.

cinemas. The Black Bull, with a seating capacity of a thousand, offered the cheapest seats at 1d for children's matinees, thus rivalling the municipal cinema, and sold the most expensive tickets for a box at weekends at 1s 6d.[39] Offering specific comforts such as this, as well as differently priced seats in the circle and stalls, the cinema competed directly with the Pavilion. The Black Bull tried to appeal to women in particular. During a February week in 1923, almost all films screened starred heroines such as *The Arizona Cat Claw* (World Film, 1919), *Why Girls Leave Home* (Harry Rapf Productions, 1921) and *The Beloved Blackmailer* (World Film, 1918), and the programme featured a live turn with a female impersonator.[40] What really stood out about the Black Bull, however, was that it staged a jazz band every Saturday night. Together with live acts and a variety of cinematograph films, jazz proved to be the key to the cinema's success and underpinned Lyle's status as an innovator who brought the latest trends to Kirkintilloch.

The Pavilion seems not to have suffered from the success of the Black Bull, but continued to run programmes on a daily basis. While these still

Figure 6.5 Advertisement Kirkintilloch Pavilion Picture House & Town Hall. *Kirkintilloch Herald*, 10 January 1923. Image via British Newspaper Archive.

contained a variety element on Saturday nights, the cinema began to focus more and more on films. The management also displayed more efforts to draw in children. During the same week that the Black Bull's films featured mainly heroines, the Pavilion opened its house for schoolchildren midweek and gave away prizes for the best essays on *Nanook of the North* (1922, Pathé Exchange), a documentary by Robert Flaherty about the life of Eskimos.[41] The municipal cinema on the other hand faltered under the influence of the new commercial rival and very quickly lost its identity as a cinema. It began to focus on live comedy, variety acts and the promotion of local talent. Its changing outlook is particularly apparent in the weekly newspaper adverts, which had shrunk back to their original size. What is most notable in the advert pictured here is that the municipal cinema was not promoted as a cinema any more, but as 'Town Hall – Pictures and Variety'. Some of the *Herald* reviews reflected this change and reported chiefly on live acts and only from time to time mentioned a film at the end. In response to the Black Bull's pricing policy, the Town Hall dropped the admission price to children's matinees to 1d. This strategy seems not to have won many children back, however, as the 'children's matinee on Saturday . . . [was] dropped for the season' in April 1923.[42] Considering that children had been a key audience for the municipal pictures, the decision to discontinue the weekly matinee hints at the depth of the cinema's troubles.

If the decline of the Town Hall had been visible throughout the first few months of 1923 it became particularly obvious in April and May when it reduced its programme to one house a night on Fridays and Saturdays. Again the size of the advert can be seen as a marker for the state of the cinema in general. By May this was reduced to a third of its original size and symbolically squeezed between the bigger adverts of the Pavilion and the Black Bull. While films had already been pushed to the margins during previous weeks, towards the end of the spring season the exhibition of moving pictures ceased entirely. A variety show on Saturday and a 'Go-As-You-Please Competition' on Friday night were all that was left, and both together received a mere two-sentence review in the *Herald*.[43] The Saturday night house was soon taken over by Lyle, who began to rent the Town Hall to stage picture shows, variety and jazz, the combination that had worked so well for the Black Bull. Only a week into his business, Lyle reintroduced the children's matinee on Saturday afternoons. Thus, the end of the municipal cinema project did not denote the end of moving pictures in Kirkintilloch Town Hall. Rather, the financial and managerial set up reverted to what it had been before 1914: the Hall was let to private showmen and continued to host many political meetings and community events. Though it retained its significance as a civic and public space, the demise of the municipal pictures put an end to the socialist ambitions that had defined the Town Hall entertainments over the preceding years.

The Municipal Pictures Committee officially ceased to exist in April 1923. Unofficially it had fallen apart much earlier, but this had not been reported at previous town council meetings, which suggests that the communication between the Committee and the rest of the Town Council had collapsed. Crucially for the reputational legacy of the project, this impasse and the fact that there was no official contract for the lease of the Town Hall had led to an accumulation of rent arrears of £240. The town council had no other option but to write off the debt; that is to make up for the loss with rate-payers' money, an illegal procedure at the time. With Johnston gone, Gibson received most of the harsh criticism from unsympathetic colleagues, who were opposed to the way the municipal pictures 'were mixed up with the Town Council'.[44] Gibson tried to defend the project but its apparent failure as a public cinema remained a topic of intense discussion at subsequent Council meetings, and in the *Kirkintilloch Herald*, over the following few months.

Municipal cinema in Kirkintilloch was a small part of a larger project to realise municipal socialism. This policy was promoted by the Independent Labour Party and implemented by local councillors such as Tom Johnston. The objective was to use the profits made by running a cinema to pay for other public services and to expand the provision of affordable amenities. A further ambition was to define municipal cinema as a site for 'responsible' entertainment and to utilise it for propaganda and educational efforts. This ambition, however, could only be partially fulfilled.

The mediation of the cinema's local function has to be seen in relation to the close proximity of commercial rivals, first the Pavilion Picture House and OK Pictures, later the Black Bull Cinema. The immediacy of commercial rivals meant that the municipal cinema's programmes were constantly negotiated with an audience that could always choose between the public and private cinemas. This limited the cinema's ability to deliver the socialist messages the councillors intended it to convey. The commitment to make an economic benefit to the community meant that the municipal cinema had to cater to the taste of its audience rather than be prescriptive in the choice of film content. Ultimately, this reflects the nascent crystallisation of cinema's social role as commercial and popular entertainment, a model that began to dominate during the later 1910s and early 1920s and which relegated alternative and aspirational uses to the margins.

This trend, coupled with a powerful recession affecting the entire economy, led to the fall of Kirkintilloch's municipal cinema and parallel schemes elsewhere in Scotland. Without supportive institutional structures, municipal cinemas were not in an economic position to subsist. A further reason relates to changes in film production and exhibition. With programmes increasingly dominated by long feature films and commercial exhibitors promoting the architectural luxuries of their cinemas, promising relaxation as well as entertainment, the lack of comfortable seating in town halls contributed to the move of film exhibition out of makeshift venues. As a result, municipal cinema as an exhibition practice that challenged commercial picture houses largely disappeared from Scotland's cultural landscape.

The idea of a public service that gave access to entertainment and information lived on. John Grierson campaigned for a public-service cinema that would be independent of commercial constraints and popular demand,[45] and the British Broadcasting Corporation, shaped by the thinking of John Reith, promoted the principles of public service broadcasting.[46] Conclusively, in its conception of the provision of entertainment as a public service and its belief that popular leisure could occupy a place within civic culture, early municipal cinema anticipated some of these arguments and developments.

Notes

1. Lebas, *Forgotten Futures*, 14.
2. Iversen, 'Norway', 106.
3. Griffiths, *The Cinema and Cinema-going in Scotland, 1896–1950*, 114.
4. 'The Municipal Cinema', *Bioscope*, 27 November 1919, p. 113.
5. Griffiths, *The Cinema and Cinemagoing in Scotland, 1896–1950*, 115.
6. Ibid., 112–14.
7. 'Ousting the Exhibitor', *Bioscope*, 19 September 1918, p. 4.
8. 'The Municipal Cinema', *Bioscope*, 27 November 1919, p. 113.
9. Ibid.
10. 'Ousting the Exhibitor', *Bioscope*, 19 September 1918, p. 4.
11. Ibid.
12. 'Councils and Kinemas', *Scottish Kinema Record*, 10 July 1921, p. 1.
13. 'The Burgh Hall Cinema, Montrose', *Bioscope*, 5 August 1920, p. 74.
14. Griffiths, *The Cinema and Cinema-going in Scotland, 1896–1950*, 115–16.
15. Hardie, *The Common Good*, 7. Available at <https://archive.org/stream/TheCommonGood_201411/> (last accessed 18 April 2016).
16. Walker, 'Johnston, Thomas (1881–1965)'. Available at <http://www.oxforddnb.com/view/article/34213> (last accessed 18 April 2016).
17. *Tom Johnston: Man of His Century*, 1.
18. Thomas Johnston, 'The Municipal Picture House in Scotland', *Forward*, 16 May 1914.
19. Ibid.
20. 'O.K. Pictures', *Kirkintilloch Herald*, 9 December 1914.
21. 'Corporation Entertainments', *Kirkintilloch Herald*, 11 March 1914.
22. Ibid.
23. Thomas Johnston, 'The Municipal Picture House in Scotland', *Forward*, 16 May 1914.
24. 'Municipal Public Entertainment', *Kirkintilloch Gazette*, 15 May 1914.
25. Thomas Johnston, 'The Municipal Picture House in Scotland', *Forward*, 16 May 1914.
26. 'Municipal Pictures Opening', *Kirkintilloch Herald*, 18 November 1914.

27. Ibid.
28. Ibid.
29. See for example 'The Picture House', *Kirkintilloch Herald*, 13 and 26 January 1915.
30. 'Municipal Pictures', *Kirkintilloch Herald*, 12 May 1915.
31. 'O.K. Pictures', *Kirkintilloch Herald*, 9 December 1914.
32. Ibid.; Jim Clark also ran shows in Paisley, which appear to have finished in 1915. See for example, 'Away up North: A few Notes from Scotland', *Bioscope*, 23 February 1911, p. 26.
33. 'The Crack at the Brig', *Kirkintilloch Herald*, 23 June 1915.
34. Thomas Johnston,'The "Crack at the Brig" and the Municipal Pictures', letter to the editor, *Kirkintilloch Herald*, 30 June 1915.
35. Advertisement: Municipal Pictures, *Kirkintilloch Herald*, 10 January 1917.
36. Advertisements: Pavilion and Municipal Pictures, *Kirkintilloch Herald*, 10 May 1916.
37. Advertisement: Pavilion, *Kirkintilloch Herald*, 6 June 1917.
38. Advertisement: Municipal Pictures, *Kirkintilloch Herald*, 6 June 1917.
39. See Advertisements: Pavilion, Town Hall Pictures and The Black Bull Cinema in the *Kirkintilloch Herald*, 10 January 1923.
40. 'Black Bull', *Kirkintilloch Herald*, 14 February 1923.
41. 'Picture House', *Kirkintilloch Herald*, 14 February 1923.
42. 'Town Hall', *Kirkintilloch Herald*, 14 March 1923 and 11 April 1923.
43. 'Town Hall', *Kirkintilloch Herald*, 9 May 1923.
44. 'Kirkintilloch Municipal Ventures – Arrears of Rent', *Kirkintilloch Herald*, 18 April 1923.
45. Caughie, 'Broadcasting and Cinema 1: Converging Histories'.
46. Briggs, 'The End of The Monopoly'; Scannell, 'Public Service Broadcasting: The History of a Concept'.

CHAPTER 7

Rob Roy: Britain's First Feature Film

Caroline Merz

In 1911, when single-reel films still dominated exhibition and production practices, the first British three-reel fiction film, *Rob Roy*, was made entirely in Scotland, by a Scottish production company. This production is usually mentioned only as an interesting footnote to the history of British cinema, and has invited little curiosity.[1] The few historians of Scottish cinema have tended to regard *Rob Roy*, like other Scottish-made films of the silent era, as an early example of producers' ambitions outstripping their abilities.[2] *Rob Roy* is a film known to be 'lost', produced by a company that is known to have failed, yet the circumstances surrounding its production invite a set of questions that need to be answered. What was this film about, and who were the people that made it? Why did they decide to embark on such an ambitious production, and what were their resources? How, where and by whom was *Rob Roy* distributed and seen?

Close study of the story behind *Rob Roy*'s production uncovers an intriguing picture of Scottish producers whose ambitions were rooted in an understanding of the maturing film industry, and extended to the production of a series of feature films based on Scottish literature. Indeed, *Rob Roy* is probably the most significant narrative film of the silent period to be made in Scotland, representing a deliberate and carefully calculated attempt to create an entertainment with the widest possible popular appeal. Although the film is lost, by tracing its genesis it is possible to get some idea of how *Rob Roy* might have played, and why it was, and remains, so central to the chequered history of early fiction film production in Scotland.

It is no surprise that the first excursion the Scots made into fiction feature production was a version of the Rob Roy story. The outlawed clan chief Rob Roy Macgregor (1671–1734) was already a legendary figure when Walter Scott wrote *Rob Roy* in 1817.[3] Scott's novel added to Rob Roy's fame, presenting him as a romantic folk hero whose exploits were caught up both in Jacobite rebellion and in modern commercial life.

Rob Roy was destined to become one of the most popular figures of the Scottish and romantic imagination long after the author's literary works had fallen out of favour with the reading public.

The image Scott created for Scotland, where historical romances were played out in Highland landscapes, was all-pervasive internationally by the time the cinema was born. It was almost inevitable that filmmakers both at home and abroad would draw on this vision when choosing 'Scottish' subjects for films. In the early silent period, between 1909 and 1914, fourteen films based on Scott novels were made in Britain, France, the USA and Italy.[4] Only one of them, based on a theatrical adaptation of *Rob Roy*, was the product of a newly established Scottish film company, United Films, Limited.

United Films, with offices at 4 Union Street, Glasgow, was incorporated on 18 November 1910. It had three directors; Thomas McKinnon and James Bowie, both listed in company records as merchants, and Robert Neilson, a draper. A private company, its nominal capital was £5,000, divided into 20,000 shares of 5s each. Six weeks after the company's incorporation, 3,930 shares had been allotted with a nominal value of £982 10s, and by February 1911 the total number of shares taken up had risen to 4,260.[5] The only shareholder with experience of the emerging film industry was Arthur Vivian, the entrepreneurial manager of one of Scotland's first dedicated cinemas, who was to play an active role in the production of *Rob Roy*.

Vivian's career in film had begun as an itinerant exhibitor and as an electrician with the Benson Shakespearean Company in the West Indies. After this he worked for A. D. Thomas and Ralph Pringle, both significant figures in the story of early cinema in Britain.[6] In June 1910 Vivian formed his own company, the Scottish Moving Pictures Company, and took over the lease of a former church, the St George's Picture Theatre in Kerr Street, Paisley. For those like Vivian who were fascinated by the business of film and the potential for return on speculative investment, the idea of backing a new Scottish film industry must have seemed an exciting prospect. Certainly he and the other investors would have had good reason to believe that United Films had every chance of success.

United Films was formed for the purpose of making *Rob Roy*, which was to be followed by *Jeanie Deans* and a series of other literary and theatrical adaptations. Six months after the company's formal inception, *Rob Roy* was already in production. While publicity for the film prominently featured the actors (all of whom were associated with the theatrical drama on which the film was based), no mention was made of the production team. *The Bioscope*'s Scottish correspondent, 'Scotty', reported in June 1911 that 'a company of leading actors and actresses has been engaged to produce the entire dramas on our native heath – right in the heart of the Highlands – and the resulting pictures ought undoubtedly to stir many audiences everywhere to the highest pitch of enthusiasm'.

> The films will be produced under the personal supervision of Mr Arthur Vivian, and this expert cinematographist will take charge of the company during the sojourn up North . . . Produced before our own Scottish audiences they are bound to create the greatest enthusiasm. Undoubtedly this is the most ambitious venture of the kind, so far promoted hereabouts, and I congratulate Mr James Bowie on his up-to-dateness and energy.[7]

Scotty's comments have led to the inference that Arthur Vivian was the film's director and/or cameraman, but in fact he held neither of these roles.[8] The term 'cinematographist' is perhaps misleading; today it would generally be understood as referring to a camera operator or director of photography. In the early days of cinema, however – when the language of cinema was still being established – it could also mean someone who projected or exhibited films. The words 'personal supervision' are also vague and suggest a role as production manager rather than director. The energetic James Bowie was the managing director of United Films.[9]

In 1946 a Scottish cinema trade veteran, Jack Kissell, wrote an article for the *Educational Film Bulletin* in which he reminisced about the early days of cinema in Glasgow. He recalled that 'Danvers Yates of Barker's was the director and camera man of a film of Rob Roy with John Clyde in the title role', adding that in this first Scottish-produced film there were 'no interior scenes'.[10] While Kissell's account was written thirty-five years after *Rob Roy* was made and cannot be verified, it is likely that Vivian and Bowie would have sought the assistance of people with wider experience in film production. *Rob Roy*, and the series of adaptations of 'great Scottish dramas' that United Films intended to make, were a serious enterprise.[11]

Frank Danvers Yates had begun his career as an actor and in 1909 moved into directing short sound films (i.e. films synchronised with a gramophone or other device) for the Warwick Trading Company.[12] Later that year he joined the newly formed Barker Motion Photography Company of London and in January 1911 (six months before filming began on *Rob Roy*) was credited as one of the cameramen on Will Barker's documentary *Fox Hunting*. Yates was also cameraman for Barker on at least one of several films made by British production companies taken to mark the most newsworthy event of 1911, the Delhi Durbar.[13] One of his two fellow cameramen on *Fox Hunting* was Walter Buckstone, who had originally been employed by Barker's as a technician. Both men went on to have long and successful careers in the film industry. Danvers Yates joined the British branch of Pathé and also worked on fiction films for G.B. Samuelson, becoming George Pearson's main cameraman on films such as *A Study in Scarlet* (1914). Buckstone worked as a British official cameraman on the Western Front during the First World War, and his career as a news and documentary cameraman continued into the 1930s.[14]

It is significant that both Yates and Buckstone worked for Barker Motion Photography, the company founded by Will Barker that in 1911 was credited with leading a revival in British cinema. In an effort to rival American imports and improve the worldwide standing of British films, Barker produced a lavish adaptation of Shakespeare's *Henry VIII*. Sir Herbert Beerbohm Tree was hired to reprise his stage triumph as Cardinal Wolsey and was famously paid £1,000 for a day's work, while the celebrated composer Sir Edward German was engaged to write music especially for the film.[15] The resulting two-reel production, which comprised five scenes from the stage play, was received with great enthusiasm by the press and by exhibitors, but whether the public was equally enchanted is unknown.[16]

United Films' decision to make a film of a theatrical version of *Rob Roy* was almost certainly influenced by the enormous publicity surrounding *Henry VIII*, which was released in British cinemas in February 1911. At this period in cinema's worldwide evolution, filmic adaptations of well-known plays were already common. An alliance with legitimate theatre brought respectability to the new medium as well as a ready supply of actors and stories that could be plundered for their most dramatic elements.[17] It is worth noting that Sidney Olcott's film adaptations from Dion Boucicault's popular Irish plays *The Colleen Bawn* and *Arrah-na-Pogue* were also released by the Kalem Company in 1911.

The company's ambition was to create a truly Scottish narrative film with national and international appeal. In this context it would seem natural to turn to Walter Scott, and a popular contemporary stage version of one of his best-loved works. It is evident from contemporary accounts that *Rob Roy* was intended to be 'the film of the play' featuring the well-known and enduringly popular cast of a production that had been performed in theatres in Edinburgh and Glasgow and had toured widely for more than a decade. The name of Scottish actor John Clyde had become synonymous with the title role of Rob Roy, while his fellow actor/singer Durward Lely was almost equally associated with the play's romantic lead, Francis Osbaldistone. The comparisons with *Henry VIII* are numerous: Scott for Shakespeare; Clyde for Beerbohm Tree, and a ready-made and very popular theatrical drama with proven power to draw in big audiences. Will Barker, of course, had two things that Bowie and McKinnon of United Films lacked: professional expertise and respectability within the emerging film industry. If United Films were to take the audacious step of producing Scotland's first feature film (and going one better than Barker's by making theirs even longer) they would need to employ a professional crew, and who better to draw on than men who had a proven track record with Barker himself?

Two documents reveal Walter Buckstone's involvement with United Films, Ltd and the production of *Rob Roy*. These relate to the registration of the film for copyright purposes with the Stationers' Company in August 1911, and the reassignment of copyright in April 1912.[18] In both documents, Walter Buckstone is named as the 'author' of 'photograph films' of *Rob Roy*. His address is given as 4 Howard Street, Glasgow – the office of United Films, Ltd. In this context, the word 'author' would have meant the person who created the 'photograph films'; that is, the cameraman. It would therefore appear that Frank Danvers Yates was *Rob Roy*'s director and Walter Buckstone its cameraman. Production of this film began only a few months after the filming of *Fox Hunting* for Barker's. While Yates's and Buckstone's film-making experience was limited, they would have brought ambition and the cachet of working for a famous London firm to this new Scottish enterprise.

The first copyright registration document referred to above had a section of the film of *Rob Roy* attached to it. This portion of the original nitrate film, a strip of six frames, survives and is held in The National Archives (TNA). A print of it which is now attached to the document shows a scene in which John Clyde as Rob Roy and another, unidentifiable, character are seen sitting outside a thatched cottage in Aberfoyle; and it is this strip of film of which Buckstone is named as the 'author'.

At this time (and until as late as 1957) films were not protected as a single entity, but as sequences of photographs. It was normal practice to attach a portion of the particular scene of the film to the registration form. By 1911, however, registration was no longer mandatory and involved paying a considerable fee. Why, then, did the producers of *Rob Roy* decide to register their film with the Stationers' Company in August 1911? The only other non-factual film to be registered in the same year – and indeed in the entire period between 1910 and 1920 – appears to have been Barker's *Henry VIII*.[19] This film was registered in May 1911, just three months before *Rob Roy*, which also suggests that McKinnon, Bowie et al. may have been attempting to emulate Will Barker in creating a Scottish production of equal standing to *Henry VIII*. But there was another, more specific, intention behind the copyright registration of *Rob Roy* and a reason for attaching to the document the strip of film showing Clyde as Rob Roy, with another character, outside a row of cottages at the Clachan of Aberfoyle. The Clachan (small village), one of the main settings of Walter Scott's *Rob Roy*, was originally a collection of houses around an inn. It was there, in Jean McAlpine's 'rude inn', that Francis Osbaldistone received an important note from the outlaw Rob Roy, and Bailie Nicol Jarvie fought off an attacker using a red-hot poker.[20]

The registration of *Rob Roy* for copyright and the significance of this portion of film is related to an issue relevant not only to this production but to most films made in Scotland in the period before the coming of sound. This is the notion of authenticity. Long before writers such as Forsyth Hardy and the *Scotch Reels* critics called for efforts to achieve an authentic and credible portrayal of Scotland, Scottish film-makers were competing over whose film was the most authentic, albeit in terms of location rather than documentary-style or social realism.[21] Nowhere is this more evident than in the publicity for two versions of *Rob Roy* that appeared in 1911; the United Films' production under discussion and another film of the same title produced in Scotland by the French company Gaumont, which was to be released almost simultaneously. The Gaumont film was much shorter at a mere 995 feet, and was based on escapades of the outlaw Rob Roy. But the fact that two films concerned with Rob Roy had been produced at the same time led to an extraordinary occurrence; a public battle played out in the trade press over which production was more authentic, and (literally) on what grounds it was said to be so.

On 15 June 1911 a full-page advertisement in *The Bioscope* for the United Films' *Rob Roy* announced 'A Great and Popular Entertainment' with 'The coming Pioneers of the Picture World of Scottish Drama' in the shape of John Clyde and 'all the best Actors in the various principal parts'. The advertisement also noted that 'Special scripts have been written, and already for weeks the plays have been under rehearsal'. But most of the page was given to the announcement that United Films, Limited 'are taking these remarkable films on the actual World Renowned historic ground at the CLACHAN OF ABERFOYLE, PERTHSHIRE, SCOTLAND'.[22] The advertisement also showed that the next of the popular plays set to go into production was *Jeanie Deans*, written by Dion Boucicault in 1860 and named after the heroine of another of Scott's Waverley novels, *The Heart of Midlothian*.

Over the following weeks the wording of advertisements for the rival films became increasingly combative, making claims for the superiority of their acting talent as well as the greater 'authenticity' of their respective

Figure 7.1 The only surviving fragment of United Films' 1911 *Rob Roy*, showing John Clyde (left) as the eponymous hero, outside the inn at the Clachan of Aberfoyle. TNA, COPY 1/565/150.

locations. Gaumont's campaign implicitly drew attention to United's inexperience in screen work and its reliance on stage actors who were famous within Scotland but unknown elsewhere. In August 1911 another full-page advertisement entreated cinema managers to 'WAIT FOR GAUMONT'S WONDERFUL FILM OF ROB ROY' which was performed by a 'First Class company of Star Artistes thoroughly experienced in picture work' and taken 'in the Macgregors Country, the actual spots in Perthshire and Argyllshire, by kind permission of His Grace the Duke of Argyll'.[23] The oblique reference to the 'actual spots' became slightly clearer in a subsequent advertisement, which stated that 'For some time the Gaumont Company have been preparing a series of Scottish historical dramas, which are being filmed on the actual ground upon which the original incidents occurred'.[24]

Both production companies appeared to believe that the key to attracting bookings was the authenticity of the Scottish locations, as if this would add authority and a sense of historical accuracy to the fictional narrative. In August 1911 United Films played its trump card by registering the scene at the Clachan of Aberfoyle for copyright and providing the visual evidence to prove that this was, indeed, the World Renowned historic ground. From now on, advertisements for United's version of *Rob Roy* bore the words 'As actually filmed at the Clachan of Aberfoyle (Registered)'.[25] Neither of the promotional campaigns made any reference to their respective films' narratives. In the case of the United Films' treatment this is perhaps understandable: renters and audiences were assumed to be familiar with the play of *Rob Roy* and its various roles. Advertisements for Gaumont, however, offered no hints about the basis for their story. By November 1911 their film had been renamed *An Adventure of Rob Roy* (to distinguish it from the United production released in August) and publicity suggested that it was a kind of Scottish Western.[26] A synopsis promoting a screening in Gisborne, New Zealand, revealed that in an action-packed single reel it presented scenes in which Rob Roy rescues a peasant about to be hanged by redcoats, and is later saved from captivity by the grateful peasant. Rob swears vengeance on the soldiery, 'and it is to do with the carrying into effect of this curse that the film has most to do with'.[27]

The fact that this international French-based company chose to travel to Scotland to film the story indicates how much importance was attached to authenticity of location. United Films must have thought its appeal to exhibitors' national sentiment was worthwhile, as it went to the lengths of paying for copyright registration and making sure that everyone knew about it. It seems unlikely, however, that audiences would care whether the film they saw was produced within or outwith Scotland, as long as they enjoyed the story and appreciated the Scottish settings.

It is curious that when United discovered the existence of the rival production, they chose not to promote the single feature which made their film stand out: its running time, which at 3,000 feet would have been around forty-five minutes. The decision to make a film even longer than *Henry VIII* showed its modernity; the 'up-to-dateness' for which Scotty of *The Bioscope* praised the company's manager, James Bowie. It was also a considerable risk, and not just in financial terms. In 1911, when *Rob Roy* went into production, the idea of a multiple-reel film constituting most of a programme, rather than a number of short films, was still quite new. Cinema managers were unsure how audiences would respond to this kind of innovation, evidenced by a lively debate in *The Bioscope*. In September 1911, for example, an exhibitor from Newcastle complained in a letter to the editor:

> Northern picture houses are mostly run on the lines of a programme consisting of about seven subjects (about 4,000 feet), interspersed with two variety turns, and this entertainment is given twice nightly. I find that my patrons are fully appreciative of their evening's entertainment . . . What should I do if ever the 2,000 feet subject became popular?[28]

Instead of focusing its promotional campaign on the modernity of its film, United Films chose to highlight other aspects: *Rob Roy*'s status as a version of the 'world renowned and dearly loved Scottish drama' and the national character of the production. In September 1911, for example, a full-page advertisement referred to *Rob Roy* as 'The Scottish Drama, produced by Scottish Actors on Scottish ground by the Scottish firm'.[29] In retrospect it is possible to see that the assumption that renters and audiences would care about the film's Scottishness was mistaken. This may have served only to emphasise its insularity and even discourage non-Scottish renters. Unlike Gaumont, United had no track record in the industry, and the fact that comments on its activities were confined to the Scottish section of the trade press may not have helped to establish it as a presence on the British let alone the world stage.

In July 1911, shortly before *Rob Roy*'s release, Scotty wrote again about the 'enterprising firm's' production:

> I have just returned from Aberfoyle in connection with the performances in the open air for cinematographic purposes of 'Rob Roy' and other famous Scottish dramas . . . I had the pleasure of witnessing a performance, and I was greatly charmed with the realism of the acting [and] the company, headed by Mr John Clyde and Mr Durward Lely.[30]

Scotty concluded that the 'resulting series of films' would be much sought-after, but there is no evidence of their production – although it appears from his comments that some scenes of *Jeanie Deans* may have been shot.[31] Perhaps coincidentally, Gaumont was also planning a series of Scottish films. A news item in *The Bioscope* noted that the French company had 'for some time been preparing a series of Scottish historical dramas', adding that these would give 'Southrons' the opportunity of seeing famous Scottish dramas 'enacted in the locality in which they were first written'.[32] Gaumont's 'Grand Coloured Historical Drama' *Mary, Queen of Scots* (another one-reel production) appeared early in 1912.[33]

An item in *To-day's Cinema* published in 1953, shortly before shooting began in the Highlands for Disney's version of *Rob Roy*, offered an intriguing insight into the techniques behind the 1911 production.[34] Noting that this 'Scottish film' had been made in the Highlands previously, the writer continued:

> Records are still intact of the shooting of the story at Aberfoyle, in the Trossachs, in 1912 [*sic*]. The prints which remain show up clearly the very simple techniques of those early film-makers. Amid the natural wooded setting at Aberfoyle, scenes of various episodes in the book were enacted against a screen painted to represent each different locale. In two of the photographs one can quite plainly distinguish actor Durward Lely.[35]

Unfortunately these prints have since disappeared. But the short paragraph in itself reveals much: not just the way that a fundamentally theatrical technique was deployed in an outdoor setting but also that the entire film was made on locations around Aberfoyle, with no studio filming involved.

Aside from this, there is little evidence of how *Rob Roy* was presented on screen or of how the original story and the theatrical version were adapted. Scotty's remarks were vague but positive: after the trade show in August 1911, for example, he assured readers that the film 'bristles with excitement and thrills everyone', adding that it would undoubtedly 'meet with the approval of every Scotsman, both at home and abroad, and of many more besides Scots'.[36] In order to understand United's *Rob Roy* better, it is therefore necessary to explore its back story; the popular theatrical production on which it was based.

As Ann Rigney has noted, productions of *Rob Roy* dominated the nineteenth-century stage, especially in Scotland.[37] The vast majority were probably based on a version first produced in 1818, in Scott's lifetime, and dramatised by Isaac Pocock: *Rob Roy MacGregor; or, Auld Lang Syne! A musical drama, in three acts, founded on the popular novel of Rob*

Figure 7.2 Full-page advertisement for *Rob Roy*, the 'World renowned and dearly loved Scottish Drama'. *The Bioscope*, 14 September 1911.

Figure 7.3 Queue for *Rob Roy* outside the Picture Salon, Sauchiehall Street, Glasgow. Photo courtesy of the National Library of Scotland's Moving Image Archive.

Roy, first performed at the Theatre-Royal Covent-Garden, Thursday March 12, 1818. The drama was set at the time of the first Jacobite uprising in 1715 and featured many of the characters from the novel: as well as the outlaw Rob Roy and his wife Helen, these included the romantic hero, Francis Osbaldistone; his sweetheart Diana Vernon, daughter of the exiled Jacobite Lord Beauchamp; Dougal (often referred to as the 'Dougal Craitur'), the wild-looking turnkey at the Glasgow tollbooth; Bailie Nicol Jarvie of Glasgow and his housekeeper, Mattie; Jean MacAlpine, innkeeper at the Clachan of Aberfoyle; and Captain Thornton, a Redcoat. In later versions it was referred to as 'A national operatic drama'.[38]

By 1911, the best-known and most frequently staged professional production of this play both within and outwith Scotland featured John Clyde as Rob Roy and Durward Lely as Francis Osbaldistone in companies variously managed by Captain W. Vernon, William Mollison and Clyde himself. Neither of the lead actors was a young man when they performed their roles for the camera: Clyde was fifty and Lely (playing the youthful romantic lead) was fifty-eight. They had been appearing together in the drama since 1892, almost twenty years before the film went into production, and continued to do so until Clyde's death in 1920. Clyde was the leading Scottish actor/manager of his generation, and, while obituaries remarked on his versatility as an actor who had performed roles in popular Scottish plays such as *Jeanie Deans*, *Cramond Brig*, *The Bonnie Brier Bush* and *The Lady of the Lake*, it was *Rob Roy* with which he was most prominently associated. *The Scotsman* remarked that over the years Clyde had 'saturated himself with the spirit of the Highlands', and that on the boards he 'always seemed to be the perfect embodiment of the MacGregor chief'.[39]

Numerous reviews of stage productions of *Rob Roy* over the decades are significant not only for what they reveal about John Clyde's acting style and his celebrity within Scotland but also for the way in which the drama was presented.[40] A review of an 1897 staging at the Town Hall, Falkirk, praised Clyde for his 'striking and commanding appearance' and 'strong, resonant voice': his portrayal of Rob Roy was said to be 'as near Sir Walter Scott's ideal of the "bold outlaw" as one could imagine'. The expensive, large-scale touring production involved the use of an 'elaborate' wardrobe, 'magnificent' scenery painted by the eminent artist William Glover and incidental music, songs, chorus and overture arranged and composed by Edward De Banzie.[41] The role of Francis Osbaldistone was primarily a musical one, and hearing Durward Lely, an operatic tenor who had been one of the original Savoyards, was one of the main attractions. On some occasions, however, other singers took his place: in a production mounted by Clyde in 1909, Francis was played by Mr J. W. Bowie, who was congratulated on his performance of the songs 'Soon the Sun', 'Though You Leave Me Now in Sorrow' and 'Old Langsyne'. This may have been James Bowie, later to become the managing director of United Films.[42]

Over the years, the 'operatic drama' *Rob Roy* evolved into a form of family entertainment similar to pantomime, with well-known songs, a series of familiar scenes rather than a flowing narrative, and featuring popular performers with strong local credentials. By 1911, a lavish production was mounted every Christmas in the major Glasgow, Edinburgh and Dundee theatres, providing what one newspaper called a 'suitably varied entertainment for this time of year'.[43] Audiences knew what to expect, but could look forward to the surprise of new and ever more elaborate staging, scenery and costumes. A review of the show performed in Dundee in 1908 remarked upon one thrilling effect:

> It is seldom we have the opportunity of seeing realism on stage, but at the Empire Theatre last night the swish of water rolling over the rock in the clachan of Aberfoyle sent a thrill through the audience.[44]

Not all such innovations were as well received. It was noted the following year that 'as the years go on "Rob Roy" undergoes certain changes which may not appeal to all as improvements', the reviewer adding that the range of music had been chosen with 'heroic disregard for the perfect fitness of things', exemplified by Diana Vernon's rendering of the Jewel Song from *Faust*.[45] It is also evident that by 1911 the stage show was considered a little tired and worn, although it could still be relied on for an enjoyable evening's entertainment. This is amply illustrated by a review in *The Scotsman* of June 1911, just two months before the film's release, of an Edinburgh production that was to run for two weeks:

> If only for its memories, 'Rob Roy' must afford pleasure to Scottish audiences. Its sentimental picture of a romantic past has become familiar by frequent repetition, and the flaws in its dramatic construction have long been obvious.[46]

The stage show was constructed around a series of tableaux, one of which took place at the clachan of Aberfoyle 'when Rob Roy falls a prey to the Sassenach troops through the treachery of Rashleigh Osbaldistone'. This scene was also central to the film, which evidently followed a similar 'tableaux' format, performed out of doors in front of painted screens rather than (as in the case of *Henry VIII*) transporting stage sets to a studio. The clash between the naturalism of the setting and the style of performance must have been considerable, a disjuncture that would have been apparent to cinema audiences.

Music was central to the stage show, but played a more marginal role in the film. A musical score written by Mr H. Henderson, a Glasgow theatre orchestra conductor, was made available to cinema exhibitors, but there are few clues as to what tunes it included and how it was performed.[47] On the occasion of *Rob Roy*'s debut screening at the St George's Picture Theatre in October 1911, Arthur Vivian had all his staff dressed in full Highland costume and 'at special parts of the production pipers played well-known airs pertaining to the drama'.[48] The substitution of this kind of musical accompaniment for live singing by the performers whose stage presence was so inextricably linked with their voices may well have proved disappointing to the cinema audience. The dramatic action would have had to be very exciting and very *cinematic* in order to compensate. As far as we can tell, this was not the case. The film strove to live up to the reputation of the stage production, transferring the action to natural settings which may have been less spectacular and thrilling from the audience's point of view. At the same time, the action of the film would have been more difficult to follow, probably depending on lengthy intertitles and certainly on previous knowledge of the story. Above all, Clyde's and Lely's mellifluous voices could not be heard.

At the time of its production, however, United Films had good reason to expect that a version of the most successful theatrical drama to have come out of Scotland would be a hit with cinema audiences. As a popular drama, *Rob Roy* would have had a wider appeal than Barker's *Henry VIII*, whose target audience was the 'acculturated' middle-class public, more used to visiting the legitimate theatre than the picture house.[49] While such filmic adaptations of Shakespeare were part of cinema's drive for respectability, *Rob Roy* had the potential to be both respectable and populist. But the very fact that the musical drama was so frequently performed may have worked against its success. In addition to regular stagings in Scotland's cities, Pocock's version of *Rob Roy* was one of the most popular choices for the many amateur dramatic societies that were springing up throughout the country. Put simply, audiences might have had enough of *Rob Roy* – and, if not, there was ample opportunity to see a stage version that might compare favourably with the film.

There is little evidence as to how *Rob Roy* was received by the viewing public; most reports were filtered through Scotty's admiring gaze. In October 1911 he described a special screening at the Picture House in Sauchiehall Street, Glasgow, in the presence of the Lord Provost and four hundred other invited guests, where the film elicited 'universal admiration'. On its public release 'large and enthusiastic audiences' were said to have crowded the Picture House in order to witness it.[50] The following week there were 'overflowing audiences at every performance' at the St George's Picture Theatre (a cinema in Paisley under the management of Arthur Vivian), while at the Burgh Hall in Pollokshaws *Rob Roy* again played to capacity houses.[51]

Riding on the success of these first performances, an advertisement claimed that 'Rob Roy is the greatest money magnet on the market' and included (apparently unsolicited) testimonials from cinema managers to this effect. In addition to the cinemas mentioned above, these included the managers of the Gaiety Theatre in Ayr and the Town Hall, Clydebank – where 'hundreds [were] turned away'.[52] Currently available evidence suggests that Ayr was the furthest this film travelled within Britain, although it is possible it was seen in England. United Films' connection with the Barker Motion Photography Company of London, mentioned above, was not just informal. It had arranged a distribution deal with Barker's, who were to handle bookings of *Rob Roy* in Leeds and the South of England, while United itself was responsible for the film's distribution in the North and in Scotland.[53] This arrangement also suggests a more ambitious exhibition strategy than was previously supposed.

Aside from Scotty's partisan reports and publicity in the trade press, the only mentions of United's *Rob Roy* from within Britain are found in retrospectively written accounts of Scottish film production. In 1918 Matt Cullen, a Scottish cinema manager, wrote an article about 'early' film production in Scotland in which he noted that every scene of *Rob Roy* had been 'taken directly on the spot', and was by no means considered an embarrassing failure.

> Comparing it with what we see now, the production was not great by any means, but it may be judged better by its success. Few pictures enjoy such a successful run as this one had, and if it had only been possible to continue the series what a following this company would have obtained![54]

Trevor Griffiths has rightly suggested that this modestly budgeted production may have struggled for attention in the wealth of 'Scottish' films that surrounded it, but *Rob Roy* fared better than he and other film historians have supposed.[55] Rather than disappearing from the scene soon after its 'much-trumpeted debut', prints of the film travelled across the world. In November 1911 *Rob Roy* was screened at the King's Theatre in Wellington, New Zealand, where, as in Scotland, advertisements noted that it was taken on the actual ground where the historic events occurred.[56] The following month the film made its way south to Dunedin, where a review remarked:

> It can safely be said that a more realistic picture drama has never been witnessed in Burns Hall, and the bagpipe music supplied assisted very materially to make lifelike the various incidents in this piece. Those who have read this work will appreciate the significance of these remarks, and those who have not would do well to spend an evening with the Haywards this week in order to see the genuine and entertaining pictures screened in connection with this work.[57]

In January 1912 it was similarly promoted at Hayward's Pictures in Wanganui, New Zealand, where the film was to be accompanied by the in-house Lyceum Orchestra. New Zealand exhibitors – in contrast to their Scottish counterparts – chose to remark upon and even exaggerate the film's length: '3000 feet of a picture story to be appreciated by everybody'.[58] This aspect was also highlighted in a promotional article for *Rob Roy* at West's Pictures in Adelaide, Australia, in late November 1911. West's (who had previously secured the rights to Barker's *Henry VIII*) was eager to satisfy a growing demand for a 'lengthy star film' in each programme, and *Rob Roy* fitted the bill.[59] At least two prints must have been in circulation at the same time, as *Rob Roy* was being screened in Australia almost simultaneously with an appearance in New Zealand. By

May 1912 it had travelled to Auckland, where it enjoyed four screenings at the Windsor Theatre in Ponsonby.[60]

The wide distribution of *Rob Roy* in the Antipodes may be partly explained by the fact that the Clyde/Lely stage production on which it was based had not been seen in either Australia or New Zealand. The film was therefore publicised as a substitute for the 'real thing'. The promotion of the film's national character would have appealed to national sentiment in the many Scottish communities of New Zealand and Australia, whose appetite for Scott and for filmic representations of Scotland, fuelled by a large diasporic community, was probably greater than it was in Britain. It is, of course, also possible that cinema managers and audiences in Australia and New Zealand were ahead of Britain in their acceptance of longer films.

The Wanganui advertisement stated that *Rob Roy* was 'produced by the Barker Co., of London', suggesting that it was Barker's who had been successful in recognising the film's potential to attract 'Scottish audiences everywhere' and in attracting overseas bookings. By this time United Films was in severe difficulties, pursued by creditors and unable to pay even for the film stock it had purchased. In December 1911 a writ was issued on behalf of the Cinés Company of Charing Cross Road, London, whose account for 'cinematograph films [film stock] to the value of £53 9s 10d' supplied between 7 October and 2 December had not been paid.[61] The fact that by October 1911 United was unable to pay this relatively modest sum shows how dire its financial situation was. Friends (or competitors) in the trade may have tried to help: A. E. Pickard, who at the time managed the Britannia Panopticon and the Ibrox Picture Palace in Glasgow, paid £21 to show *Rob Roy* in his venues, although it is unclear whether the print was hired or purchased.[62] Either way, in January 1912 the company went into voluntary liquidation due to the weight of liabilities incurred.[63] Three months later, copyright in *Rob Roy*, together with the company's assets, was reassigned to Alexander Hendry Turnbull of Dalveen, Cardonald.[64] Turnbull, who may have been a creditor, was at the time an employee of the manure makers Robert Johnston & Sons of Anderson Street, Glasgow.[65]

Rob Roy was in many ways a very modern production as an early example of a 'long' film. The United Films, Ltd was a short-lived company whose plans for a series of Scottish dramas may have come to nothing, but it should not be written off as an enterprise that was destined to fail. As it claimed in advertisements for *Rob Roy*, United Films appeared indeed 'pioneers of the picture world of Scottish drama'. Its intention to make a 'great and ambitious work that will stir the heart of every Scotchman throughout the world' may not have been realised but, as outlined above, the rationale behind the production of *Rob Roy* was sound.[66] The reasons for its (heroic) failure are evident today: under-capitalisation of the company, the absence of an indoor studio, a film that was too hidebound by the stage version from which it was drawn and a lack of experience in feature film production. Many other production companies made the same mistakes, but for this Scottish company there was no second chance.

Notes

1. Cloy, 'Scottish Film Production in the Silent Period', 7.
2. Griffiths, *The Cinema and Cinema-going in Scotland, 1896–1950*, 282.
3. A fictionalised account of Rob Roy's life possibly written by Daniel Defoe, *The Highland Rogue or the Memorable Actions of the Celebrated Robert Macgregor, Commonly Called Rob-Roy* (1723), was published during his lifetime.
4. Dolin, 'The Great Uncredited: Sir Walter Scott and Cinema'.
5. NRS, BT2/7704/1 and 3, The United Films Limited, Memorandum of Association, 17 November 1910; Return of Allotments, 28 December 1910.
6. 'Opening of New Glasgow Hall', *Bioscope*, 1 August 1912, p. 363.
7. *Bioscope*, 8 June 1911, p. 467.
8. See, for example, Gifford, *The British Film Catalogue Vol. 1, Fiction Film, 1895–1994*, 105; McBain, 'Scotland in Feature Film: A Filmography', 235.
9. *Scottish Post Office Annual Glasgow Directory 1911–12*, p. 112. Available at <http://digital.nls.uk/directories> (last accessed 31 October 2016)
10. *Kinematograph Weekly*, 7 February 1946, p. 30. In an article called 'Trade Makes Merry at Cinema Ball', Jack Kissell was described as the employee with the longest service, suggesting he was active in the cinema trade as early as 1908.
11. *Bioscope*, 8 June 1911, p. 467.
12. These included *Apache Dance*, *The Taximeter Cab*, *Sneezing* and *Land of Hope and Glory*. *News on Screen*, 'Frank Danvers Yates'. Available at <http://bufvc.ac.uk/newsonscreen/search/index.php/person/1022> (last accessed 5 November 2013).
13. The most famous of these is a set of films produced by Charles Urban, who took four or five cameramen with him to film the entire royal visit to India in Kinemacolor.
14. *News on Screen*, 'Walter A. Buckstone ("Wally")'. Available at <http://bufvc.ac.uk/newsonscreen/search/index.php/person/124> (last accessed 31 October 2016).
15. Sir Edward German (1862–1936) was one of the most popular English composers of the early twentieth century; a successor to Arthur Sullivan in the

field of comic opera, and the composer of light classical music and incidental music for stage productions.

16. Robert Hamilton Ball suggests that Barker's film was not a popular success. Ball, *Shakespeare on Silent Film: A Strange Eventful History*, 84.
17. Street, *British National Cinema*, 44.
18. TNA, COPY 1/559/172, Photograph film (for cinematographs) of the play of 'Rob Roy' as actually produced at Aberfoyle, originally registered on 31 August 1911; COPY 1/565/150, Photographs registered at the Stationers' Company. Bundle of forms applying for copyright.
19. TNA, COPY 1/556/340: Photograph (cinematograph) of Henry VIII as played by Sir Herbert Tree and Company. Portion of print attached depicting Wolsey in Cloisters.
20. Until recently the Bailie Nicol Jarvie Hotel stood on the site of the inn, but little of the original clachan remains. The hotel building has been converted into private housing.
21. McArthur, *Scotch Reels*; Hardy, *Scotland in Film*, 221.
22. *Bioscope*, 15 June 1911, p. 566.
23. *Bioscope*, 31 August 1911, p. 454.
24. *Bioscope*, 14 September 1911, p. 579.
25. *Bioscope*, 14 September 1911, p. 535.
26. *Bioscope*, 16 November 1911, Supplement p. ix.
27. *Poverty Bay Herald*, 21 February 1912, p. 9.
28. *Bioscope*, 28 September 1911, p. 667.
29. *Bioscope*, 21 September 1911, Supplement p. xxii.
30. *Bioscope*, 13 July 1911, p. 75.
31. *Bioscope*, 15 June 1911, p. 566.
32. *Bioscope*, 14 September 1911, p. 579.
33. *Bioscope*, 23 November 1911, p 75.
34. *Rob Roy, the Highland Rogue* (dir. Harold French), 1953.
35. *To-Day's Cinema*, 21 October 1953, p. 10.
36. *Bioscope*, 24 August 1911, p. 397.
37. Rigney, *The Afterlives of Walter Scott*, 6.
38. For example Pocock, *Rob Roy Macgregor; or, 'Auld Lang Syne;' a National Operatic Drama Extended with an Intr. & C. by a Glasgow Playgoer*.
39. *Scotsman*, 3 November 1920, p. 3.
40. *Arbroath Herald*, 23 September 1897, p. 4.
41. The landscape painter William Glover (1836–1916) was also director of the Theatre Royal, Glasgow, in the 1870s; the conductor and light opera composer Edward De Banzie (1858–1916) was, at various times, musical director of the Empire and Gaiety Theatres in Glasgow.
42. *Evening Telegraph*, Dundee, 9 March 1909, p. 6.
43. *Courier*, Dundee, 26 December 1909, p. 7.
44. *Evening Telegraph*, Dundee, 5 May 1908, p. 5.
45. *Evening Telegraph*, Dundee, 9 March 1909, p. 6.

46. *Scotsman*, 6 June 1911, p. 10.
47. *Bioscope*, 19 October 1911, p. 157.
48. Ibid.
49. Burrows, *Legitimate Cinema*, 46.
50. *Bioscope*, 19 October 1911, p. 155,
51. *Bioscope*, 26 October 1911, p.233,
52. *Bioscope*, 26 October 1911, p. 272,
53. *Bioscope*, 14 September 1911, p. 535,
54. M. Cullen, 'Film Production in Scotland', *The Cinema*, Scottish Section, 3 January 1918, p. 67.
55. Griffiths, *The Cinema and Cinema-going in Scotland, 1896–1950*, 283.
56. *Dominion*, 20 November 1911, p, 1.
57. *Otago Daily Times*, 26 December 1911, p.6.
58. *Wanganui Chronicle*, 15 January 1912, p.7.
59. *The Advertiser*, Adelaide, 27 November 1911, p. 11. In 1911, T.J. West controlled Australia's largest chain of purpose-built cinemas.
60. *Auckland Star*, 23 May 1912, p. 2.
61. NRS, CS46/1912/1/85, Decree for payment, Cinés Co, otherwise called Società Italiana "Cinés" Rome against The United Films Limited.
62. Letter from The United Films Limited to A. E. Pickard, 30 November 1911. Letterbook, *Pickard's Papers*, available at <http://pickardspapers.gla.ac.uk/items/show/2406 > (last accessed 1 November 2016).
63. NRS, BT2/7704/15, The United Films, Ltd, Extraordinary General Meeting of Members, 29 January 1912.
64. TNA, COPY 1/565/150.
65. *Post Office Annual Glasgow Directory, 1911–1912*, pp. 354 and 676. Available at <http://digital.nls.uk/directories/> (last accessed 1 November 2016).
66. *Bioscope*, 14 September 1911, p. 535.

CHAPTER 8

Local Films for Local People: 'HAVE YOU BEEN CINEMATOGRAPHED?'

John Caughie and Janet McBain

In October 1936, the week before the BBC launched the first public television service to an audience living within twenty-five miles of its production centre in Alexandra Palace, London, Gerald Cock, the first Director of Television, published an article in a special television issue of the *Radio Times*, 'Looking Forward: A Personal Forecast of the Future of Television'. Arguing that television '*from its very nature*' was better adapted to the dissemination of information than to entertainment, he states his case:

> I believe viewers would rather see an actual scene of a rush hour at Oxford Circus directly transmitted to them than the latest in film musicals costing £100,000 – though I do not expect to escape unscathed with such an opinion.[1]

Even as late as the 1930s, even with the evidence of cinema's movement from side shows and one-reel actualities to its classic period of feature-length narration and spectacle, early television, like early film, put its faith in the attractions of the local, the familiar and the everyday: a version of the local topical peculiar to the immediacy of television. This chapter considers the scope and nature of local topical film-making and its exhibition in Scotland. By 'local topical' we mean short non-fiction films made or commissioned for local exhibition, and which captured moments of everyday life, such as street scenes and factory exits, or specific local events and ceremonies. We argue that the local, the familiar and the everyday were not simply transitory attractions, peaking in the period of travelling shows and itinerant exhibition, but were central to the appeal of early cinema and had a greater importance in new technologies of the moving image than historians or existing narratives often allow. (Think, in passing, of the uses to which Facebook, YouTube and Instagram are put.)

The appeal of the local topical was not lost on the trade. A handbook published by *Kinematograph Weekly* circa 1912 opined: 'There can be no two opinions as to the value of the local topical film as a means of filling your theatre.'[2] Or *Cinema Exhibitors Diary* writing as late as 1928:

> Local topicals are still one of the best means of bucking up business and filling the local picture theatre. It is the biggest business booster the wideawake manager can employ to increase his profits.[3]

For understanding the history of exhibition and movie-going before and after the arrival of sound, the trade press offers evidence throughout the period that the local topical enjoyed a valued place in the bill of fare offered by exhibitors, was popular with audiences and was a key tool in building business. More than that, in many instances, particularly perhaps in small towns, the local topical gives some indication of the civic status of cinema, recording the key events of the town, its pageants, ceremonies and sports as well as the everyday lives of its people. The local topical engaged its audience both as paying customers and as members of a community: it was good for business, and, at the same time, the recognitions and familiarity it offered were one of the distinctive pleasures of cinema-going.

The local topical was a feature of the cinema programme from the earliest days of the travelling shows and fairground cinematograph booths. The recovery in the 1990s by Peter Worden of the eight hundred or so Mitchell and Kenyon films, their donation to and preservation by the British Film Institute, their contextualisation by the University of Sheffield's National Fairground Archive, and their transmission as a three-part series, 'The Lost World of Mitchell & Kenyon', by the BBC, raised the profile of early local actuality films and prompted a reassessment of our understanding of the nature of early British film-making and exhibition.[4] Mitchell and Kenyon, however, did most of their business with travelling cinematograph operators, and ceased making films in 1913, just as cinema was moving into fixed locations and purpose-built cinemas. While the recovery of their work is critical for the history of early cinema in Britain, the significance of local topicals to exhibition was not confined to the early decade of the itinerant moving picture show. The topical and its inclusion in the cinema programme endured the sea-change in the nature of exhibition in the years leading up to the Great War as cinema came off the road and 'settled down' in fixed site shows, as the full-length feature film – the so-called 'super-film' – became the anchor for the programme, and as Hollywood features began to change the nature of distribution and exhibition and to encourage various forms of 'block-booking'. Throughout this period of change and consolidation, the local topicals remained a familiar and appealing element of the cinema programme. Critically, while cinema moved more and more towards a cinema of narrative absorption and spectacle, the topicals continued to exercise the attractions of recognition, familiarity and the everyday, offering the pleasures of a participant audience, actively engaging rather than passively consuming, and maintaining the diversity of experience that the early film programmes offered over the course of an evening. They constituted part of what it meant to have a 'good night at the pictures'.

Definitions are important, and the boundaries of the local topical sometimes need to be flexible. By the first decade of the twentieth century, the 'topical' was the term given to an actuality film which came to be embedded in the film programme as an early form of newsreel. Exhibitors could be supplied with two topicals or newsreels or 'animated gazettes' per week to match the change of programmes, with each gazette comprising around five items per issue each running for approximately one minute. Originally produced by film-makers such as James Williamson or Will Barker, their production was consolidated by the British offices of Pathé and Gaumont as Gaumont Graphics or Pathé Gazettes, joined in 1911 by the British company Topical Budget.[5] Typically, they featured major sporting events, national celebrations and appearances of the Royal Family, and they had particular prominence during periods of war or conflict: the Boer War of 1899–1902; the Balkan crisis of 1908–9 (some of which was filmed by one of very few women cinematographers, Jessica Borthwick);[6] or the First World War. The gazette was imagined as a way of not simply recording an event but bringing it before you in moving images, and making it real: emotionally, and, in wartime, often fictitiously. As early as 1899, the *Campbeltown Courier* reported the response of the audience to a screening of a topical of the Boer War by Robert Calder's concert and cinematograph company:

> The cinematograph has not yet lost its attraction of novelty, and when it keeps pace with the times its success is assured . . . The photo of Paul Kruger was greeted with hoots and howls of indignation, but the portrait of Mr Chamberlain elicited shouts of approbation.[7]

If the topicals or gazettes or animated graphics were an opportunity to reproduce the national newspaper in moving images, music and whatever commentary the exhibitor chose to offer, the local topical was a little more like what we now think of as the local newspaper. (The analogy is not precise as local newspapers in the early decades of the twentieth century were a major source of national news.) While in the first decade or so these short elements made up the bulk of the programme, even after the arrival of the full-length feature film the 'shorts' – scenic, interest, newsreel and local topicals – continued as key supporting elements of a full programme. The subject matter of the local topical would typically be an event taking place in the vicinity of the picture house itself, or on the streets and in the public spaces in the catchment area of the cinema, spaces occupied by the cinema's regular patrons. Stephen Bottomore makes an important distinction:

> We need to be quite careful about a definition, because several kinds of film may be called 'local' for different reasons. For my purposes here, local doesn't just mean a film which is made about a local area. I define a film as 'local' only if there is a considerable overlap between the people appearing in the film and those who watch it or are intended to watch it.[8]

This allows him also to make a distinction between 'municipal advertising' films (*Blackpool: The Wonderland by the Waves* (1912)) which were made locally but were intended for an audience outside the area, and local topicals, made for local cinema-goers (*Lochgelly at Work and Play* (1922)). Interestingly, it also allows Tom Gunning to make a distinction between Lumière's *Sortie de l'Usine* of 1895, a film of the workers leaving their factory, commonly seen as the progenitor of many later 'factory gate' films, and similar 'factory gate' films made by Mitchell and Kenyon and others. Lumière's film was intended for the upper-middle-class audience that attended the early screenings of the Cinématographe in Lyon or Paris whereas Mitchell and Kenyon's films were filmed to attract the factory-workers to the cinema.[9] They were 'local' in the sense that there was a substantial overlap between the people in the film and the people in the audience. As well as 'factory gate' films, local topical films feature civic celebrations, galas, parades, festivals, sports competitions: a range of community activities in which potential cinema patrons would be participants or spectators. The key element of the content is an activity that attracts the local people – 'Local Films for Local People', the advertising tagline for Mitchell and Kenyon – out in public view so that they can be captured on camera.

Unlike the gazettes which were fragmentary items, a local topical was usually around one reel in length: about 1,000 feet of 35mm film, or fourteen minutes on screen. (Seven to ten minutes is the standard length of the topicals held in the National Library of Scotland Moving Image Archive.) These local topicals could be shot by a professional cameraman engaged for the day, sometimes in Scotland engaged from the Glasgow office of Gaumont; or they could be made 'in house' by the manager, projectionist or other member of the cinema's staff. The camera operator would be clear that the editorial goal was to include generous shots of faces in the crowd in order to maximise the intended audience – members of the public who were there that day, saw the cameraman at work and would shortly afterwards be enticed into the picture house with the prospect of seeing themselves on the big screen – recognising not just oneself but friends, family, workmates and neighbours. The classic trope of the local topical is the panning shot, the camera slowly passing across faces in a crowd, along rows of football spectators in the stands, or capturing the mass of workers streaming out of the factory gates. The camera operators or their assistants often encouraged people to wave to the camera, highlighting the immediacy of the moment. 'Come and See Yourselves As Others See You' was the hook to pull in the customers. On special occasions, using the available technology of the day, the interval between the filming of the activity on the street and the showing of the film in the cinema could be as little as three or four hours. This afternoon's parade could be seen in the cinema that evening. As television would later recognise, part of the attraction in this 'cinema of attractions' was indeed the immediacy of the relay. This immediacy may have limited the shelf-life of the exposed film – the event had lost much of its impact a week later – but it increased the urgency of seeing it now.

In Scotland, as elsewhere in Britain, audiences in the major cities and in small towns were exposed from the earliest days of the cinematograph to local topicals through the travelling showmen, touring companies and concert parties of the 1890s and 1900s. Scottish showmen, exhibitors and renters, operating substantial circuits across Scotland and the North of England, and local entrepreneurs with a more geographically circumscribed audience were quick to adopt the practice of including local films in their programmes, making them themselves, commissioning them, hiring them or purchasing them.

One of the pioneers was William Walker, a bookseller and optical lanternist in Aberdeen, whose company toured Scotland, often featuring in his concert party the famous Aberdeenshire dance master, composer and fiddle player Scott Skinner. Walker's company became Walker's Royal Cinematograph Company after screening his programme to Queen Victoria in October 1898. His programme included local films for local people throughout the North-east of Scotland, and he travelled as far south as Bo'ness by 1904. The significance of Walker is not simply as a pioneer but as a recruiting agent and training ground. Paul Robello and Joe Gray, employed by Walker to photograph and process his local films, and present the shows, were to become leading cinematographers (or 'cinematographists') in the field of topical production after Walker's company ceased trading in 1911. Similarly the ubiquitous Robert Calder formed his own touring party in 1896, and, like William Walker, developed a local circuit in and around Aberdeen before expanding to other localities. By 1900, the *Campbeltown Courier*, advertising Calder's Grand Cinematograph and Pictorial Concert Party, was asking

> HAVE YOU BEEN CINEMATOGRAPHED?
> See the Local Pictures: *MacGregor's Gathering, Clyde Trip, Arrival at Campbeltown Pier.*
> With Concert Party.[10]

This was followed by an editorial comment the following week: 'A feature of the concert is the cinematograph exhibition, the films being all up-to-date and well chosen, and including a number of local views which should prove a great attraction.'[11] So, like Walker, Calder was engaging the local audience with the familiar tagline, 'Have You Been Cinematographed?', to bring them into his travelling shows.

It is striking that the once prominent concert parties and cinematograph companies began to fade from the programmes of major venues between 1911 and 1913: Walker, Calder, Lizars, Dr Ormonde, 'the Great Hypnotic Clairvoyant Rosicrucian Psychognomancy' and his family concert party, Lely's Limited Gigantic Cinematograph Carnival and Pictorial Festival, all of them with their roots in the fairground, had gone out of business by 1913 or 1914 as purpose-built cinemas began to dominate the market. Companies, some of which had offered local topicals as an attraction in their programmes, retired from the road, and other companies, like Mitchell and Kenyon, which had supplied topicals, ceased to make films after 1913.

Travelling exhibitors, however, were not the only ones making and showing topicals. Local entrepreneurs, often with the technical skills of optics or photography and some with experience in lantern shows, offered topicals within their regional territories, showing them as part of their own programmes or providing a service for other showpeople. Peter Feathers in Dundee had been an optician and photographic dealer before moving to cinematography in 1896 with a programme of his own films offered in a small circuit around Dundee, locally based rather than part of an itinerant showmanship. He established himself as one of the city's most successful exhibitors and continued to include local topicals in his programmes into the 1910s and 1920s. In 1901 he advertises Feathers' Animated Panorama show in direct competition to William Walker's 'World-Famous Cinematograph'. Within the same newspaper column Walker's advert offers 'cinematograms by the mile', including local actualities of Harris Academy scholars exiting the school, while Feathers gives top billing to his 'Extensive series of magnificent animated pictures illustrating Life In Dundee' with an impressive list of ten subjects including the 'phantom ride', *Tayport to Dundee in Front of an Engine*.[12]

Similarly, David Gaylor and his son W. P. Gaylor ran an optician's in Hawick, before making lantern shows and bioscope entertainments around the Borders towns, showing in church halls and schools. By 1899 they had established the Borders Kinematograph Company to make films of local interest for their catchment area, billing them as 'Borders Newsreels' and focusing particularly on local events or sports. There is a regular annual programme of the various Borders Ridings, a continuing tradition of Border towns like Hawick and Selkirk. Twenty-three of these Borders Newsreels are held in the National Library of Scotland (NLS) Moving Image Archive.

Around 1910 and 1913, with the proliferation of purpose-built cinemas throughout Scotland, in major cities and in small- to medium-sized towns, topicals were made or commissioned by cinema managers, engaging with the everyday life or the annual ceremonies associated with their own community. The topical continued to be commercially attractive: people still liked to see themselves as others saw them, and it continued to be good for business. At the same time, there is a growing sense that the local topical becomes part of the communal life of the town or the 'urban village', cementing cinema into its civic identity. The cinema manager who makes the films or commissions them begins to develop a municipal profile, not just as an entrepreneur but as a prominent community figure who now has a civic standing.

This developing civic profile could be enhanced by personal appearance on screen. James Gillespie, manager of the Palace in Rothesay, can be seen in shot in each of the surviving topicals he commissioned in the 1910s and 1920s. In *Lady Lauder in Rothesay* (1922) his daughter Jenny is foregrounded holding the bridle of a seaside donkey bearing a placard, 'Everybody goes to the Palace but me!'

In a sense, this is the 'classic' period of the local topicals: *Coronation Parade, Broxburn* (1910), *Laying the Foundation Stone at Kirkintilloch Parish Church* (1913), *Great Western Road* (1915 and 1922), *Lochgelly at Work and Play* (1923). Titles like these circumscribe the local topical: like items in the local newspaper, they may have little or no interest outside their own community, but at the same time they affirm the local identity of that community.

Many of the films that are held in the NLS Moving Image Archive are associated with individual cinema managers. Louis Dickson, for example, the proprietor and manager of the Hippodrome in Bo'ness, filmed a number of local topicals in the town, including, most famously, the annual Bo'ness Children's Fair Festival and the parade of the Festival Queen. Tommy Timmons, the proprietor of the Cinema de Luxe in Lochgelly, made a number of local topicals in the 1920s including *Lochgelly Old Age Pensioners' Drive to Crook O' Devon* (1928). In his civic role, Timmons was a member of the organising committee for the outing, and he was still making local topicals in the 1950s.[13]

In Glasgow, James Hart, employed as projectionist at the Hillhead Picture Salon (opened in 1913), became a topical cameraman. In Glasgow's fashionable West End in September 1915, he filmed the Sunday morning promenade along Great Western Road from the back of a moving car. *The Entertainer* reported on 2 October 1915 that the film had been completely successful, albeit with 'the usual trouble of youngsters wanting to be in the picture all the time'.[14] And indeed, the dignity of the sober Sunday parade is undermined by boys, who clearly know something about cinematography, running ahead of the camera to stay in frame, seeing and being seen. In 1921 Hart moved to the neighbouring Grosvenor Cinema, newly opened, where he continued with his topical production, returning again to Great Western Road in 1922 to film the parade again. Becoming one of the most prolific topical film-makers in the trade, his locals were presented under the title Grosvenor Topical News. In 1928 Hart was promoted to management, and cited for his meritorious services, as 'in addition to his duties in the operating chamber, [he] has been the cameraman responsible for the taking of local topicals, which form practically a weekly attraction at the popular Hillhead house".[15]

In Aberdeen Joe Gray similarly enjoyed local celebrity as a topical film-maker. Having been one of Walker's Cinematograph staff cameramen until the firm's demise in 1911, he went to work as projectionist for J. J. Bennell, who had taken the lease of the Coliseum in Aberdeen (opened in 1910 by William Walker) for his B.B. Pictures. Continuing as projectionist, Gray also shot topicals for Bennell. By 1914 he had moved to Green's newly built La Scala Photo Playhouse on Union Street as projectionist but he continued to make topicals dealing with wartime events in the city. In the 1920s he moved around various halls in the city continuing with his filming activity, and became staff cameraman for Green's Scottish Moving Picture News.

On the Clyde coast, Harry Kemp had taken over a cinema in Saltcoats for which he produced a number of topicals. Harry was the son of George

'President' Kemp, who had been a travelling showman since 1882 and a pioneer of fairground bioscope exhibition with his majestic 'Dreamland' booth, where he showed topicals commissioned from Mitchell and Kenyon. Harry Kemp brought this showmanship flair to the La Scala in Saltcoats. Married to Susan Green, Kemp commissioned topicals from Green's Film Service. These include a local campaigning animation film, *Vote for Harry Kemp* (1922), to support his candidacy for the Saltcoats Burgh Council.

Not far from Saltcoats, Fred Randall Burnette had invested in a number of cinemas around the Clyde Coast, including the Theatre de Luxe in Rothesay (opened in 1912) and the Picture House in Campbeltown (opened in 1913). Burnette had toured in the United States before opening the Argyle Electric Theatre in 1910, one of the first purpose-built cinemas in Glasgow. At Campbeltown, he was responsible for some of the most fascinating local films kept at the National Library's Moving Image Archive. On 18 July 1914, he advertised in the *Campbeltown Courier*: 'Campbeltown Invaded, by F. R. Burnette, Managing Director, and his Staff and Cine Operator, to take a picture at the Pierhead of the Argyll and Sutherland Highlanders.' Inauspiciously, the arrival of the Argyll and Sutherland Highlanders for a training camp preceded by days the outbreak of the First World War, and the march past of cheerful soldiers, filmed by an operator from Gaumont, now seems rather poignant.

From the record, it is a characteristic of the known local topicals that they seem to congregate around small towns – Lochgelly, Saltcoats, Hawick or Bo'ness. The difficulty is that the record is constituted to quite a large extent by what is held in the NLS Moving Image Archive, or what can be gleaned from the catalogues of Mitchell & Kenyon. Unlike feature films, or even to some extent scenics and interest films, local topicals were not given trade shows and therefore did not appear in the trade press, and, by and large, they were not advertised, and only occasionally were they mentioned in editorial page comment in the local press. It is reasonable to assume that the archive or the record is by no means complete, that what remains is the result of the happenstance of what has been preserved or recorded, and that the appeal of the topicals extended well beyond the handful of towns where clusters of films can now be identified. We know, for instance, that J. D. Ratter, a well-known and still collected photographer in Shetland at the turn of the century, showed a programme of films of a 'kirnin' (butter churning) and birdlife on Noss at the North Star Cinema in Lerwick in 1916, but no record remains other than a passing mention on the editorial page of the *Shetland News*.[16] So we can assume that there were many more local topicals than those of which we now have a record. What is interesting, however, is that, even allowing for the incompleteness of the record, the local topicals seem to offer an insight into the ways in which cinematography was integrated into its communities. In a period when cinema in the UK and in Scotland was moving towards the global, and the feature film set in the Highlands was likely to be filmed in Los Angeles or Devon, the local topical preserves this foothold of attraction for the local and the everyday.

The trade press was actively providing the local exhibitor with information and advice on the practice and costs of making local topicals. The exhibitor, the trade papers suggest, had a choice in how he acquired his film and could either commission a specialist producer or purchase the film-making apparatus to shoot the film in-house. In 1912, *How to Run a Picture Theatre* estimated the cost of a topical as anything up to £10 to £15 according to length and value of the subject: 'on average 5d a foot if your own man takes it' or 6d a foot if you were to commission a production company.[17] The Williamson Kinematograph Company offered an operator and camera for hire at 12s 6d a day. With negative and print costing 2d per foot each, a 100 ft topical shot in one day would cost £1 13s 4d.[18]

The manufacturing sector was similarly responding to the needs of the exhibitor. In *The Bioscope* in 1913 two companies are advertising for sale a camera for topical use – equipment specifically aimed at the exhibitor or his camera operator. The Williamson Company offered 'a camera which costs the same as two weeks' Gazette and which will provide Your Own Weekly Local Gazette', at a cost of £10 10s.[19] Jury's Kine Supplies were marketing a complete photographic outfit that comprised a camera which could be converted into a film printer, along with accessories that allowed processing and developing of the film negative in situ. Jury's camera and lens was priced from £7 to £13 whilst the complete camera/printer/developing package ranged from £14 to £20.[20] The presumption both in adverts and in the trade manuals is that the cinema's projectionist is the person best qualified to become the camera operator: It was claimed that anyone who has operated a projector and taken a photograph with an ordinary camera can also operate a kinematograph camera: 'Every operator a film producer . . . Your Operator Can use it', claimed Williamson.[21]

The trade and its specialist press were also engaging management readership with articles on marketing and promoting local topicals and noting in their regional news sections examples of imaginative and proactive publicity stunts and successes. The inclusion of a topical, with its exclusivity, could give an individual exhibitor an edge over their rival, something special and unique to that cinema's programme of fare, particularly in towns where several cinemas could be in keen competition for patrons.

Unlike the national gazettes these reels were not shared across several cinemas in the one town. Exclusivity was a key component and could be flagged up in the advertising through posters, fly aways and local press adverts: 'Specially taken for this theatre'.

The publicising of the topical fell into the pool of showmanship skills and attributes that were recognised by the cinema trade as a valued element of the profession, as seen in *Kinematograph Weekly*'s awarding of Certificates of Showmanship to individuals who had shown a flair for the task.

Typical of many topicals postwar is the inclusion of a shot of the exterior of the sponsoring cinema itself, sometimes with the manager as the host in the entrance, identifying the film strongly with the place of its exhibition and reinforcing the film's exclusivity to that place. The camera's gaze could fall on the cinema itself, and its role in civic life. Films of the queue for the children's Saturday matinee, for the first talkie or for the appearance of a film star at the hall made the cinema patron a screen protagonist. On occasion reels would be brought out for reshowing decades later. The 1925 topical of Annan's Riding of the Marches shot by Gaumont for Victor Biddall's cinema at Gracie's Banking was followed on the same reel by an earlier film of the Riding prefaced with a new intertitle 'We shall now take you back to 20th September 1913 to compare the event of 12 years ago'.[22]

At the same time, some of the major cinema circuit owners and entrepreneurs were engaged in producing topical films for their own use or for commission. Gaumont, the international production and distribution company, had opened an office in Glasgow in 1912, and it brought the expertise of their camera operators to the production and supply of local topicals, often supplying managers in small towns who did not have access to equipment or expertise. With Jack Harris, their resident news cameraman, and with their own film laboratory facilities available for the production of actualities, Gaumont became major producers of sponsored and topical films for local clients.

J. J. Bennell, who had started as a Temperance lecturer in the North of England, owned one of the major circuits in Scotland with cinemas in Glasgow, Dundee, Aberdeen, Airdrie, Perth and Greenock. B.B. Pictures (B.B. is variously Bright and Beautiful, Bennell's Brilliants or the initials of J.J.'s wife), established in 1907, was one of the early companies in Scotland to realise that Bennell could offset the cost of hiring films by becoming a film renter, and B.B. Film Services was set up to rent films and to produce them for local use with a film production department created in 1911. As well as renting, B.B. Film Services claimed that 'The

BB budget of Scottish news is the only cinematograph journal published in Scotland'.[23]

The most concerted effort to produce a Scottish newsreel came from the Green family, an established family of travelling showpeople. Originally from Lancashire, George Green had commissioned Mitchell and Kenyon topicals for his fairground bioscopes.[24] This was the start of a prosperous circuit of cinemas. George's sons, Fred and Bert, established Green's Film Service in 1912 to rent films and produce local topicals for local managers. Its distribution business had offices in Glasgow, London and Newcastle, from which it rented films to hundreds of clients in Scotland and the North of England, and it had a mechanical department selling projectors and a music department renting sheet music. Green's was producing local topicals in the West of Scotland from around 1910, branching out to other cities as it extended its circuit. By 1917, it aimed to consolidate the production side of the business by producing not just local films for a local audience, thus fragmenting the market, but to produce Scottish topicals for a Scottish audience, creating a national market for their topical films. Scottish Moving Picture News, as it was called, would be available for purchase or hire to exhibitors across Scotland: *The Scottish Grand National* (1919), for instance, or *Julian, the Tank Bank* (1918), a topical of a tank filmed in Edinburgh, Dundee and Aberdeen whose purpose was to raise money for the war effort. In 1919 the Scottish Moving Picture News briefly became the British Moving Picture News, indicating a desire to broaden the market even further, but indicating also a commercial drift of Green's Film Service away from the local topical to the national news gazette. If definitions are indeed important, there is a boundary, however flexible, between the local topical – 'local films for local people' – and newsreels or gazettes – items of news or national interest wherever you happen to be.

If major distributors like Green's or J. J. Bennell had ambitions for a programme of national topicals, there is also limited evidence that local topical film-makers may occasionally have had ambitions to cross the boundary from topicals to drama. On 8 August 1912, 'Scotty' in the 'Away Up North' column in *The Bioscope* reports on leaflets distributed by Bert Foulger, the Manager of B.B. Film Services, including a leaflet which

> gives particulars regarding four new exclusive films which have been issued by the same Service, and these include *Tam O'Shanter's Ride* and *Land of Burns* – the former to be first featured at the Ayr Picture Palace on August 5th, and the latter to be shown at the same house a week later. This is quite a new line for the B.B. Service – the producing, photographing, and printing of their own special films – and I am sure that Mr. Foulger, with his accustomed business ability, will make this scheme a great success.[25]

In 1912, the *Ayr Post* reported on a forthcoming programme that would include *The Last of the Mohicans* and a variety act of vocalists and dancers:

> For next week the management have shown commendable enterprise in securing a film for the week of the scenes depicting Tam O' Shanter and his famous ride past the haunted kirk of Alloway. Some time ago the scenes were enacted here, and Ayr people wondered at the time what the picture would look like when completed. Their curiosity will be satisfied if they go to see the film some night next week.[26]

Subsequent issues reported that 'the audience has shown its appreciation in no half-hearted manner, and the fact that the film has been taken locally added to the enjoyment'.[27] Little is known about either *Tam O'Shanter* or *Land of Burns*, but it is worth recording that a company, B.B. Film Services, and a manager, Bert Foulger, who are associated with film rental and the production of topicals had used their experience to stray into the territory of a kind of local drama. There is no evidence that the films were ever shown anywhere other than the Ayr Picture Palace, and like the topicals, their appeal seems to have been to local interest and local exhibition.

A number of threads can be distinguished in this: the appeal of the local in a touring 'cinema of attractions' in which the 'attraction' was precisely the local; the development of an interest in local actualities as managers recognised the appeal of local interest to the communities in which they lived; the beginnings of an overlap between local topicals and newsreels; and the difficulty of 'graduating', if that is how it was seen, from local topicals to feature films. The boundaries between the threads are permeable, but what persists is the appeal to audiences and exhibitors of the local topical. Throughout the period, before and after the emergence of purpose-built cinemas, before and after the rise of the feature film, and, indeed, before and after the arrival of sound, it seems clear that there was a continuing interest in the local and the everyday. While this may have moved from the attraction of novelty – seeing yourself moving on the screen – to the appeal of local interest – seeing the everyday life of the community recorded – local topicals continued to exercise an appeal.

What is the significance of local topicals for the history of cinema, and what is the particular significance for a history of Scottish cinema? Routine and amateur as they may be, these films of the everyday now seem a great deal more 'modern' than many fictions of the period and most fictions of Scotland. What is striking in scanning the trade press in Britain and America is that, while the cinema industry is modern, a great proportion of its early films appeal to a society that is still imagined as premodern.

Characters, themes and places recur that belong to an earlier age – the village, the forest, gypsies, smugglers, fisher-folk, lighthouse keepers, the squire – and place twentieth-century cinema somewhere in an imagined nineteenth century. Feature films set in Scotland seem particularly rooted in the eighteenth and nineteenth centuries: in a longing for the mythology of the Highland wilderness or in a nostalgia for the small pre-industrial town.

Walter Benjamin speaks frequently of the 'dream' of the nineteenth century in which we slumber. Of his massive unfinished work, *The Arcades Project*, he says that it 'deals with awakening from the nineteenth century'.[28] In Scotland, in the history of its early films and film-making, the local topical seems to awaken from the nineteenth and, indeed, the eighteenth centuries. The topicals record the accidental detail of everyday life that the modernity of early cinema seemed to promise but never quite deliver. In Francesco Casetti's terms, they, rather than the feature films, seem to offer the possibility of 'the popularization of modernity and the modernization of popularity',[29] wakening up from the dream of the nineteenth and eighteenth centuries with everyday films that are both geographically and historically located in the here and in the now. Without idealising the primitive, by accident *and* by design they give a licence to their subjects to look back at the camera, sometimes because they cannot prevent small boys from chasing the camera, but sometimes also because they want to capture as many faces as they can to deliver on the promise of seeing yourself as others see you. This gives an immediacy and an intimacy to the figures on the screen which resists the objectifying and interrogative gaze of the documentary camera. People return the look of the camera. The Lochgelly old age pensioners who look back at the camera have not yet learned to be objects of this new visual apparatus and deal with it with a dignified but distant interest. The soldiers on their way to a war from which many will not come back memorialise a historic moment without being aware of its history or its tragedy. The look of these people, and the small boys who continually intrude on their space, gives them a sense of presence and materiality, a kind of 'matter-of-factness' – which is increasingly difficult to recognise on the various screens we now use.

In his autobiographical essay 'Autobiography of a historian', written in 1949, the liberal/Whig historian G. M. Trevelyan describes the 'poetry of history' thus:

> The dead were and are not. Their place knows them no more and is ours today . . . The poetry of history lies in the quasi-miraculous fact that once, on this earth, once, on this familiar spot of ground, walked other men and women, as actual as we are

today, thinking their own thoughts, swayed by their own passions, but now all gone, one generation vanishing into another, gone as utterly as we ourselves shall shortly be gone, like ghosts at cockcrow.[30]

This suggests, somewhat poetically, the legacy of the local topicals. It is conventional, but somewhat dry and prosaic, to say that they are important social and historical records. They are that, of course, but the popular appeal and fascination which the local topicals still seem to offer to audiences who are seeing them now for the first time is not just as records of social customs, local events or workplace rituals. It is partly that the films make few if any gestures towards posterity; they are recorded for this audience, here and now, and will be shown hours or days after the event. Some of their historical appeal is that they are, precisely, transitory and

Figure 8.1 People leaving church in a still from local topical 'Great Western Road 1922', Glasgow. National Library of Scotland's Moving Image Archive.

Figure 8.2 Territorial Army parade in a still from 'Arrival at Whitehart Hotel, Campbeltown' (1914). National Library of Scotland's Moving Image Archive.

Figure 8.3 Still from 'Lochgelly Old Age Pensioners' Drive to Crook O'Devon' (c.1928), National Library of Scotland's Moving Image Archive.

Figure 8.4 Still from 'Lochgelly Old Age Pensioners' Drive to Crook O'Devon' (c.1928), National Library of Scotland's Moving Image Archive.

ephemeral. We see them by chance – and through careful curation – rather than as documents of historical record. What seems most important is the disconcerting look of these people back at the camera. The documentary look at the object becomes reversible, and its objects become subjects.[31] The unselfconscious look back at the camera of these old age pensioners, the soldiers, the workers leaving the factory, the children on parade and the small boys being boisterous is both intimate and distant. It seems to individualise them within the mass, making them both present and absent, familiar and strange at the same time. The directness of their look at the camera – and therefore at us – gives them a material presence which is so much their appeal in the cinematographic memory.

Notes

1. Gerald Cock, 'Looking Forward: A Personal Forecast of the Future of Television', *Radio Times* (Special Television Issue), 23 October 1936, p. 7.
2. Kinematograph Weekly, *How to Run a Picture Theatre: A Handbook for Proprietors, Managers, and Exhibitors*, 21.
3. *Cinematograph Exhibitors' Diary*, 71.
4. Toulmin, Russell and Neal, 'The Mitchell and Kenyon Collection'; Toulmin, Popple and Russell, *The Lost World of Mitchell & Kenyon*.
5. See McKernan, *Topical Budget*.
6. See McKernan, 'A Girl Cinematographer at the Balkan War'.
7. *Campbeltown Courier*, 21 October 1921. (Paul Kruger was President of the South African Republic; Joseph Chamberlain was British Secretary of State for the Colonies.)
8. Bottomore, 'From the Factory Gate to the "Home Talent" Drama: An International Overview of Local Films in the Silent Era', 33.
9. Tom Gunning, 'Pictures of Crowd Splendor: The Mitchell and Kenyon Factory Gate Films', 50–1.
10. *Campbeltown Courier*, 20 August 1900.
11. *Campbeltown Courier*, 1 September 1900.
12. *Evening Post* (Dundee), 20 September 1901.
13. See *St. Patrick's Church, Lochgelly* (1952–3), National Library of Scotland Moving Image Archive, ref. no. 0963.
14. *Entertainer*, 2 October 1915.
15. *Bioscope*, 15 August 1928, p. 43.
16. *Shetland News*, 6 April 1916.
17. Kinematograph Weekly, *How to Run a Picture Theatre*. According to the National Archive's 'Currency Converter', £10 0s 0d in 1910 would have the same spending worth of £570.60 in 2005. See <https://www.nationalarchives.gov.uk/currency/results.asp#mid> (last accessed 29 January 2016).

18. Williamson House advertisement, *Kinematograph Year Book (1914)*, 48.
19. Williamson Company advertisement, *Bioscope*, 27 February 1913, pp. 622–3.
20. Jury's Kine Supplies advertisement, *Bioscope*, 27 February 1913, p. 618.
21. Williamson Company advertisement, *Bioscope*, 27 February 1913, pp. 622–3.
22. *Riding of the Marches in the Royal Burgh of Annan, September 12th 1925* (1925), National Library of Scotland Moving Image Archive, ref. no. 3738.
23. *Aberdeen Daily Journal*, 16 September 1911.
24. See McBain, 'Mitchell and Kenyon's Legacy in Scotland: – The Inspiration for a Forgotten Film-Making Genre'.
25. *Bioscope*, 8 August 1912, p. 413.
26. *Ayrshire Post*, 2 August 1912.
27. *Ayrshire Post*, 9 August 1912.
28. Benjamin, *The Arcades Project*, 464.
29. Casetti, 'Filmic Experience', 58.
30. Trevelyan, 'Autobiography of an Historian', 13.
31. On 'reversibility', see Daney, 'La Remise en scène', 58–9.

CHAPTER 9

Depicting Scotland: Scotland in Early Films
John Caughie

In *Distant Reading*, Franco Moretti poses the problem for the historian of world literature:

> Knowing two hundred novels is already difficult. *Twenty thousand?* How can we do it, what does 'knowledge' mean in this new scenario? One thing for sure: it cannot mean the very close reading of very few texts . . . A larger literary history requires other skills: sampling; statistics; work with series, titles, concordances, incipits.[1]

For Moretti, 'the trouble with close reading (in all its incarnations, from the new criticism to deconstruction) is that it necessarily depends on an extremely small canon'.[2] The solution that he proposes is 'distant reading' where distance is 'a condition of knowledge': learning how *not* to read the 0.5 per cent of texts that constitute the canon of nineteenth-century novels in favour of a sampling from the other 99.5 per cent through tracing systems, patterns, movements and mappings.

For the historian of early cinema, the problem of the number of film texts is compounded by another problem: the problem of survival. In a report for the American Council on Library and Information Resources and the Library of Congress, David Pierce calculates that of the 10,919 feature films produced in the United States between 1912 and 1929 only fourteen per cent still exist in their original format and another eleven per cent exist in foreign-release versions or in inferior formats.[3] So for American cinema, and for world cinema more generally, the question is not simply of knowing eleven thousand feature films but of knowing eleven thousand films of which seventy-five per cent no longer exist. For early Scottish films and Scottish-themed films the numbers are much lower (about two hundred fiction films, and many more 'scenics' and 'topicals') but the extinction rate is a great deal higher: rather than forming a canon the films that are available for viewing or screening constitute a survivors' list; treasured because they have survived rather than because they are 'great'.

The solution that I have adopted in charting Scottish-related films from 1908 to 1927 is not so much 'distant reading' as 'remote reading': in a period before the practice of film reviewing or film criticism had been established, my 'knowledge' of the films is acquired remotely from a reading of the accounts of the films and the synopses of the plots delivered in the trade press, or occasionally in the local press where 'reviews' were customarily written by exhibitors for potential paying audiences. The focus of the trade accounts tended to be advisory for potential exhibitors – *The Fair Maid of Perth* (1923) is 'Purely a title booking that may get over with suitable music and effects'[4] – or on marketing and exploitation: for *Bonnie Prince Charlie* (1923),

> Bagpipes, even in an English town, always attract a considerable amount of attention, and you might do well to have a man attired in full Highland dress wearing a Stuart tartan parading the streets with his instrument a week or so prior to your screening. He could be accompanied by a boy also in Highland costume, who could distribute handbills regarding the showing of the picture.[5]

This is not to say that the trade accounts were completely void of a critical vocabulary, and the traces of an aesthetics of atmosphere and authenticity do emerge, but critical judgement seems principally directed towards what a paying audience will value or tolerate. While one may regret the absence of the films themselves on which criticism depends, remote reading offers a route to understanding the ways in which Scotland was represented – and marketed – in early cinema: like distant reading, the remoteness is a condition of knowledge. It allows us to see the commercial attractions of Scottishness – or, more appropriately for the period, 'Scotchness' – and where Scotland sat in the world market of images.

As is argued in the previous chapter, what is striking in scanning the trade press in Britain and the United States is that while the cinema industry – its mode of production and distribution, its appeal to the democratic audience – is modern, a great proportion of its early films appeal to a society that is still imagined as premodern. Scotland fits quite comfortably into this imaginary past. It is not singled out as a premodern state, isolated from twentieth-century modernity, with an antique and romantic past. Rather, this imagined Scotland is part of a pattern of representation in early popular cinema which, until the urban realism of the 1930s, is still rooted in nineteenth-century literature and culture. The gypsies, fisher-folk and squires of early American cinema are as much a cultural anachronism in the twentieth century as the kilts and glengarries of Scotland.

Scottish audiences, like American audiences, did not necessarily receive these images passively, and did not necessarily confuse cinematic representations with national or cultural identity. In 1917, the Scottish correspondent for *The Bioscope* writes:

> I am going to advocate that every American producing company which attempts to produce a Scottish picture should have a Scotsman on their staff to keep them right as to what is the correct wear for the ladies and gentlemen of the land o' cakes. We do not all wear kilts and Glengarry bonnets . . . We have had *Peggy* [1916], now are given *A Daughter of Macgregor* [1916], and, in the near future, are to have Mary Pickford in *The Pride of the Clan* [1917], and the Scottish dress in each will be a laughing stock to every Scottish man and woman who sees them. As Mr Waddell would say, 'The worst of it is that we know they are doing their best'.[6]

Representations of Scotland in early cinema, and indeed of England or the United States, are most commonly a kind of romance, inhabiting an imagined land in which received images are played out as masquerade. The question that this poses, of course, hangs over the point at which this imagined land becomes an imagined community, in which people recognise, or misrecognise, themselves as a nation.

Scotland is prolifically, and sometimes notoriously, represented in early cinema. The works of Walter Scott were staples for European and American companies, and the romance of Scottish history – Mary Queen of Scots, Rob Roy and Bonnie Prince Charlie – became part of the diet of global cinema; 'Scotch' comedies and comic sketches featuring kilts, bagpipes, Highland cows and whisky (usually in combination) follow the popularity of music hall and Harry Lauder; and 'Scotch songs' like *Annie Laurie* and *Auld Robin Gray* were part of the international repertoire in parlour singing which could form a pretext for a film. Some geographically unfixed and temporally dislocated 'Highlands' became the location for a whole corpus of 'Scottish' films, and the relationships between wild Highland maidens and the refined gentry of London and New York, or between metropolitan ladies and untamed Highland squires, formed the 'border-crossing narrative' of many English and American romances.

This points to the paradox that may make Scotland truly distinctive in early cinema: compared with other small countries where cinema was being invented and developed as a narrative form, Scotland had a world literature, and, in some sense, a world popular culture. In the

English-speaking world and for much of Europe in the nineteenth and early twentieth century, Sir Walter Scott is a world literary figure, rivalled only in English by Dickens and Shakespeare: an influence on Hugo and Dumas; on Jules Verne, with three of his novels set in Scotland; translated into opera in Italy; and, for Ralph Waldo Emerson, Scott was 'the delight of boys', whose aristocratic sensibility was tempered by his democratic humanity.[7] Notoriously, Mark Twain blamed Scott, and particularly *Ivanhoe*, for the outbreak of the Civil War: 'Sir Walter had so large a hand in making Southern character, as it existed before the war, that he is in great measure responsible for the war.'[8] Common readers in English, as part of their patrimony in the English-speaking world, were familiar not only with *Ivanhoe* and *Rob Roy* but also with *The Lady of the Lake* and *Marmion*. Scott, along with Robert Burns, and later joined by R. L. Stevenson and J. M. Barrie, placed Scotland, small in size but disproportionately large in world literature, within an internationally shared reading culture. They provided a shared narrative heritage for the new generation of cinema-goers, but also a repository of stories and settings and historical romance, some of it copyright-free, that could be adapted and filmed as easily in Rome, Los Angeles or London as in Aberfoyle or Kirriemuir. Similarly, at a time when parlour music was an important domestic entertainment, *Comin' Through the Rye*, *Annie Laurie* or *Auld Robin Gray* were sung by people who had never set foot in Scotland. The paradox is that in early cinema, with the growth, first, of England, France, Italy and Germany as dominant forces within Europe, and the growth, later, of Hollywood as the dominant world force, there is a tension between having an internationally available world literature and having an indigenous and sustainable film industry. Scottish producers did not successfully exploit their own literary heritage or their own popular history precisely because it was internationally available and because better capitalised producers, hungry for 'content', had already exploited it from elsewhere.

Scenic films were an established category in film production, renting and exploitation. By the 1910s and 1920s, the short 'scenic' was an expected part of the standard programme in cinemas around the world, which included comedies, newsreels, local topicals and a feature film. Table 9.1 gives an illustrative list of the diversity of Scottish subjects covered as 'scenics' by a range of British and international production companies.

This list of scenics, filmed in Scotland and produced by companies such as Kineto, Urban, Barker, Pathé and Gaumont, is by no

Table 9.1 Examples of early Scottish scenic films

Year	Film title	Production company
1910	Travelling Through Scotland	Urban
1910	A Holiday in the Highlands	Barker Motion Photography
1910	The Island of St Kilda	Pathé
1911	Scenes from Bonnie Scotland	Milano
1911	Scenes in Shetland	Urban
1911	High Scotland	Nordisk
1911	Motoring Over Ben Nevis	Kineto
1911	Highland Games at Oban and Dunoon	Kineto
1911	Gems of Scottish Scenery	Gaumont
1912	Herring Fisheries at Loch Fyne	British and Colonial
1912	Scenes in the Land of Bonnie Prince Charlie	Clarendon
1913	The River Clyde	Pathé
1913	A Trip Through the Highlands of Scotland	Pathé
1913	Oban on Regatta Day	Kineto
1913	In and Around Scotland	Kineto
1913	Rambles in the Inner Hebrides	Kineto
1913	The Lowlands of Scotland	Kineto
1913	The Bonny Isle of Skye	Kineto
1913	Through the Caledonian Canal	Kinemacolor
1913	Highland Waterfalls	Gaumont
1913	Beauty Spots and the Highlands	Gaumont
1914	Scottish Scenery	Gaumont
1914	Haafnet Salmon Fishing	Dart
1914	The Historic Borderland and the Home of Sir Walter Scott	Kineto
1914	Prince Charlie's Country and the Western Highlands	Kineto
1914	Herring Fishing	Pathé
1914	Scenes in Highlands of Scotland	Turner
1914	Scottish Shepherds at Work	Turner
1915	Historic Stirling	Pathé
1915	Mountains and Glens of Arran	H&B
1915	A Trip up the Clyde	Kineto
1916	Around Braemar in Bonnie Scotland	Éclair
1917	The Western Highlands	Kineto
1918	Glimpses of North Scotland	Kineto
1921	The River Clyde from its Source to the Sea	Square Film Company
1922	A Tour Through the Land of Burns	Gaumont
1924	The Love Isle	Ideal
1924	Bonnie Scotland Calls You	Scottish Film Academy
1925	Highland Games	Stoll
1925	A Trip to the Beauty Spots of Scotland	H. E. Hayward
1926	The Open Road	Claude Friese-Greene
1927	Scottish Historical Pageant	Pathé

152   JOHN CAUGHIE

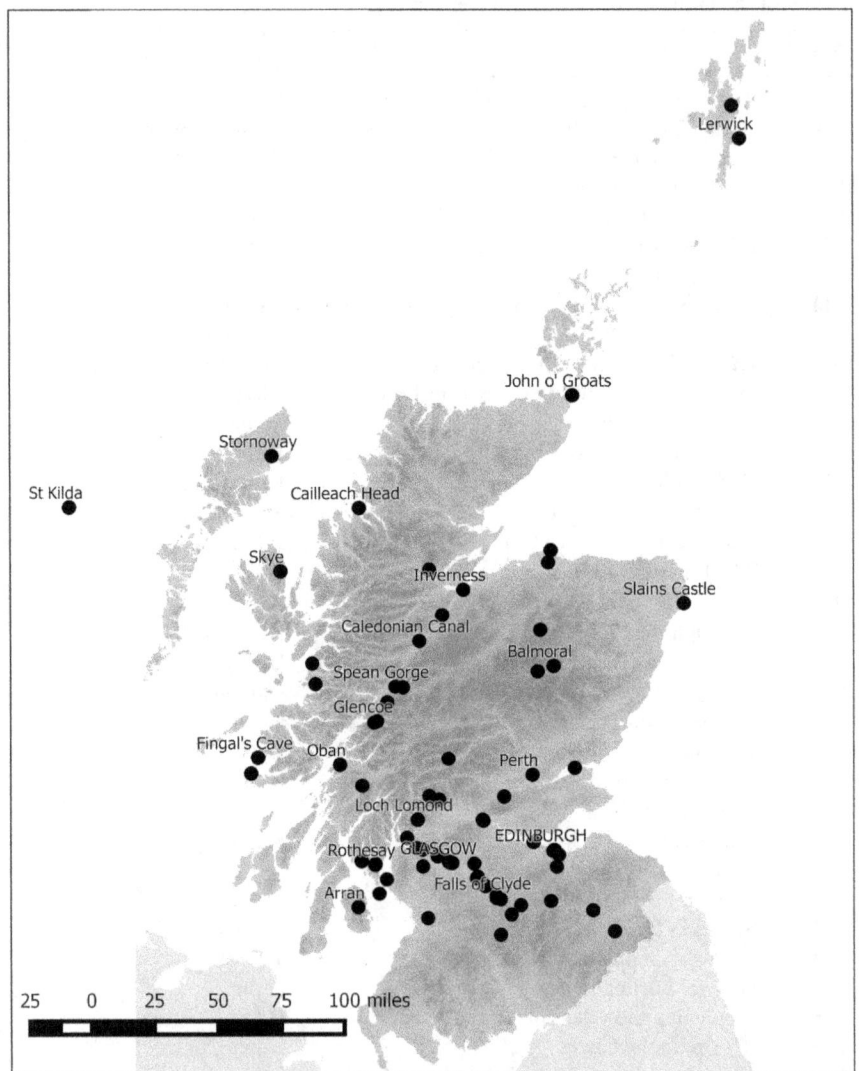

Figure 9.1 Locations of scenic films given in trade reviews.

means comprehensive. Many more titles appear in the trade press in both British and American trade journals. It is rather an indicative list, based on titles that were reviewed or noted in *The Bioscope* between 1910 and 1927 on the basis of trade shows. The titles give some sense of the particular attraction of the place, and the map above shows the locations which can be drawn from most of these reviews. The map, however, shows only locations that are specifically mentioned in the reviews, and does not include broad areas indicated in such films as *Glimpses of North Scotland* (1918) or *Scenes in the Land of Bonnie Prince Charlie* (1912).

Scotland as a scenic landscape preceded, and may have informed, the production of Scotland as an imaginative landscape by Scott and later novelists. Most famously, Thomas Pennant toured Scotland in 1769 and again in 1772,[9] Boswell and Johnson toured in 1775,[10] Robert Burns in 1787,[11] Elizabeth Diggle in 1788,[12] and Dorothy and William Wordsworth in 1803.[13] In the earlier part of their tour, the Wordsworths were accompanied by Coleridge, and in the latter part, in what would become 'Scott country', by Walter Scott. These were the most celebrated of more than thirty published accounts of travels in the Scottish Highlands between the middle of the eighteenth century and the middle of the nineteenth, which varied from scientific and ethnographic accounts to the reminiscences of her life in the Highlands by Queen Victoria,[14] or to the tour taken by J. M. W. Turner in 1831 for his paintings and watercolours for Scott's *Poetical Works*.[15] Pennant's extensive tour of 1772, on which he was accompanied by a botanist and a Gaelic-speaking minister, was dedicated to Joseph Banks. He had corresponded with Linnaeus and met Voltaire, and, as a traveller in the age of Enlightenment, his travels are part of an attempt to understand better the natural world and natural history. Other tours may have been more romantically inspired by Burns, Scott and Byron, and to some extent replaced the fashionable grand tours of Europe at a time when Europe was riven with international wars and national revolutions.

These tours begin to map Scotland in a way which is replicated in the scenics of early cinema. Johnson's tour, like Pennant's, is an enlightenment tour. He visits the major cities and their universities, stays with landed gentry and visits such notables as Flora MacDonald at Kingsburgh on Skye, recording her charms in such a way that confirms the suspicion that he was, at heart, a Jacobite. Pennant had also stayed with the MacDonalds at Kingsburgh, but was more impressed by the antiquities shown him by Mr MacDonald than by the charms of Flora. Like Pennant, Johnson develops an almost anthropological account of the Western Islands: agricultural methods, the clan system, life expectancy, post-1745 disarmament, dining habits and female beauty. Though, like Pennant, he is less concerned with landscape than with people, he maps a topography which becomes familiar.

Predictably, Dorothy Wordsworth's recollection of the tour she made with William is romantically, rather than scientifically, inspired, though she is astute in recording the people she meets and the more humble

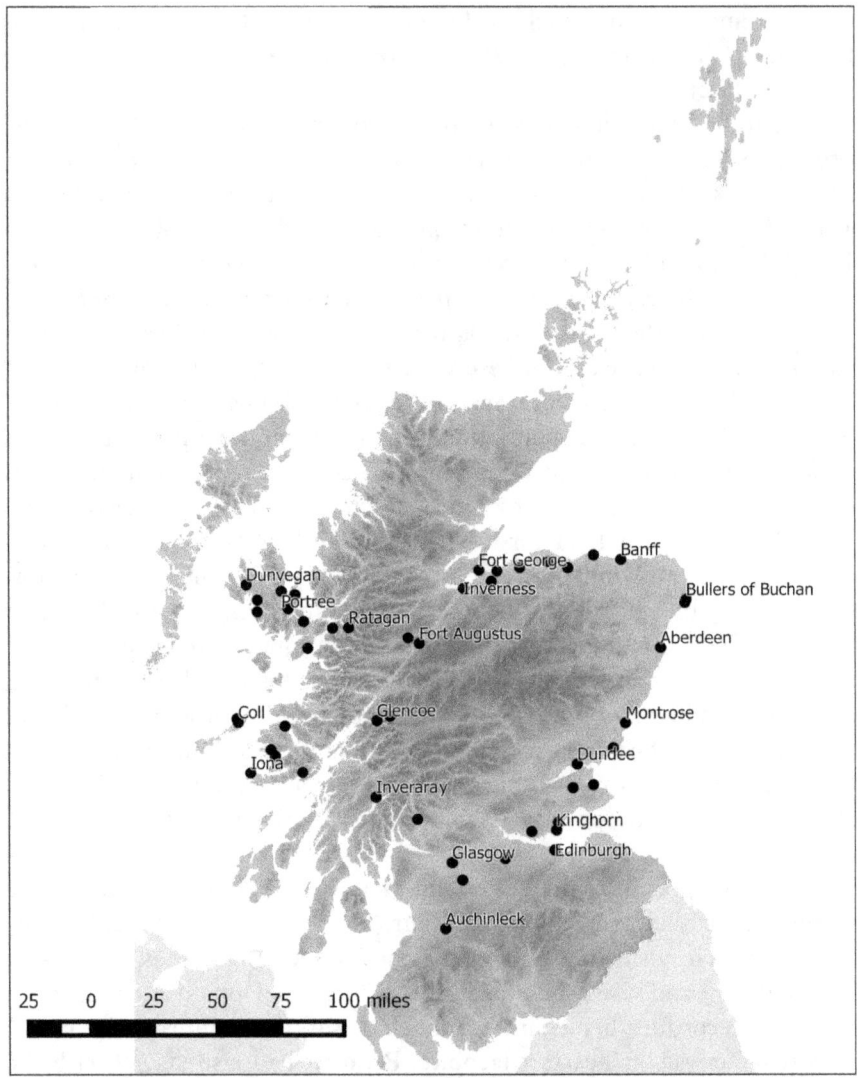

Figure 9.2 Places mentioned in Samuel Johnson's *Journey to the Western Islands of Scotland* (1775).

living quarters in which they stay. Dorothy and William are constantly drawn back to the Trossachs, passing through parts of it two or three times, and they stay not with the landed gentry but in wayside inns or with Gaelic-speaking 'natives'. (Even in the Trossachs, thirty miles north of Glasgow, Gaelic seems to have been the dominant language.) Constantly comparing Highland Scotland with the Lake District they know, there is a real sense of strangers in a strange land. '[W]e', says

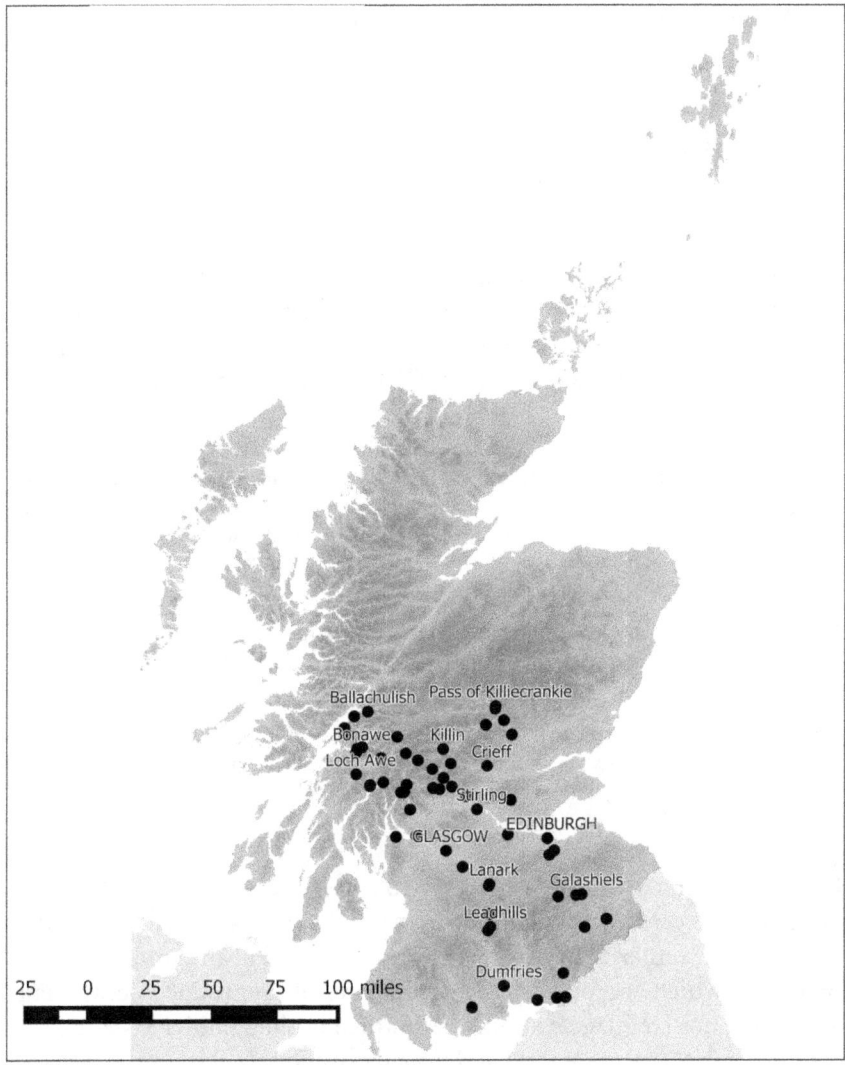

Figure 9.3 Places mentioned in Dorothy Wordsworth's *Recollections of a Tour Made in Scotland, A.D. 1803*.

Wordsworth in 'Stepping Westward', 'who thus together roam, In a strange Land, and far from home'[16] – a land as strange, indeed, as North America. 'What I had heard of Loch Lomond', says Dorothy, 'had given me no idea like what we beheld: it was an outlandish scene – we might have believed ourselves in North America.'[17] They visit Rob Roy country and see his grave, but this is fifteen years before Scott wrote his novel and

Rob Roy was still remembered as a folk hero: 'We mentioned Rob Roy', she says at Loch Katrine,

> and the eyes of all glistened; even the lady of the house, who was very diffident, and no great talker, exclaimed: 'He was a good man, Rob Roy! He had been dead only about eighty years, had lived in the next farm, which belonged to him, and there his bones were laid.'[18]

What makes Dorothy Wordsworth's account most interesting is, firstly, that she is by far the most sensitive in her descriptions to landscape, and to landscape in its wildness rather than Pennant's or Johnson's interest in 'improved' landscape as cultivation. Of Loch Lomond, she says,

> The whole was indeed a strange mixture of soothing and restless images, of images inviting to rest, and others hurrying the fancy away into an activity still more pleasing than repose. Yet, intricate and homeless, that is, without lasting abiding-place for the mind, as the prospect was, there was no perplexity: we had still a guide to lead us forward.[19]

And of Glencoe she expresses a little disappointment, shared with her brother:

> we found that though the expectations of both had been far surpassed by the grandeur of the mountains, we had upon the whole both been disappointed, and from the same cause: we had been prepared for images of terror, had expected a deep, den-like valley with overhanging rocks.[20]

The eye is pulled upwards towards the still majesty of the mountains, while her preferred landscape is drawn to waterfalls and gorges, to nature in movement rather than nature at rest: a Scotland of the sublime and the imaginary which the physical Scotland can only reproduce occasionally, and which her language can only reproduce in the familiar vocabulary of the Sublime, 'restless images' and 'images of terror'.

Like the Wordsworths, early scenics share the fascination with waterfalls and gorges. There is a film on *Highland Waterfalls*, and the Spean Gorge and the Falls of the Clyde are points of constant return. Nature in movement is indeed the proper matter of moving pictures. Where cinema has difficulty, however, is with Dorothy's 'sublime' fascination with the changing light of the weather, and with the romanticised landscape, characteristic of nineteenth-century landscape painting, dominated by cloud and sky. Early cinema can only reproduce this sublime mechanically, chemically, in ungraded blacks and whites and in frames that might shake and might suffer from frequent use. Technically, early 'blue-sensitive' film stock and filters cannot capture the effects of clouds, and the romantic epiphanies and fantastic imaginings of poetry and painting are washed out in an even greyish white. The landscape of early scenics becomes referential to an imaginary sublime landscape that it cannot reproduce, a record of where the sublime might be, but in a cinematic language, a little like Dorothy's prose compared to William's poetry, which cannot yet quite represent the unrepresentable.

Importantly, in place of a language of the sublime, Dorothy Wordsworth seems frequently to use the trope which in film would later be called the cutaway: she cuts away from the landscape to root it in some detail of everyday life. At Wanlockhead, they meet three boys, one with a fishing rod, all with honeysuckle in their hats: 'I cannot express', she says, 'what a character of beauty these few honeysuckles in the hats of the three boys gave to the place: what bower could they have come from?'[21] The force of the place is condensed in its inhabitants, a frequent trope of scenics and travelogues which constantly jump between the landscape and the details of everyday life – the local peasantry, children playing or maybe just Highland cows. This cutaway or condensation to human dimensions was anticipated by her brother in poems like 'Stepping Westward', 'To a Highland Girl' or 'The Solitary Reader'.

My argument is that the scenic in early cinema is drawn to locations that are already imbued with romance and imagination and are memorialised in an earlier travel literature. Technically, it cannot represent the sublime landscape or capture its romance, but it can reference it: a topographic marker for an imaginary landscape that has been memorialised elsewhere. By the beginning of the twentieth century, many of these landscapes had been mapped by a travel literature that can be traced more directly to Thomas Cook's tour of 1846 and to subsequent travel guides, but the memorialisation of the rural landscape owes something to the tours of Johnson and Wordsworth, and to the many literary accounts from the eighteenth and nineteenth centuries. It is there that not only are the locations established and the imaginary landscape mapped, but also that some of the grammar of observation is written. What is striking, at the beginning of the twentieth century and at the height of Scotland's industrial world power, is that industry is simply missing. While the Clyde is celebrated in scenics, the camera is drawn to the upper reaches and to the Falls of Cora Linn or Boniton or to the Firth of Clyde opening out into the Argyllshire Highlands. Only Claude Friese-Green's *The Open Road* (1926) passes through the industry of the shipyards on its way to the open estuary and Loch Lomond. Unlike the films of the documentary movement from the 1930s that celebrate heavy industry, what Scotland brings to the international screen in the 1910s and 1920s is rural or coastal livelihoods and a landscape that has already been imbued in refined and popular travel literature with romance, imagination and the sublime.

For its fictions, some of that common culture on which early cinema draws is not the narratives of literature but the familiar lyrics of poetry and song, a poetry made internationally familiar both through Burns and Scott and transmitted to popular verse and parlour music: *Auld Robin Gray*, for instance, or *On the Banks of Allan Water*. In the filmography in Chapter 11, there are twenty-nine adaptations from songs, lyrical poems and narrative poems. In some instances, a narrative poem may provide the outline of a fiction which is adapted more or less literally: *Young Lochinvar* and *The Lady of the Lake*, for instance, provide the story, and Young Lochinvar is adapted as a historical romance, as a comedy or as a 'modern' story six times before 1927. Rather more typically, however, a popular song like *Auld Robin Gray* is the pretext in 1910 for a narrative about an old man about to marry a young woman when her young lover returns; is then readapted to be a story of the First World War (1917); and then is given a sequel in *The Master of Grays* (1918). *Annie Laurie* begins life in 1913 as a tale of the American Civil War in which the song itself provides a motivating narrative link; is reset in Scotland as a rural romance by Hepworth in 1916; becomes a Great War story in *Bonnie Annie Laurie* for Fox in 1918; and ends up in 1927 as a story of the Glencoe Massacre by MGM, with Lilian Gish, as Annie Laurie, almost but not quite stopping the massacre. Familiar poetry or song, therefore, becomes a pretext, appealing to familiar lyrics, or even just a familiar title, as part of a common culture: a commonality in which the titles and, perhaps, the spirit, form a currency of exchange, and a culture so common that it may be dislocated geographically from its context. *Comin' Through the Rye*, for example, adapted by Hepworth in 1916 and again in 1923, becomes a classic English bucolic. (The appropriation of lyric titles as points of reference to a shared culture is still common: Ken Loach, for example, titles his 2004 Glasgow romance *Ae Fond Kiss*.) Importantly also, however, in a so-called silent cinema, the songs become the key and distinctive element of the musical accompaniment. The trade show of *Annie Laurie* in 1916 is advertised with appropriate music accompaniment: 'Miss Kate Holbrook, of the Royal Opera House, has been engaged as soloist for the occasion.'[22] For *Young Lochinvar* in 1924, exhibitors are encouraged 'to dig up the famous poem which bears the same title as the film, and which we believe is being made into a song'.

Have a chat with your musical director regarding this, and, if possible, arrange for a number of Scottish melodies to be played, giving your patrons a small multigraphed slip on which they should enter the names of the various selections played.[23]

The appeal of adapting songs and poems, then, is not simply a commercial opportunity to tap into a common frame of cultural reference, but is also a means of engaging the community, offering them the possibility of 'singing along' to a familiar song, of participating in the show, keeping alive the inheritance of variety and music hall which is part of the experience of cinema-going in cinema's early decades.

Adaptation from novels and successful London or Broadway plays provided a ready-made store of narratives that early cinema exploited, sometimes repeatedly and sometimes mercilessly. On my count, of the 223 fiction films listed in the filmography, forty-four are adapted from novels or short stories, and twenty-four are adapted from theatre plays. *The Little Minister* was adapted four times in the silent period before the famous Katherine Hepburn version of 1934, and within the period there were nine versions of *Macbeth*, the 'Scottish play': two from Germany, two from France, two from England, two from the USA and one from Italy.

It is interesting to note the spectrum which these adaptations cover, from the historical romances of Scott and his European counterparts, Balzac (*A Calvinist Martyr* (1913)), Heine (*William Ratcliff* (1909 and 1922)) and Schiller (*Maria Stuart* (1927)), to the more parochial landscape of J. M. Barrie, S. R. Crocket and Ian MacLaren. It is also interesting to note what is missing: while Scott is clearly a central figure, his central novel, *Waverley*, was not adapted (and has never been adapted), and *Old Mortality* is also missing. The ambivalence of the young hero in both novels may have blunted the edge of the romance. Similarly, though *Treasure Island* (1912), *The Suicide Club* (1914), *The Bottle Imp* (1917) and *Dr Jekyll and Mr Hyde* (1920) were all adapted from Robert Louis Stevenson, his quintessential Scottish Jacobite novel, *Kidnapped*, was adapted by Edison in 1917 but does not appear to have been released in the UK and does not become part of the canon of 'Scotch' films.

It is also important to recognise that many of the adaptations are from play versions of the original novel. *The Little Minister* of 1921, for example, was an attempt to exploit the success of the theatre adaptation at the Haymarket Theatre in London and on Broadway. Many of the other titles of the 1920s were themselves adaptations of adaptations: films adapted from stage plays adapted from novels or short stories. As one might expect, production companies were attracted to stories that had already demonstrated that they could attract popular audiences, and that could quite easily, appropriately and economically be translated from a stage set to a studio set. Aesthetically, this seems to return film to the theatrical tradition, the narrative turned from the novelistic to the dramatic and the theatrical. Film scripts were commonly still referred to as 'dramatic plays'. For Scott, as subsequently for Dickens, this meant an emphasis on the dramatic or melodramatic action and on dramatic types like Meg Merrilees, Jeanie Deans, Bailie Nicol Jarvie and Rob Roy himself, rather than on the voyages of discovery and transformation of Frank Osbaldistone, Henry Morton or young Edward Waverley.

Finally, and most dramatically, of the forty or so adaptations of Scottish literature and Scottish stories reviewed in *The Bioscope*, only one was produced by a Scottish company: the United Films production of *Rob Roy* in 1911 (discussed in Chapter 7), which was released almost at the same time as Gaumont's 1911 *Rob Roy*, based on the legend rather than the novel. Competition was swift and ruthless. The mere production of a film did not guarantee that it would find an audience, particularly if it had to compete with a major international company.

The precariousness of early film production in Scotland is striking, and, given the popularity of cinema-going in Scotland, still defeats easy explanation. Caroline Merz gives a detailed and sympathetic account of Scottish attempts at production, with particular attention to the case of United Film's *Rob Roy*. Fundamentally, however, making films is difficult in a nation that does not have a large enough domestic audience to underwrite the risks of investment. This has been a historic problem for Britain as a whole, and for Scotland even more sharply. The result is that productions tend to be 'one-off' entrepreneurial ventures, dependent on the success or failure of a single film, and this does not provide the base on which an infrastructure can be built. Equally, investors and entrepreneurs in the period may have been more attracted to the apparent security of investing in exhibition, often on quite a grand and ambitious scale, than in the high-risk business of investing in production when the world market was increasingly dominated by the USA.

There are traces of film production companies being established in Ayr or in Montrose or in Aberdeen, and there are indications from trade reports in the Scottish Section of *The Bioscope* that they had got as far as beginning the filming of screenplays. In 1920, 'Scotty' reports on a film studio in Montrose in which C. F. Partoon, a Dundee photographer who had made a number of local topicals for Dundee cinemas, had produced what had the makings of a feature film, *The Greater Riches*, using a local writer and local actors, and filmed around Dundee and in a 'well-equipped' studio in

Montrose. Ever optimistic, 'Scotty', having read the scenario and on the basis of what he has already seen, predicts success: 'the Trade may look with confidence to his first work, which will only lack one thing, and that is the stamp of amateurism'.[24] But then there is silence, later accompanied by disappointment: 'By the way,' says Scotty in December 1921, 'what has come over that company that was producing in Dundee and Montrose? Are the pictures they partly took ever to be finished, or must the venture be written down as abandoned?'[25] It is hard to avoid the conclusion that exhibition was where profits were being made with a minimum amount of risk, and production from a small country in the English-speaking market where competition was fierce did not make economic sense.

What is in some ways equally interesting is the use of Scotland as a location for Scottish stories. In 1921, *The Bioscope* reports on a company established in Forres, in North-east Scotland, whose purpose was to market local landscape as film location:

stretches of sand dunes, suitable for desert scenes; hills and dales, woodland and charming river scenes of the Findhorn, and near at hand massive and beautiful rock formations which would delight the heart of any location manager.[26]

There is, unfortunately, no record of its success. A handful of films was made by English and American companies on Scottish locations: the various versions of *Rob Roy* seem to have been filmed in and around Aberfoyle; the 1923 *Bonnie Prince Charlie* was filmed in the accessible highlands of the island of Arran in the River Clyde; *Christie Johnstone* spent ten days filming in Auchmithie and its star, Stewart Rome, became a major celebrity in the neighbouring town of Arbroath; and *The Romany*, after considerable time spent researching gypsies by Victor McLagen, seems to have spent some time filming in and around Atholl. For *Robinson Crusoe*, however, there may or may not have been scenes in Largo showing his earlier life, and for *The Little Minister* in 1915 the only shots of Kirriemuir were of the Manse and the village well.

Film-makers visited Scotland to soak up atmosphere – 'I have just been up to Scotland for atmosphere', says Charles Calvert of his 1921 production, *In His Grip*. 'I can assure you it would have been impossible to get the Scotch atmosphere down here', but, having secured the atmosphere, he shot the scenes in London.[27] For the practicalities of film-making, accessibility outweighed authenticity, and atmosphere could be created cinematically rather than reproduced photographically. The Highland seascape of Maurice Tourneur's *The White Heather* (1919) was shot in Los Angeles harbour, and Jeanie Deans's arduous journey to London in

A Woman's Triumph (1914) (a version of Scott's *The Heart of Midlothian*) was shot in Cuba. Of *The White Heather*, says *The Bioscope*, 'The scenes in a spacious Scottish castle, the Highland exteriors and the wonderful London Stock Exchange interiors could scarcely have been better done in England.'[28] Or *Huntingtower* (1928), with Harry Lauder starring as Dickson McCunn, and with six Glasgow youths to play the Gorbals Diehards, set near Carrick in South-west Scotland in John Buchan's novel, was shot in the Cricklewood Studios in London and in Bamburgh Castle in Northumberland.

This move from authenticity to atmosphere, from photographic realism to constructed realism is significant aesthetically, but it is also important economically. A comparison with Ireland is instructive. In 1910, and again the following year, the Kalem company brought their crews and their inward investment to Ireland for a number of films that came to be known as the O'Kalems.[29] This inward investment did not happen in Scotland, and did not form the infrastructure on which something like a sustainable film industry could be built.

While adaptations in one form or another constitute almost half of the films which I have identified as Scottish, a little more than half are, as far as can be determined, original productions. These are films which have Scottish narratives, Scottish locations or prominent Scottish characters. Many of the films are set in Scotland, almost invariably in small towns and villages or in 'the Highlands'. The imaginary map of Scotland is one in which cities, urban life and industry are barely visible behind the hills and glens, villages and castles, peasantry and nobility of a geographically and historically dislocated 'Highlands'. At a time when Glasgow was one of the leading industrial cities in the world, accounting for twenty per cent of the world's shipbuilding, and with a heavy industry infrastructure to support it, we know of only two widely distributed films set or filmed in Glasgow: the locally produced comedy *Football Daft* (1921) and one episode of the Eddie Polo picaresque serial, *The Vanishing Dagger* (1920), which has one scene set in a Glasgow shipyard. Other films are set in London or the United States or Canada, tracking the diaspora with Scottish characters relocated to the American South or Canadian logger camps. Though the Scottish elements in many films seem incidental – *The Wolf* (Vitagraph, 1919), for example, is a set in a Canadian trapping camp – they are highlighted as distinctive in the trade reviews and synopses: *The Wolf*'s plot is motivated by the 'cruel father' who 'typifies well the traditional Scottish male parent'.[30] Adopting a trade definition of Scottishness, these are films that have, in a sense, been 'Scotched'. As imaginary as the landscapes, 'Scotch' characters may be the stern and unbending Presbyterian father who cannot adjust to new ways; the mother longing for her diasporic son, or the diasporic son longing for home; the dispossessed aristocrat seeking new money and a return to social dignity; or the winsome lass who may be the dispossessed aristocrat's best hope; or soldiers from the Highland, bagpipe-playing regiments, relieving towns under siege in the colonial wars (*The Campbells Are Coming* (1915)), or saving villages in the European war of 1914–18 (*Bravo Kilties!* (1914)): 'At the moment when our Scottish regiments are exciting universal admiration any film recording their prowess on the battlefield is certain of success.'[31]

Many of the US 'Scotch' films were not distributed in the UK or had limited release in Scotland. To the extent that these films were aimed at a folk memory it was not necessarily a Scottish folk memory. It is even worth considering that Scotland was not a good market for ersatz 'Scotch' films, or Scotch themes. *The Call of the Pipes* (1918) is advertised in the *Bo'ness Journal* as

All Scotch – Produced on the Bonnie Banks of Loch Lomond
Not an American idea of Scottish Scenery and Character,
but the 'Real Mackay'.[32]

The appeal to the 'Real Mackay' suggests a recognition by the publicist of a clear and sceptical perception on the part of the audience of the 'unreal Mackay', imagined from the other side of the Atlantic.

The issue, then is not one of identity but of the way in which Scotland functioned in the imaginary; a question not just of the recognition or misrecognition on which subjectivity depends but of a refusal to recognise. Scotch locations, Scotch characters and Scotch narratives map Scotland's place within the international imagination both as a repository of the wildness of the Highlands – a European equivalent of the American West – or as a memory within a diasporic and urbanised culture of a lost past of the rural, the home, a vanishing and romanticised nobility, and a secure and simplified morality.

Finally, however, there is no very clear evidence that the failure to represent Scotland constituted a failure to meet demand. The really popular films in Scotland seem to have been Westerns, particularly Tom Mix, or Chaplin comedies, or serials. 'Scottish' films, however, like the 1911 *Rob Roy* that did claim to be made for Scots by Scots, do not appear to have enjoyed enough commercial success, even in Scotland, to sustain a stream of production. Scottish-produced films did not necessarily travel, and they often disappeared without trace outside the city-centre cinemas. For the Scottish experience of film-going, it may be that Scottish spectators, who crowded the cinemas week after week, despite the attempts of the industry and the trade press to woo their support for British, if not Scottish cinema, would rather identify with Tom Mix or would rather be subject to the perils of Pauline. They would rather watch the sophisticated industrialisation of cinematic narrative, spectacle and stardom which the Hollywood studios were now perfecting than watch the occasional and sometimes quite amateur productions of a cinema that seemed to make every film as a one-off.

I am increasingly sceptical of the view that some of us took in the 1980s that the so-called deformities of Scottish popular culture represented, or were derivatives of, deformities in Scottish identity.[33] The evidence from the 1920s is that audiences were themselves sceptical, and were, on the one hand, drawn to the landscapes, but dismissive of the parodies of dress, language and custom with which Scotland was encrusted. Hollywood films of the American West seemed more up-to-date than films of the Scottish Highlands. At the same time, I am interested both in the continuities of the imaginary from literature to film, and in the ways in which cinema is caught in that ambivalence of modernity between the shock of the new and the desire for the past. As suggested in the previous chapter, and somewhat curiously, it is when one comes to look at the local topicals that are held in the National Library of Scotland's Moving Image Archive that cinema seems new again. It is in these local topicals, in the fascination of the amateurs with the new technology, in the experience of seeing their lives recorded, in the immediacy of their localities caught on film, in the commonplace and the everyday, that cinema, again, seems most modern.

Notes

1. Moretti, *Distant Reading*, 67.
2. Moretti, *Distant Reading*, 48.
3. Pierce, *The Survival of American Silent Feature Films, 1912–1929*, 1.
4. *Bioscope*, 15 October 1925, p. 37.
5. *Bioscope*, 13 January 1924, p. v.
6. *Bioscope*, 1 February 1917, p, 507.
7. Emerson, 'Tribute to Walter Scott on the One Hundredth Anniversary of His Birthday, 15 August 1871'.
8. Twain, *Life on the Mississippi*. On Scott, see Chapter 46, 'Enchanters and Enchantment'.
9. Pennant, *A Tour in Scotland and Voyage to the Hebrides, 1772*.
10. Johnson and Boswell, *A Journey to the Western Islands of Scotland*.
11. Burns, 'Journal of a Tour in the Highlands Made in the Year 1787'.

12. Diggle, 'Journal of a Tour from London to the Highlands of Scotland, 19 April–7 August 1788'.
13. Wordsworth, *Recollections of a Tour Made in Scotland*.
14. Victoria, *Queen Victoria's Highland Journals*.
15. Ardill and Imms, 'Tour of Scotland for Scott's Poetical Works 1831'.
16. Wordsworth, 'Memorials of a Tour in Scotland, 1803. VII. Stepping Westward'.
17. Wordsworth, *Recollections of a Tour Made in Scotland*, 87.
18. Wordsworth, *Recollections of a Tour Made in Scotland*, 99.
19. Wordsworth, *Recollections of a Tour Made in Scotland*, 88.
20. Wordsworth, *Recollections of a Tour Made in Scotland*, 154.
21. Wordsworth, *Recollections of a Tour Made in Scotland*, 48.
22. *Bioscope*, 16 June 1916, pp. 1042–5. This is the London trade show at the West End Cinema, Coventry Street.
23. 'British Film Weeks: Selling Angles for All Pictures', *Bioscope*, 3 January 1924, p. xii.
24. 'New Studios at Montrose: Production already commenced', *Bioscope*, 12 August 1920, pp. 78–9.
25. *Bioscope*, 8 December 1921, p. 73.
26. *Bioscope*, 30 June 1921, pp. 55–7.
27. 'Studio Notes', *Bioscope*, 26 May 1921, p. 45.
28. 'Criticism of the Films: The White Heather', *Bioscope*, 19 June 1919, 83.
29. See *The O'Kalem Collection, 1910–1915*, a DVD collection of eight Kalem films made in Ireland, including *Rory O'More* (1911) and *The Colleen Bawn* (1911), with an accompanying documentary *Blazing the Trail: The O'Kalems in Ireland* (Irish Film Institute and BIFF Productions, 2011).
30. 'The Wolf, *Moving Picture World*, 16 August 1919, p. 1023. Via *Media History Digital Library*, http://archive.org/stream/movingpicturewor41chal
31. 'Bravo Kilties!', *Bioscope*, 12 November 1914, p. 668.
32. *Bo'ness Journal*, 8 March 1918.
33. See, for example, McArthur, *Scotch Reels* – to which the present author contributed.

CHAPTER 10

The Talkies Triumphant: Scottish Cinema and the Coming of Sound

Trevor Griffiths

For the cinema industry across Scotland, the move to replace silent with sound film was extensive and abrupt. An exhibition sector which, by the later 1920s, appeared stable, profitable and increasingly popular was suddenly confronted by the necessity of undertaking significant re-equipment and reorganisation. Within twelve months of the talkies' debut north of the border, the screening of Warner's *The Singing Fool* at the Coliseum in Glasgow in January 1929, some hundred houses across the country had converted or were expected to convert to sound, so that for the trade press at least the talkie house had become a commonplace.[1] So ubiquitous had it become that in submissions to Scottish courts it quickly came to be advanced, as had the silent film before it, as an explanation in mitigation of acts of criminality. At Ayr Sheriff Court in June 1929, a sixteen-year-old boy pleaded guilty to a charge of assault, but claimed that he had been seeking money to take his girlfriend to the talkies in Kilmarnock.[2] By early 1930, the onward march of sound appeared so relentless that a Cinema Exhibitors' Association (CEA) questionnaire found only seventy-five members determined to remain silent.[3] The implications of this change were many and varied, but were particularly profound for those hitherto employed to add sound to the silent image. As the silent era approached its end, Edwin Evans, musical correspondent of *The Bioscope*, had claimed that some three-quarters of all paid employment for musicians across Britain was provided by cinemas.[4] At the same time, the Glasgow branch of the Musicians' Union (MU) recorded a membership of 1,122, close to the highest enrolment yet recorded. Yet within three years, membership was down to 510, union officials estimating that only fifty members were still engaged in cinemas, with most of those located outwith the city.[5] The decline was so marked that the Ministry of Labour noted that the wage agreement concluded as recently as 1925 between the MU and the CEA was now redundant, 'as there are practically no musicians now employed in cinemas'.[6] Nor was Glasgow in this regard exceptional, going some way towards justifying the MU's claim that the impact of the switch to sound had been more severe in Scotland than anywhere else in the British Isles.[7]

The fate of cinema orchestras marked an important change in the manner in which films were exhibited, live performance becoming effectively marginalised if not wholly removed as the standard programme came to revolve around a double bill of features with short subjects in occasional support. The cost of mounting the programme now fell increasingly on film producers, the role of the exhibitor in offering bespoke music, speech or sound effect, so contributing materially to the way in which the movies were experienced, being substantially reduced.[8] So widespread were the changes that resulted, the silent film increasingly confined to screenings by interested minorities such as film societies, that in retrospect it carries an air of inevitability. For exhibitors pursuing the highest possible return, the take-up of sound appeared little more than a rational business decision. As an advertisement for the British Acoustic sound system had it, in September 1930, 'Silence was Golden, but Talkies mean Profits!'[9] For contemporaries, however, the position was less clear-cut than this suggests. In the months immediately preceding the advent of sound, doubts were repeatedly expressed that an audience long attuned to silent modes of storytelling would have the patience to engage with an extended narrative conveyed largely through dialogue, and so some role for live performers, be they orchestra or variety turn, was considered crucial if the programme were to remain attractive. For many, the precise form that film presentations would take appeared more open to question than at any time since the advent of the moving picture. The format for an effective evening's entertainment was subject to debate, with some advocating a programme made up of a series of short subjects interspersed with live variety turns.[10] That such expectations were so rapidly and comprehensively dashed does not mean they should be discounted. Rather, they point up the need for a close investigation of the circumstances in which exhibition strategies developed in the early sound era. Far from being ineluctable, the eventual outcome for audience, exhibitors and performers appears the result of a series of contingent developments and decisions that linked the industry in Scotland to production companies centred on Hollywood and London, legislators at Westminster, officials at the Treasury and the Board of Trade, and the mass of cinema-goers locally.

Before tracing their impact, attention is first directed to the soundscape of silent cinema in Scotland, providing a context for assessing thinking in the trade during what turned out to be the last full year of the silent era. Sound had long played a key role in the presentation of silent film.[11] Musical accompaniment was capable, through its relevance to the subject matter, to encourage an enhanced appreciation of and engagement with the film. During time of war, patriotic sentiments were quickened by appropriate vocal and instrumental support. In October 1914, a performance of patriotic airs was mounted to enhance the screening of *Britain's Call* at the Palace in Edinburgh, while in July 1916 the Lyceum, also in Edinburgh, employed the brass and pipe band of the Argyll and Sutherland Highlanders to accompany the first official war film, *Britain Prepared*.[12] Where possible, Scottish associations were emphasised through the deployment of appropriate music. The pipes were once more employed in early 1917 to boost shows including *The Battle of the Ancre and the Advance of the Tanks*.[13] More rarely, the juxtaposition of silence and music was used to heighten the effect of the visuals. For one wartime subject involving an enemy submarine, shown at Glasgow's Picture House in 1919, silence was maintained until the final sequence depicting the surrender of the boat's crew, at which point the orchestra struck up a rendition of *Rule Britannia*.[14] The human voice could also be deployed to manage abrupt changes in subject matter or to root the film in a local and familiar context. At a number of Aberdeen cinemas, 'elocutionists' performed behind the screen, often lending the material a Doric inflexion.[15] Even into the 1920s, lecturers were employed on occasion to offer personal insights into the events depicted. In 1924, at Poole's Synod Hall in Edinburgh, home of annual Myriorama shows, the screening of *Crossing the Great Sahara* was enhanced by the accounts of Captain Angus Buchanan, Military Cross and Fellow of the Royal Geographical Society, leader of the expedition, accompanied by two Arab guides, one of whom entertained audiences further by performing native dances and offering reflections on a visit to the Empire Exhibition at Wembley.[16] The following year, the same venue played host to Captain J. B. Noel, also Fellow of the Royal Geographical Society, and 'The Famous Seven Lamas' for screenings of *The Epic of Everest*, an account of the unsuccessful 1924 expedition.[17] Here, cinema's continuation of the long-established practice of conveying enlightenment and uplift through the medium of entertainment and spectacle was evident.

Attempts to synchronise sound with the footage being shown were more intermittent but recurred through the period from cinema's first decade to the end of the silent era. Before the First World War, a variety of devices were promoted that claimed to achieve effective synchronisation. In the final months of peace, the Edison Kinetophone was adopted in at least two Edinburgh cinemas. The Silver Kinema in the city's Nicolson Square stressed that it was 'The only Photo Playhouse in Edinburgh where Genuine Talking Pictures are to be Seen and

Heard'.[18] An alternative approach was essayed by the Clarendon Speaking Pictures at the nearby Palace, which employed an unseen speaker to recite passages from the literary works depicted on the screen, including in February 1914 Robert Buchanan's poem 'Phil Blood's Leap'.[19] Mechanical methods of synchronisation functioning without the need for live performers promised significant returns and encouraged Scots to move into sound technology. That which progressed furthest was based on a design by a mechanic based at the Royal Naval Torpedo Works in Greenock and was promoted by the Vocal Cinema Co. Ltd, registered in January 1914.[20] The company produced a number of 'Singing and Talking Pictures' that included dramatised scenes to accompany song texts. Even in the few months leading up to the outbreak of war, the firm struggled to see a return on its investments and attempts were made to sell the patent rights.[21] The fate of this and other innovations may have discouraged further attempts at the mechanical marriage of sound and pictures. Such at least is suggested by the comparatively few references to such innovations across the 1920s. In their place, an older means of synchronisation was revived, so that, at Edinburgh's St Andrew Square Picture House in September 1924, the exhibition of the Graham-Wilcox production of *Chu-Chin-Chow* involved two members of the original London cast singing the musical numbers as they appeared on the screen, matching the words to the lip movements of the actors.[22]

A final brief experiment in synchronised sound was attempted in the mid-1920s. Phonofilms made use of the de Forest and Case sound on film technology, and played at Edinburgh's Synod Hall in the later months of 1926. One of the subjects, receiving what was claimed to be its first ever showing, was a forty-five-minute sketch of Scottish life in the nineteenth century, *Till the Bells Ring*, written by and featuring that 'most humorous of Scotsmen', the actor and playwright Graham Moffat. Reviews following the screening were complimentary about the quality of synchronisation and the clarity with which words were reproduced.[23] The latter in particular made demands on the audience who, in advance of the show, were

> particularly requested to refrain from entering the Auditorium within 45 minutes after the above times [4, 6.15, 7.15 and 9.30 p.m.], so that the dialogue may not be interrupted.[24]

How far such unfamiliar injunctions may have worked to limit the film's appeal is not known. It is however clear that the impact of the film quickly faded, so that within a few years it had disappeared from popular memory. The appearance of *The Singing Fool* in the city in the summer of 1929 was reported to be Edinburgh's first encounter with sound film.[25] From the perspective of 1928, then, experiments in synchronisation appeared short-lived and of limited appeal. As a result, the arrival of the latest attempt at sound pictures, even when backed by a major Hollywood studio, occasioned little comment and that which was offered was, for the most part, sceptical.

In June 1928, *The Bioscope* in an editorial headed 'Golden Silence', expressed doubts that audiences would tolerate sound for other than the occasional short or interest item used as interludes to break up the programme.[26] The readiness of patrons to sit for long periods following extended narratives driven by spoken dialogue seemed most unlikely. As late as October of that year, the view continued to be that the appeal of the talkies would be limited: in a world in which sound was encountered willingly or otherwise on an everyday basis, the attraction of an escape into silence would remain real.[27] Equally, audiences, it was felt, would be alienated by the restrictions imposed to ensure audibility. A quality that added gilt to silence was the discretion allowed patrons to pay as much or as little attention to the screen as they deemed appropriate. In November 1929, with the talkies a rapidly growing presence, the Kingsway in Levenshulme, Manchester, made a virtue of its continued reliance on silence: 'No Talkies Here – At the "Talkies" you can't talk – you have to remain Silent. We remain Silent but don't compel you to keep silent or talk.'[28]

Surveys of audience preferences, mostly conducted outwith Scotland, reinforced doubts as to the appeal of sound. The second Bernstein questionnaire of patrons attending his Granada chain of cinemas revealed an equal divide on the question of sound versus silents among male picture-goers, while women, making up the bulk of the adult audience, divided seventy to thirty in favour of silents.[29] A further investigation across northern counties of England canvassed views from 54,366 cinema-goers and found that 62.85 per cent of those questioned preferred silent films.[30] Where different opinions were encountered, a key variable was found to lie in experience of sound films: where the talkies were encountered, support for silence was often seriously compromised.

A comparable progression was encountered north of the border and can be traced through the diary of one young female cinema-goer in Glasgow. Kitty McGinniss celebrated her twenty-first birthday in 1929 and across the year, the first in which sound films figured on local bills, she recorded forty-seven visits to local picture houses.[31] Significantly for the purposes of this inquiry, she was one of 292,182 picture-goers who

LOOKING FOR THE MAN WHO INVENTED THE " TALKIES."

Figure 10.1 'Looking for the man who invented the "talkies"', *The Musicians' Journal*, July 1929, p. 27. Courtesy of the Musicians' Union Archive, University of Stirling

saw *The Singing Fool* (1928) across three-and-a-half weeks at Glasgow's Coliseum. Such was the enthusiasm generated by this Jolson vehicle that, while nearby houses were said to be struggling for business, the Coliseum opted to cancel a screening of MGM's *The Garden of Allah* (1927) in favour of retaining *The Singing Fool* for a further week than had originally been planned. Kitty McGinniss's verdict provided further endorsement for this decision as she adjudged it a 'splendid show'.[32] From that point, her diary chronicles a recurrent exposure to talkies, including *Showboat*, *Blackmail* and *The Broadway Melody* (all 1929). While all encouraged favourable comments, experience overall may not have been uniformly positive, so that it was only towards the end of November, when *Broadway Babies* (1929) played at the New Savoy, that she felt able to confide that she was 'liking talkies better now'.[33] Overall, the diary reveals a readiness to seek out talkies, even though the form was unfamiliar and occasionally of variable quality. There was little trace here of the scepticism anticipated by *The Bioscope* just a few months earlier.

Additional evidence of the talkies' early popularity can be gained from the performance of houses that initially opted to remain silent. In October 1929, directors of the Crosshill Picture House in Glasgow appealed against the company's assessment for rates before the local Valuation Court, arguing that business had fallen by some fifteen per cent, a trend traceable in part to the proximity of two large talkie houses.[34] The finances of another cinema offer more sustained insights into the speed and extent of any impact. At the end of the silent era, the Palace, located at the east end of Edinburgh's Princes Street, showed consistent profitability. In the black in every week across 1928, the last full year for silents in Scotland, the house returned each week an average profit of £120 6s on takings of £471 1s.[35] Little occurred to alter that pattern through the first half of 1929, receipts averaging £468 13s weekly. Thereafter, trading became more difficult, so that takings towards the end of the year, rather than showing the customary upturn following a summer lull, remained consistently lower, over twenty per cent down on the previous year at £371 13s a week. Key to the change in fortune was the opening in quick succession of houses either converted to or built for the showing of sound films: the New Picture House further west along Princes Street opened as a talkie house in June, as did Poole's Synod Hall on Castle Terrace the following month, while in August the Playhouse, a cinema wired for sound from the outset and with a capacity of over three thousand, opened for business.[36] For the Palace, the impact quickly became clear as the fall off in custom continued into the following year. In the final fourteen weeks of operating as a 'silent' house, receipts were only just over half the figure of two years before and the balance sheet on average showed a weekly loss approaching £30.[37] Demand, as expressed through the box office, showed an almost immediate and unambiguous preference for sound.

Other aspects of the Palace's performance in those final weeks point to simultaneous problems on the supply side. Profits remained elusive despite marked reductions in the cost of hire. In 1928, an average of £90 17s a week had been spent constructing the programme. By contrast, in the last fourteen weeks prior to conversion, spending on films had fallen to nearer £40 a week. The low point came in late August, when £16 was paid for a double bill headed by the German drama *Their Son* (*Sensation im Wintergarten*, 1929), supported by a reissue of the 1924 Stoll romance *The Love Story of Aliette Brunton*. Despite its low cost, takings of £190 produced a loss overall for the week of £68.[38] While still unusual, the inclusion of a European film on the bill became a more frequent feature of programming at the Palace as 1930 progressed. In the more benign circumstances of 1928, only three programmes had included productions that were not either American or British in origin, whereas that was true of six out of the last fourteen weeks of the house's career as a silent cinema.[39] If this ensured that local picture-goers gained access to artistically significant productions, such as Fritz Lang's *Frau im Mond* (1929), and Carl Theodor Dreyer's *La Passion de Jeanne d'Arc* (1928), weekly profits of £54 and £12 respectively remained modest and were the result primarily of the low cost of hire: £40 and £48 in each case.[40] This may be compared with the £465 spent on average each week across 1930 to supply the nearby Playhouse.[41]

All this is suggestive of increasing problems which silent houses encountered in attempting to secure attractive product, as the availability of new silent features declined sharply. The contrast with the Playhouse also draws attention to the cost of hiring sound compared to silent subjects. Both would have major implications for the pace and pattern of the take-up of the talkies across Scotland. The first drove many otherwise sceptical or reluctant exhibitors to abandon silents. The very month that the talkies made their bow in Glasgow, John Maxwell, head of Associated British Cinemas and its production arm British International Pictures Ltd and himself a Scot, predicted, in a speech to the CEA in Manchester, a shortage of silent films by the end of 1929 as major Hollywood studios began first to privilege sound production and then to abandon silents altogether.[42] By March, Fox had announced its intention of focusing on sound production, a decision echoed the following month by Universal.[43] So, more than a month before Edinburgh had its first sustained encounter with talkies, Jesse Lasky of Paramount had declared 'Silent Films Dead for All Time'.[44] The following year, reports from the USA suggested that fewer than 350 silent titles were available, a number insufficient to satisfy even the limited demand identified by the CEA as coming from the cinemas across Britain that intended to remain silent. Even this modest pool mostly comprised re-releases or silent versions of sound productions released in 1929–30.[45] Developments in the British production industry offered little promise of relief. Major studios, including BIP, were outlining ambitious programmes for sound films early in 1929.[46] Their decisions were encouraged by the greater security offered by quota legislation, which obliged cinemas across Britain to show a minimum percentage of footage that was 'British' in origin. Improved prospects for the British industry anticipated from the Act had encouraged the creation of large, vertically integrated concerns, modelled on the lines of the Hollywood majors. Both Associated British Cinemas and the Gaumont-British Picture Corporation had devoted resources across 1928 to acquiring cinemas across the country that would provide guaranteed outlets for their productions.[47] The former, thanks to Maxwell's own Scottish Cinema and Variety Theatres chain, already had a strong presence north of the border. With major producers tying their cinemas into acquiring sound films, the pressure on independent exhibitors to do likewise in order to secure marketable British product was great. At CEA meetings, such as that held in Edinburgh in October 1929, proprietors of small houses were complaining of being forced into adopting sound, regardless of their own preferences.[48] The iron law of supply was such that even those most vociferous in claiming the necessity of the silent film for smaller halls, such as Baillie Timmins of the Theatre De Luxe, Lochgelly, had by January 1931 moved to install sound equipment.[49]

It would appear therefore that a potent combination of demand- and supply-side pressures worked to force Scottish exhibitors to engage with the talkies. It also worked to shape the manner in which the sound film was presented. Until the advent of the talkies, the expectation had been that the contribution of live performers would grow rather than diminish with the coming of sound. *The Bioscope* across 1926 and 1927 noted an increasing readiness to include variety turns in the bill, as short film subjects were often found to be in short supply and comparatively expensive, so that even if the quality was often doubtful 'Still, even one singer means two reels less!'[50] As a consequence, the variety act remained a staple of programmes for many large as well as small exhibitors, their importance to the house's overall appeal reflected in the prominence accorded them in accompanying publicity. Up to the end of the silent era, advertisements for Poole's Synod Hall highlighted the presence of variety artistes and were careful to specify their place in the daily schedule. So, in one week in February 1929, when the bill was headed by Fox's *None But the Brave* (1928), with screenings at 2.30, 4.30, 6.50 and 9.15 pm, supported by the same studio's Western *Girl-Shy Cowboy* (1928), at 3.30, 5.30 and 7.45 pm, audiences were diverted at 6.30 and 9 pm by live performances of Charles Ancaster and his 'Waltzing Bottles and Boomerangs'.[51] Live performances also worked to enhance the appeal of the main feature, through staged prologues, the popularity and effectiveness of which were confidently asserted by the trade press through the 1920s.[52] Prologues could vary in nature, from the straightforward, such as the performance of the ballad 'Annie Laurie' prior to the screening of the MGM production of the film of the same name at the Coliseum in Glasgow in May 1928, to the elaborate: a staged cabaret with twenty-one performers, comprising a full jazz orchestra and two dancers, being employed to precede shows of MGM's *The Taxi Dancer* (1927) with Joan Crawford and Owen Moore at Green's Playhouse in January the same year.[53] The future of variety was debated within the pages of *The Bioscope* in the late summer of 1928. If some were inclined to dismiss cine-variety as 'this formless cuckoo', others including S. Cruickshank, former manager of a Green's cinema, argued that it represented the future of the industry, to the extent that it would soon be offered by seventy-five per cent of all houses. A. S. Albin of Edinburgh's Regent Picture House agreed, noting that new houses, including the planned Playhouse had included provision for a stage, suggesting that 'Vaudeville is bound to appear as a permanency on picture house programmes in the near future'.[54]

That the transition to sound would result in a retrenchment rather than the envisaged expansion in the provision of live entertainment was a consequence, in large measure, of the costs attending the switch. Two factors were influential here: the expense involved in installing and maintaining the equipment, but also the enhanced and less predictable cost of film hire. To take the first, the Coliseum was said to have spent some £7,000 in installing both the Vitaphone sound on disc and the Movietone sound on film systems late in 1928, an outlay well beyond the means of most houses operating at the end of the silent era.[55] Prices would fall quickly as the interchangeability of systems encouraged many producers on to the market to satisfy the burgeoning demand. By early 1930, sets were available for less than £1,000, Klangfilm offering installation for a down payment of £150, with the balance payable over one or two years.[56] Western Electric, the largest single producer of talkie equipment and the company responsible for the Coliseum installation, was, by 1931, advertising a set suitable for small exhibitors at a total cost of £785 plus service.[57]

As had been the case three decades earlier, when methods of projection had proliferated as a way of avoiding payments to existing providers, innovations of seemingly questionable technical merit circulated: one such, the Mihaly Tone Film Apparatus, which proclaimed itself 'The Salvation of the Smaller Theatres', claimed to obviate the need for rewiring by utilising an 'invisible ray'.[58] Scotland had its own alternative to English and American systems with Bestalk, a development by Malcolm Irvine of Scottish Film Productions (1928) Ltd and an offshoot of his attempts at film production from a studio in India Street, Glasgow. Bestalk was taken up by several smaller cinemas and was the standby system used at the Regent in Glasgow.[59] Variation went further: individual cinema managers, on occasion drawing on earlier experiments with the mechanical reproduction and amplification of music, developed their own bespoke methods of sound projection, in the process bringing the talkies earlier than might have been anticipated to smaller urban centres such as Elgin, Polmont and Musselburgh.[60] The economies promised by cheaper systems were often outweighed by substandard reproduction. The Regent in Glasgow opted in 1929 to adopt the Powers Cinephone system, employing Malcolm Irvine to oversee the installation, but quickly repented of the decision when patrons repeatedly complained of poor sound quality. In September 1930, the manager was reporting that many had 'left the House after waiting to hear only a small part of the programme'.[61] The directors had already approached Western Electric in search of an alternative, and discussions were renewed in August 1931. By then, the terms included a down payment of £187 12s, followed by 156 payments of £12 10s 9d weekly, a total outlay of £2,118 9s plus a weekly service charge of £3 10s.[62] The Regent's experience was not unusual. Green's purchased the British Talking Pictures and the Klangfilm systems for the Playhouse before opting for Western Electric.[63] The readiness of exhibitors to persist in seeking the most effective system indicates the degree to which talkies had come to be seen as the only option available to the trade and that in competing for business the quality of sound was a paramount consideration.

There remained the cost of the film, hired on terms different from those which had prevailed in the silent era. Then, most subjects were acquired on payment of a flat-rate fee which applied regardless of the film's subsequent box-office performance. In part, such arrangements reflected the exhibitor's role in ensuring that productions appealed to local audiences, through the provision of suitable sound accompaniment. They also ensured that fluctuations in rental charges were predictable and could therefore be minimised. At the Palace in Edinburgh across 1928, expenditure on programmes varied between £57 and £122 a week, while in forty of the fifty-two weeks in the year the magnitude fell within the range £75 to £105.⁶⁴ With the talkies, greater responsibility for the overall appeal of a picture fell on the producer, who now bore a greater proportion of costs represented in the final product and in the process incurred a higher risk. In such circumstances, it was inevitable that the rewards of boxoffice success would be reallocated to some degree. Payments were now more often on a percentage basis, with a proportion of takings claimed by distributor and producer. For potentially attractive star-studded vehicles, this could involve up to fifty per cent of receipts, an arrangement that applied for Chaplin's *City Lights* (1931), and MGM's *Grand Hotel* (1932). The desire to maintain amicable relations with producers and so sustain access to what promised to be highly lucrative product encouraged acceptance of such terms by exhibitors. In November 1932, the Aberdeen Picture Palaces Ltd agreed to take *Grand Hotel* on a fixed fifty per cent basis for two weeks.⁶⁵ More often, films were hired on a sliding scale, the percentage claimed by distributors rising as takings exceeded a certain figure. Rental charges thus became more variable, coloured as they were by the fluctuating state of the box office. In 1932, payments at the Palace ranged from £30, for a programme headed by a British documentary with the unpromising title, for Scottish audiences at least, of *England Awake* (1932), to £212 for the Greta Garbo vehicle *Mata Hari* (1931).⁶⁶ Charges were also generally higher than had been the case for silents. The Palace's spending thus exceeded the 1928 average of £91 on thirty-three occasions in 1932, although in the interval it had moved from being a first-run silent house to a second-run (to the nearby Playhouse) talkie cinema, an arrangement that should in theory have limited the rental bill.⁶⁷ The prospect of higher rentals raised by declining output from Hollywood studios and the enhanced competition for a limited pool of attractive British product encouraged the CEA to explore the possibility of forming a company to act as a booking agent for small, independent exhibitors, the pooling of booking arrangements enhancing their market power.⁶⁸

The implications of increased charges were registered in company accounts. For first-run houses in the silent era, films made up the business's largest single outlay. In six months to June 1926, the Regent in Glasgow spent £3,925 on film hire, compared to £1,667 on staff wages and £2,186 on the orchestra.⁶⁹ For smaller second-run houses, the wage bill, including payments to musicians, outstripped the cost of films. At the Torry Cinema Ltd in Aberdeen, wages were almost double the hire charge.⁷⁰ Yet, by the early 1930s, reduced musical provision and the higher cost of sound films had almost precisely reversed that pattern. At other houses nearby, balance sheets underwent a comparable recalibration.

Table 10.1 Torry Cinemas Ltd: expenditure on films and wages, 1926–33

Year	Wages	Films
1926	£1,302 16s 2d	£722 17s 3d
1927	£1,329 9s 8d	£846 3s 8d
1928	£1,577 2s 10½d	£801 10s
1929	£1,604 16s 2d	£900 17s 6d
1930	£1,790 8s 7d	£1,033 13s
1931	£1,242 13s 4d	£1,840 17s 5d
1932	£1,033	£2,196 0s 4d
1933	£1,097 0s 3d	£1,795 11s 8d

Source: CM, Torry Cinemas Ltd Accounts

At the Aberdeen Playhouse, a rise of almost two-thirds in spending on films between the financial years 1928–9 and 1930–1 was accompanied by a fall of 64.5 per cent in wage costs.[71] Cinema staffs bore the brunt of any retrenchment enforced by the enhanced costs of film rentals, with live performers the prime casualties.

That outcome was not immediate. In January 1929, the Coliseum orchestra continued to figure on the bill alongside *The Singing Fool*, providing two interval performances, each of thirty minutes.[72] Later that same year, management at Synod Hall when publicising the decision to wire for sound also stressed that the orchestra would be retained, 'In deference [it was claimed] to the expressed desires of the vast majority of . . . patrons'. From that point it would provide full accompaniment for silent films, but would otherwise play twice-nightly interludes of fifteen minutes each.[73] At the Playhouse, much was made of the orchestra and its mode of entry into the auditorium via an electric lift. The 'rising orchestra' of sixteen players would provide musical prologues for each evening's entertainment and offered extended concerts on Sundays.[74] Decisions elsewhere to reinstate or install orchestras where they had not originally been planned offered justification for the Musicians' Union's claim that live music would remain an integral part of the cinema programme. Staying in Edinburgh, the New Caley Picture House reopened after wiring for sound in 1929 with the RCA Photophone system, augmented for silent subjects by one of the many gramophone systems on the market.[75] The absence of an orchestra, given prominence on its opening as a talkie house, was ended in July of the following year when twelve instrumentalists were taken on.[76] To the west, the Rialto in Cathcart and the Paisley Picture House also moved to restore their orchestras.[77] While providing occasional grounds for optimism, such instances could do little to alter the general downward trend in orchestral provision. Two months after the opening of *The Singing*

Fool, four members of the Coliseum orchestra were given notice.[78] It was a prelude to wider losses elsewhere, which accelerated in the autumn, the point in the year at which orchestral players were re-employed after a brief summer layoff. In September 1929, the MU noted that over seventy musicians had been dismissed from fourteen cinemas in which the talkies now prevailed. Even when they were retained, their tenure proved short-lived and, just four weeks after renewing its contract, the Regent in Glasgow moved to disband its orchestra in mid-October 1929.[79]

That same month, its early optimism long dissipated, the MU was agitating for a boycott of talkie houses. With all first-run cinemas across Glasgow set to convert to sound by August 1929 and with profits squeezed by the additional costs imposed first by the hire of the talkies and also by the acquisition and maintenance of the equipment used to project them, that sound would prevail appeared unquestionable.[80] By May 1930, the MU's Glasgow branch noted that some seventy talkie houses were active within and around the city, affecting the employment of 368 musicians.[81] The plight of these and others had the previous month been debated at the annual conference of the Scottish Trades Union Congress through a motion submitted by the MU calling for trade unionists to boycott talkie cinemas. Despite a counter-resolution from the Amalgamated Engineering Union, which stressed the employment benefits for its members of the widespread conversion to sound, the MU's call was endorsed by sixty-eight votes to forty-eight.[82] In practice, the impact of the motion was nugatory, to the extent that, seven months after it was carried, the Glasgow branch of the MU was noting the marginal presence its members had in cinemas across the city.[83] That considerations of cost had won out over the aesthetic appeal of live music-making became apparent as previously agreed rates of pay were questioned. In October 1929, the Imperial Picture House in Glasgow proposed a reduced salary of £2 a week when sound pictures were screened, full union rates to apply only when silent footage played. Equally, at Possilpark, the wage of the house pianist was reduced by fifteen shillings a week to meet, it was claimed, the challenge of the talkies.[84]

By the second half of 1931, the economies enforced by the transition to sound had brought the Glasgow cinema orchestra to the verge of extinction. Further east in Edinburgh, if the position was not quite so parlous, musicians remained on the endangered list. By then, according to the CEA, four houses continued to employ instrumentalists, their survival owing much, in the view of the MU, to intensive competition for custom among cinemas in close physical proximity.[85] In such circumstances, the provision of entertainment additional to the film was deemed essential. Along with its Rising Orchestra, the city's Playhouse cinema offered patrons a café and an eighteen-hole miniature golf course, open on all seven days of the week.[86] If instances of orchestral survival remained few, they helped feed continued optimism within the MU as to the future of live music in the cinema programme. Much significance was attached to the decision by the Gaumont-British Picture Corporation to employ musicians at houses equipped with stages. This latest example in what posterity would judge to be an act of collective straw clutching culminated in the confident assertion that 'Variety and the Band is going to be the mainstay of the kinema of the future'.[87] Yet decisions the previous month at Westminster were already working to render the prospects of the few orchestras still active even more precarious. The emergency budget of September 1931, designed to restore the nation's finances and so secure the confidence of international creditors, raised the level of Entertainments Tax, so that payment of the duty would commence on seats priced 2d rather than the previous threshold of 6d and a more sharply graduated rate was imposed on higher-priced tickets.[88] For an industry already facing the challenge of escalating costs at a time of economic uncertainty which worked to reduce the spending power of its main working-class customer base, the additional burden of higher taxes complicated the picture further. Two options were open to exhibitors, both of which threatened existing levels of business: to pass the higher tax rate on to patrons via increased seat prices or to absorb any rise and so pay over to the Treasury a higher proportion of takings. Both pointed to a squeeze on profit margins, the first through reduced business, the second as a result of a declining share of existing levels of custom. The decision to pass the increased duty on to consumers also required an unusual level of collaboration in a highly competitive business. Nevertheless, in October 1931 houses across Glasgow's south side agreed to raise prices in line with the higher tax burden.[89] In many cases, unity of action proved more elusive, so that at Bo'ness Louis Dickson's decision to raise prices at the Hippodrome was quickly reversed when his main local competitor, the Picture House, failed to follow suit. In such circumstances, businesses were obliged to shoulder the burden themselves. The Playhouse in Edinburgh opted to freeze prices on most of its higher-priced seating.[90] On all sides, a further squeeze in profits was anticipated late in 1931. The Aberdeen Picture Palaces Ltd projected a loss of £20 a week from the change.[91]

As early as November 1931, a marked fall in receipts at small cinemas located in working-class districts was being reported.[92] Later surveys offered statistical precision in support of such claims. In March 1932, returns from 1,204 cinemas across Britain suggested a decline in attendances of 11.45 per cent, which translated into a fifteen per cent fall in takings as patrons opted to fill the cheaper seats.[93] At a mass meeting organised by the Scottish CEA to call for a lifting of the tax burden, A.B. King reported that, over twelve weeks, attendances were 38,773 down at cinemas located in shipbuilding areas. Where unemployment was highest, the fall-off was even more marked at 44,949.[94] If the absence of an indication of proportionate loss limits the value of such observations, the broader trend towards reduced business and depressed profits was caught in company ledgers, such as those available for small houses in and around Aberdeen. With no alleviation from the Treasury in prospect, businesses were more likely to seek further economies, precluding the further investment in live entertainments which the MU had anticipated a few months earlier. At the Playhouse, the craze for miniature golf quickly faded, and, with profits sharply down on its first year of operations, the house had little option but to dispose of its orchestra; it rose for the final time in April 1932.[95] As the orchestra was shared with the Playhouse's sister house, the Palace, Edinburgh's cinema orchestras were immediately halved in number. Musical tastes continued to be satisfied by the Playhouse's resident organist, a reminder that live music remained a feature of cinema-going into the sound era. That said, less than four years after the talkies' Scottish debut, orchestral music north of the border was confined to just two of close on six hundred cinemas: the Rutland and the New Victoria, both Gaumont houses located in Edinburgh, where its survival owed much to regular access to the airwaves via BBC broadcasts.[96]

The fate of cinema orchestras lends the coming of sound an aura of loss, a view which hindsight has, to an extent, endorsed: many have been the lamentations concerning the demise of a fluid and mature visual method of storytelling, which constituted an art with potentially universal appeal, and its replacement by initially studio-bound, dialogue-driven narratives that embedded linguistic barriers to communication. Yet the reaction at the time was not uniformly unfavourable. Cinema-goers voted with their pennies and did so almost invariably in support of sound, and even some cineastes could regard the new technology as an advance in, rather than an eclipse of, cinema's cultural potential. In December 1930, members of the Edinburgh Film Guild debated the proposition that the coming of sound represented no gain to the filmic art and concluded by rejecting such a pessimistic view.[97] By that point, the onward march of the talkies appeared unstoppable. The speed and extent of the change gives the process an air of inevitability. Yet, as this chapter has sought to argue, there was nothing pre-ordained about the pace of take-up, nor the manner in which sound films would be presented to Scottish audiences. The outcome was the

Table 10.2 Business at two Aberdeen cinemas, 1928–9 to 1933–4

Star Picture Palace

Year	Takings	Entertainments tax	Profit
1928–29	£5,251 1s	£64 17s 7d	£1,359 16s 5½d
1929–30	£5,637 1s 10d	£78 8s 11d	£991 2s 9d
1930–31	£5,765 5s 7d	£91 9s 4d	£1,271 9s
1931–32	£7,300 6s 11d	£394 10s 9d	£2,014 9s 9½d
1932–33	£5,607 2s 4d	£968 11s 11d	£504 4s 9d
1933–34	£5,527 4s	£979 18s 4d	£817 17s 10½d

Globe Cinema

Year	Takings	Entertainments tax	Profit
1928–29	£6,187 18s 10d	£26 11s 3d	£2,225 4s 9½d
1929–30	£5,441 1s 10d	£13 2s 6d	£1,481 10s 9d
1930–31	£5,245 19s 9d	£19 7s 6d	£1,073 8s 3d
1931–32	£6,284 0s 5d	£302 17s	£1,815 14s 7d
1932–33	£5,310 19s 8d	£919 14s 8d	£857 19s 3½d
1933–34	£4,720 10s 9d	£849 14s	£487 2s 1½d

Source: CM, Aberdeen Picture Palaces Ltd Accounts

Table 10.3 Torry Cinemas, Ltd, accounts 1928–9 to 1933–4

Year	Takings	Entertainments Tax	Profit
1928–29	£5,603 8s 2d	£301 6s 6d	£1,029 8s 3½d
1929–30	£6,251 18s 8d	£334 14s 8d	£1,124 9s 6d
1930–31	£6,913 16s 1d	£433 13s 5d	£1,227 18s 7½d
1931–32	£7,812 2s 8d	£788 18s 3d	£1,519 1s 6½d
1932–33	£6,778 9s 8d	£1,034 4s 8d	£1,034 1s 3½d
1933–34	£6,406 3s 7d	£966 9s	£549 1s 6d

Source: CM, Torry Cinemas Ltd Accounts

result of the actions of individual exhibitors rarely acting in concert, determined by decisions taken by actors operating outwith Scotland itself: by film producers in Hollywood, and at Elstree and Lime Grove studios (the production bases of the two major British film combines) in London; and by legislators at Westminster, through measures which consolidated the market position of those committed to investment in the talkies and which saw mass leisure as a legitimate source of revenue in financially straitened times. Exhibitors were thus obliged quickly to abandon the policy of wait and see initially recommended by the CEA and to invest in sound equipment, even, in sharp contrast to the claims of British Acoustic, at the cost of reduced profitability. By November 1930, *The Bioscope* was offering a rather more sober view of the trade's prospects: 'between apparatus costs, renter's percentages and patron's grouses the exhibitor's lot is not a happy one'.[98]

There is a sense, then, that the transition to sound provides evidence of the degree to which Scotland's principal means of popular entertainment was being shaped by forces beyond its national boundaries. At the same time, the capacity of exhibitors to put a local slant on the programme through the provision of 'appropriate' music and variety support was increasingly muted. Yet the local was never entirely eliminated from the cinematic experience. Traditions of showmanship endured, encouraging managers to continue to invest in the production of topical subjects of relevance to their patrons and to employ variety turns to boost business when required. However subject to global forces, cinema continued to thrive where it acknowledged its place in the local community, a point confirmed by the marked increase in Sunday concerts for charitable causes as the 1930s progressed.[99] In one respect, however, sound did work to still the Scottish voice. The costs associated with the production of talkie films ensured that attempts to produce Scottish features on the lines of the 1911 *Rob Roy* were abandoned from 1928. Instead, Scottish creativity was increasingly channelled in the direction of the new alternative cinema developing around the production of sponsored documentaries, which would prove a particularly productive outlet for film-making ambitions over the next half century. To that extent, the transition to sound represented a real departure from Scotland's cinematic past.

Notes

1. *Bioscope*, 16 January, p. 47; 18 September 1929, p. 23 (for the estimate of 100 talkie houses); 8 January 1930, p. 32.
2. *Bioscope*, 19 June 1929, p. 31.
3. *Bioscope*, 28 May 1930, p. 48.
4. *Bioscope*, 19 December 1928, p. viii.
5. UoS, SC, MU/4/2/1/3/3, Musicians' Union, Glasgow Branch, General Meetings Minutes, Special Summoned General Meeting, 11 November 1928; General Meeting, 9 November 1930; MU/1/4/10, MU, Monthly Reports, Statement showing Membership, Balances and Income of Branches for Year Ending 31 December 1931.
6. TNA, LAB 83/3315, Extract from Enquiry dated 19 June 1930, minute 27 June 1930.
7. UoS, SC, no cat., *Musicians' Journal*, January 1930, p. 20.
8. Hanssen, 'Revenue Sharing and the Coming of Sound'.

9. *Bioscope*, 3 September 1930, pp. 16–17.
10. *Bioscope*, 19 December 1928, p. i; 2 January 1929, pp. 34–5.
11. Brown and Davison, *The Sounds of the Silents in Britain*.
12. *Scotsman*, 20 October 1914, p. 8; 25 July 1916, p. 7.
13. *Entertainer*, 10 February 1917, p. 10, although in this case the effect was held to be limited.
14. *SC*, 1 December 1919, p. 4.
15. *SC*, 6 October 1919, p. 12; see also Griffiths, 'Sounding Scottish: Sound Practices and Silent Cinema in Scotland', 79–81.
16. *Scotsman*, 2 December 1924, p. 9.
17. *Scotsman*, 29 September 1925, p. 9.
18. *Scotsman*, 29 December 1913, p. 1.
19. *Scotsman*, 21 January, p. 1; 10 February 1914, p. 10.
20. *Entertainer*, 20 December 1913, p. 16; 17 January 1914, p. 12; NRS, BT2/8946/2, The Vocal Cinema Co. Ltd, Memorandum of Association.
21. Merz, 'Why Not a Scots Hollywood?: Scottish Fiction Film Production in Scotland, 1911–1928', chapter 2; NRS, BT2/8946, Strang and Weir, Writers, to Registrar of Joint Stock Companies, 9 February 1921.
22. *Scotsman*, 2 September 1924, p. 6.
23. *Scotsman*, 9 October 1926, pp. 2, 7.
24. *Scotsman*, 11 October 1926, p. 1.
25. *Scotsman*, 10 June 1929, p. 7, where the arrival of talking pictures was held to mark a 'fresh chapter in the cinema history of Edinburgh'.
26. *Bioscope*, 6 June 1928, p. 32.
27. *Bioscope*, 17 October 1928, p. i.
28. *Bioscope*, 6 November 1929, p. xii.
29. *Bioscope*, 3 April 1929, p. 21. By contrast, a survey in the United States at the same time found that a majority of female picture-goers favoured sound.
30. *Bioscope*, 27 November 1929, p. 21, reporting on the survey by the *Manchester Evening Chronicle*.
31. C. McGinniss, Diary for 1929 (in possession of Mrs Rita Connelly).
32. *Bioscope*, 30 January, p. 48; 6 February 1929, p. 44; C. McGinniss, Diary, entry for 24 January 1929.
33. C. McGinniss, Diary, entries for 15 August, 24 October, 18 November, 30 November 1929.
34. *Bioscope*, 2 October 1929, p. 38.
35. NRS, GD289/1/3, Palace Cinema, Profit and Loss Ledger, 1925–55, weeks ending 7 January to 29 December 1928.
36. NRS, GD289/1/3, weeks ending 5 January to 28 December 1929; *Scotsman*, 8 June, p. 1; 22 July, p. 1; 30 July, p. 11; 10 August 1929, p. 9; *Bioscope*, 21 August 1929, p. 44.
37. NRS, GD289/1/3, weeks ending 5 July to 4 October 1930.
38. NRS, GD289/1/3, week ending 30 August 1930.
39. NRS, GD289/1/3, weeks ending 17 March, 30 June, 8 September 1928;

weeks ending 9 August, 16 August, 30 August, 6 September, 13 September, 20 September 1930.
40. NRS, GD289/1/3, week ending 13 September (*Frau im Mond*), 20 September (*La Passion de Jeanne d'Arc*), the latter supported by a re-release of the 1925 Stoll production *The Qualified Adventurer*.
41. NRS, GD289/1/1, Playhouse Cinema, Profit and Loss Ledger, 1929–68, weeks ending 4 January 1930 to 3 January 1931.
42. *Bioscope*, 23 January 1929, p. 23.
43. *Bioscope*, 27 March, p. 26; 17 April 1929, p. 32.
44. *Bioscope*, 8 May 1929, p. 24.
45. *Bioscope*, 17 September 1930, p. 14.
46. *Bioscope*, 24 April 1929, p. 13.
47. *Bioscope*, 2 June 1927, p. 21; 1 March 1928, p. 25, for the acquisition of the Graham Youll circuit of houses in Edinburgh by British Gaumont. The sale of the Regent in Glasgow to an unnamed London syndicate was agreed early in 1928, but was reversed following a revolt by shareholders which resulted in the replacement of the directors, NLS, MIA, 5/22/4, Glasgow Picture House Ltd, Minute Book, Meeting of Directors, 28 January; printed minute, Meeting of Directors, 13 July 1928. The board of Aberdeen Picture Palaces Ltd was courted by both ABPC and Gaumont, in each case unsuccessfully, CM, Aberdeen Picture Palaces Ltd Minutes, Meetings of Directors, 16 March 1928; 10 January 1929.
48. *Bioscope*, 2 October 1929, p. 40.
49. *Bioscope*, 7 January 1931, p. 40.
50. *Bioscope*, 16 September 1926, p. 26; 3 March 1927, p. xi.
51. *Scotsman*, 12 February 1929, p. 1; NLS, MIA, 5/4/15, Poole Family, Diary of Attendances, records variety turns at Synod Hall until the final week of silents, when Lucille and Trevor were hired for the week.
52. Brown, 'Framing the Atmospheric Film Prologue in Britain, 1919–1926'; *Bioscope*, 7 January 1926, p. 73, 'Prologues in cinemas are the order of the day'; 13 January 1927, p. xv.
53. *Bioscope*, 26 January, p. v; 24 May 1928, p. vi.
54. *Bioscope*, 5 September, p. 36 (Albin); 29 August 1928, p. 26 (Cruickshank).
55. *Bioscope*, 9 January 1929, p. 65.
56. *Bioscope*, 21 May 1930, p. 22.
57. *Bioscope*, 25 March 1931, p. 7.
58. *Bioscope*, 9 July 1930, p. 11.
59. Griffiths, *The Cinema and Cinema-going in Scotland, 1896–1950*, 291–2.; *Bioscope*, 26 March 1930, p. 47, by which point twelve halls were said to be using the system; NLS, MIA, 5/22/5, Glasgow Picture House Ltd, Minute Book, Meeting of Directors, 8 April 1930.
60. *Bioscope*, 5 June 1929, p. 52, for the work of J. S. Souter at the Elgin Picture House; 12 November 1930, p. 23, for Polmont; *Scotsman*, 9 May 1930, p. 9, for George Renouf of the Central Picture House, Musselburgh.
61. NLS, MIA, 5/22/4, Meetings of Directors, 10 October; 6 November;

17 December 1929; 5/22/5, Meeting of Directors, 24 September 1930, for the walk-out.
62. NLS, MIA, 5/22/5, Meetings of Directors, 4 August 1931; 28 May 1930 for the earlier approach. Over eleven weeks between June and August 1930, in eight of which the cinema made a profit, this outlay would virtually have eliminated profits in one week and severely reduced them in three others, making the business increasingly reliant on securing attractive features capable of generating high profits, sheet attached to Meeting of Directors, 19 August 1931.
63. *Bioscope*, 19 December 1928, p. 54; 15 May, p. 42; 31 July 1929, p. 34.
64. NRS, GD289/1/1, weeks ending 7 January to 29 December 1928.
65. CM, Aberdeen Picture Palaces Ltd, Minutes, Meeting of Directors, 3 November 1932; for *City Lights*, NRS, GD289/1/1, week ending 14 November 1931; *Bioscope*, 8 April 1931, p. 36.
66. NRS, GD289/1/3, week ending 10 September; 12 November 1932.
67. NRS, GD289/1/3, weeks ending 7 January to 29 December 1928; 9 January to 31 December 1932.
68. *Bioscope*, 26 February 1930, p. 39.
69. NLS, MIA, 5/22/4, Meeting of Directors, 22 November 1926; CM, Aberdeen Picture Palaces Ltd, Accounts, for the position at the Aberdeen Playhouse, where spending on films was half as high again as that on wages.
70. CM, Torry Cinemas Ltd, Accounts, in 1928 £801 10s was spent on film hire compared to a wage bill of £1,577 2s 10½d.
71. CM, Aberdeen Picture Palaces Ltd, Playhouse Cinema Accounts.
72. UoS, SC, MU/4/2/1/2/5, Musicians' Union, Glasgow Branch, Committee Meetings Minutes, Committee Meeting, 22 February 1929.
73. *Scotsman*, 22 July 1929, p. 1.
74. *Scotsman*, 5 December, p. 1; 30 December 1930, p. 6.
75. UoS, SC, no cat., *Musicians' Journal*, April 1929, p. 13; MU/4/2/1/3/3, Special Summoned General Meeting, 8 September 1929, for early expressions of optimism; *Scotsman*, 24 December 1929, p. 10, for the opening of the New Caley.
76. *Bioscope*, 2 July 1930, p. 33.
77. UoS, SC, MU/4/2/1/3/3, General Meetings, 12 January; 9 February 1930.
78. UoS, SC, MU/4/2/1/3/3, General Meeting, 10 March 1929.
79. UoS, SC, MU/4/2/1/3/3, Special Summoned General Meeting, 8 September 1929; *Bioscope*, 16 October 1929, p. 27.
80. UoS, SC, MU/4/2/1/3/3, Special Summoned General Meeting, 13 October 1929; *Bioscope*, 28 August 1929, p. 25.
81. UoS, SC, MU/4/2/1/3/3, General and Special Summoned Meeting, 11 May 1930.
82. UoS, SC, no cat., *The Musicians' Journal*, Monthly Report, July 1930, p. 3; *Scotsman*, 18 April, p. 11; 19 April 1930, p. 11.
83. See above, n. 5.

84. UoS, SC, MU/4/2/1/2/5, Committee Meetings, 11 October; 4 December 1929.
85. UoS, SC, MU/1/4/10, *Musicians' Journal*, April 1931, p. 1; January 1932, p. 1.
86. *Scotsman*, 29 September, p. 1; 22 December 1930, p. 1. Courses were also installed at the La Scala, Paisley, and the New Picture House, Kirkwall, *Bioscope*, 22 October, p. 37; 19 November 1930, p. 38.
87. UoS, SC, MU/1/4/10, *Musicians' Journal*, October 1931, p. 1.
88. *Bioscope*, 16 September, p. 25; a slight revision of rates was made in October, so that the tax would begin on prices above 2d, 7 October 1931, p. 18.
89. *Bioscope*, 28 October 1931, p. 29.
90. *Bioscope*, 9 December 1931, p. 28.
91. CM, Aberdeen Picture Palaces Ltd, Minutes, Meeting of Directors, 25 September 1931.
92. *Bioscope*, 25 November 1931, p. 16.
93. *Bioscope*, 16 March 1932, p. 26.
94. *Bioscope*, 23 March 1932, p. 28.
95. *Scotsman*, 10 February 1931, p. 1, reporting a reduction in the opening hours for the golf course; 9 April 1932, p. 11.
96. Both were advertised as Broadcasting Orchestras by late 1933, *Scotsman*, 26 December 1933, p. 1.
97. *Bioscope*, 3 December 1930, p. 40.
98. *Bioscope*, 30 January 1929, p. 51, for A. B. King's advice against rushing in to the talkies; 19 November 1930, p. 38 for the assessment of their impact in practice.
99. Griffiths, *The Cinema and Cinema-going in Scotland, 1896–1950*, 154–7.

CHAPTER 11

Filmography of Scottish-themed Fiction Films

John Caughie

This is intended as a comprehensive catalogue of Scottish-themed fiction films, produced in Scotland, England, Europe and the USA until 1927 and reviewed in the British and American trade press or on the Internet Movie Database (IMDb) or, on a few occasions, in local newspapers. There are a few criteria for being identified as 'Scottish-themed': the film is set (though not necessarily filmed), in whole or in part, in real or fictional Scotland; the film has, in whole or in part, a significant Scottish story or draws on a Scottish story (the 1913 *Annie Laurie* is set in the American south, but draws on the Scottish song as a narrative link); a significant character is Scottish (Vitagraph's *The Wolf* (1919) is set in a Canadian trapper camp, but the heroine's 'cruel father', according to the *Moving Picture World* review, 'typifies well the traditional Scottish male parent'). Thus films may be wholly or partially Scottish, but the Scottish element is clearly identified in press comment or reviews. That is to say, the identification of Scottishness – or, commonly, 'Scotchness' – draws on a trade definition, and those films are included which contain a Scottish element as a significant defining characteristic. In this way, the filmography points to the ways in which Scotland figured as an imagined, and marketable, landscape imbued with meaning. On the basis of these criteria, the filmography suggests a list of 223 fiction films.

In one or two places, the information is scant and I have relied on inference: neither *The Gypsy and the Laird* nor *Mary, Queen of Tots* is identified as Scottish-themed in the brief review, but I have inferred from the title a Scottish connection. In most cases, the Scottish element forms a major or significant item in the synopsis, comment or review. It is important to note that this is a period when film criticism was not yet an established practice, and the trade comment is often concerned as much with the ways in which the film is marketable as the ways in which it is a reliable depiction or an aesthetically achieved work. I have tried to identify the ways in which the films are identified as Scottish by quoting extensively from the trade press. In the UK, I have relied on *The Bioscope* (whose first issue was in 1908, and is not digitised), and in the USA I have relied on *Moving Picture World* (which is digitised from 1907 to 1926) and *Motion Picture News* (which is digitised from 1913 to 1930).[1] This has been supplemented by reference to IMDb and, occasionally, to local newspapers. I have also included such information about length, country of origin, production company, cast and crew as is available. For those who wish to pursue a film in more detail, further information, including reviews, synopses and reports, is available at the 'Early Film in Scotland' website.[2]

It is worth pointing out that the filmography does not include films that have a Scottish actor or a Scottish member of the production crew, and it does not include films that are derived from the work of a Scottish author or producer but do not have a significant Scottish element. Thus, R.L. Stevenson's *Kidnapped* (1917) and *The White Circle* (1920 – adapted from *The Pavilion on the Links*) are included because they retain significant Scottish elements, but *The Bottle Imp* (1917) or *Treasure Island* (1918 and 1920) are not. Neither *Ivanhoe* (1913) nor *Peter Pan* (1924) is included, despite their Scottish authors. *Macbeth*, Shakespeare's 'Scottish play' is striking: it was adapted in ten versions in France, Germany, Italy, England and the USA, including a parody, *The Real Thing At Last* (1916) by J. M. Barrie.

Of the 222 titles, thirteen were produced in Scotland by Scottish companies. The criteria, unfortunately, do not allow the inclusion of two significant Scottish-produced films identified by Caroline Merz in her PhD thesis: *The Unsleeping Eye* and *The Twilight Kingdom*.[3] These two films, released in 1928 and 1929, were made by Alexander Macdonald, a Scottish explorer and author and Fellow of the Royal Geographical society, for what seems to have been an entirely Scottish company, Seven Seas Productions. While the story of their production is fascinating, however, they were set in Papua New Guinea and Australia, and do not seem to have had a Scottish theme. Of the thirteen films catalogued here, only two, *Rob Roy* (United, 1911) and *Football Daft* (Broadway Cinema Production, 1921), seem to have had much distribution which went beyond the local, and there is reason to doubt that some of them were ever released at all. Caroline Merz has given a full and detailed account of the production context in Scotland, and is sympathetic to the challenges it posed and to the energy of those who attempted to step into the breach. The filmography, however, highlights the fact that, however much it was represented in European and American film productions, it was very difficult for a small country like Scotland with a small domestic market and without the subsidies and tax incentives that accompanied the invention of the cultural industries in the 1980s, to sustain a stream of production that would allow it to lay claim in any consistent way to its own stories and mythologies.

Notes

1. See Media History Digital Library, led by David Pierce and Eric Hoyt at http://mediahistoryproject.org/earlycinema/.
2. See 'The Early Cinema in Scotland Research Project' at http://earlycinema.gla.ac.uk.
3. Merz, 'Why Not a Scots Hollywood?: Scottish Fiction Film Production in Scotland, 1911–1928', 239–51.

Title	Year	Country of origin	Length (ft) where known	Production company	Director/producer/writer	Actors	Summary
Adventures of Sandy McGregor, The	1904	UK	300	Clarendon	Percy Stow		Scotsman tries to undress on beach without being seen.
Adventures of Wee Rob Roy, no. 1	1916	UK	175				Animated film of comic adventures of Wee Rob Roy. [Available online at Moving Picture Archive (NLS)]
All for the Sake of Mary (aka I Love a Lassie)	1920	Scotland	1,405	Page/Harry Lauder Productions	Harry Lauder (w.)	Harry Lauder, Effie Vallance and local actors	A shepherd vies for the attention of the fair Mary (a Scots bluebell) but is passed over for a rival following an unfortunate incident with a bull. Filmed in Glenbranter, Argyllshire. [In National Film and Video Archive]
All Scotch	1909	UK	380	London Cinematograph Company	S. Wormald (d.)		'A most humorous incident of a Scotch figure being removed from outside a shop by some comic and humorous thieves, one of whom makes up to assume the figure and take its place. The extraordinary instances and cunning method of thieving is most cleverly depicted, articles being stolen from all passers-by, even including a lady's skirt. This film possesses a powerful plot in addition to being the wittiest of witty pictures ever placed upon the market.' *The Bioscope*
Amorous Scotsman, The	1909	UK	135	Empire Film Manufacturing Company			'A Scotsman flirts with a farmer's fat cook.' IMDb
Annie Laurie	1913	USA	971	Reliance Film Company			Set in the US Civil War, the song becomes the link for a story of a rich man, favoured by the father, and a poor man, favoured by the young girl. The song recurs, and softens the father's heart.

Title	Year	Country of origin	Length (ft) where known	Production company	Director/ producer/ writer	Actors	Summary
Annie Laurie	1916	UK	4,000	Hepworth	Cecil Hepworth (d.), Alma Taylor (w.)	Alma Taylor, Stewart Rome, Lionelle Howard	Not obviously Scottish in setting, though it features a Scottish doctor. A tale of a rural schoolmistress loved in turn by the young Squire's nephew and the older Squire. Annie remains true to the Squire.
Annie Laurie	1927	USA	7,000	Metro-Goldwyn-Mayer	John S. Robertson (d.)	Lilian Gish, Norman Kerry	'Stirring story of a feud between rival Scottish clans, of which Annie Laurie is made the heroine, with the massacre of Glencoe as the climax. Though no pretension is made to historical accuracy, this is a stirring story of love and treachery, handsomely mounted amidst beautiful natural scenery.' *The Bioscope*
At the Torrent's Mercy	1915	UK	3,444	British & Colonial Kinematograph Company	H. O. Martinek (d.)	Percy Moran, Ivy Montford, A.V. Bramble	'In Scotland a gamekeeper's daughter saves her lover when a poacher throws him into a river.' IMDb 'The scenery is beautiful and the dresses are correct.' *The Bioscope*
Auld Lang Syne	1911	USA	1,824	Vitagraph	Laurence Trimble (d.)	Maurice Costello, Florence Turner, Harry T. Morey	Two farmer lads, Tammas and Geordie, are firm friends and both in love with Jenny. Jenny chooses Tammas, and Geordie is estranged. Much later, Geordie, with his dog, Jean, rescues their infant son. Jenny brings a flask, from which they 'drink a cup of kindness', and are reconciled to the words of 'Auld Lang Syne'.
Auld Robin Gray	1910	USA	905	Vitagraph	Laurence Trimble (d.); Lady Anne Lindsay Barnard (poem), Van Dyke Brooke (sc.)	William Shea, Florence Turner, Ralph Ince	'Sentimental tale of a young Scottish girl forced to marry an elderly gentleman for financial reasons when her lover is thought lost at sea. The lover returns to claim his betrothed but discovers that she intends to remain loyal to her kind but aged husband.' Available on site at Moving Image Archive (NLS). [Also held in National Film and Television Archive]

Auld Robin Gray	1917	UK	4,400	Ideal	Meyrick Milton (d.); Kenelm Foss (w.)	Langholm Burton, Miss June, R. Roberts	'A sailor returns from a shipwreck in time to save his fiancée from marrying a farmer.' IMdB
Bachelor Brides	1926	USA	6,000	DeMille Pictures Coprporation	William K. Howard (d); C. Gardner Sullivan and Garrett Fort (adaptation) from the play by Charles Horace Malcolm	Rod La Rocque, Elinor Fair, Eulalie Jensen	Adapted from a Broadway play, an American heiress about to marry the Laird of Duncreggan Towers castle is involved in theft of jewels and claims by another woman that Laird fathered her child. Character names, and name of villain – Glasgow Willie – suggest a Scottish theme, though it is not featured in review.
Bagpipe Player, The (aka Le joueur de cornemuse)	1910	France	607	Pathé Frères		Eugénie Nau, Jean Angelo	Douglas, the bagpipe player, is marooned by the jealous father of his lover, Flora, on a barren island. His attempt to escape is thwarted by Flora's even more jealous sister. Apparently drowned, Douglas is magically brought back to life by Nancy, a wandering gypsy witch who owes Flora a debt of gratitude. Filmed, allegedly, in the Scottish Highlands: 'Some of the scenery is exceptionally good, many picturesque views, photographically perfect, being included in the film.' *Moving Picture World*
Beloved Imp, The	not released?	USA		Universal			'It is a story of Scotch domestic life, the scene of which is laid in the mountain region of Northern Scotland.' *Moving Picture World* in August 1916 reports that it was awarded the highest fee then known – $1,200 – for an eight-page scenario. However, there is no record of the film being completed or released.

Title	Year	Country of origin	Length (ft) where known	Production company	Director/ producer/ writer	Actors	Summary
Beside the Bonnie Brier Bush (aka The Bonnie Brier Bush)	1921	USA	5,000		Donald Crisp (d.) from Ian MacLaren's novel	Donald Crisp, Mary Glynne, Alec Fraser	'Stern Scottish father disowns his lovesick daughter.' *The Bioscope*. An adaptation from Ian McLaren's 'kailyard' novel. It is reported that Crisp sought locations in Killin, but the film seems to have been shot mainly in Devon.
Best of Luck, The	1920	USA	6,000	Screen Classics, Inc.	Ray C. Smallwood (d.) from the play by Henry Hamilton & Cecil Raleigh	Kathryn Adams, Jack Holt, Lila Leslie	Story of the persecution of a beautiful Scottish girl by a rich and unscrupulous Spaniard, General Lamazana, and her protection by the poor but gallant Lord Glenayr. Adapted from successful Broadway melodrama – with startling scenic effects including fight at the bottom of the sea for buried treasure.
Black Roderick, the Poacher	1914	UK	2,025	Big Ben	H. O. Martinek (d.)	H. O. Martinek, Ivy Montford	Romance of Highland Lord and gamekeeper's daughter is interrupted by the villainy of Roderick the Poacher. Having been shot, the gamekeeper recovers in time to save the name of the Lord.
Blasted Ambitions	1922	Scotland		Arc Film Company	Max Leder (p.)		One of three 'Delightful, Refined, All–Scottish Comedies' produced by Max Leder after the failure of *The Harp King* and *The Referee's Eye*. A two-reeler, apparently seen in Dundee with some approval for *The Weekly News*, but lambasted in *The Bioscope*. Disappeared without leaving much trace.
Bonnie Annie Laurie	1918	USA	5,000	Fox	Harry F. Millarde (d); Lela E. Rogers, Hamilton Thompson (w.)	Peggy Hyland, Henry Hallam, William Bailey	'A Scottish Tale of Love and Patriotism' (Fox advertisement). Set in First World War, with Annie torn between love of her local gallant soldier and of a mysterious stranger. 'A Love Story of the War. Trench life revealed. Daring "dash over the top". Base Hospital glimpses. Tremendous storm scene.' (Fox advertisement)

Title	Year	Country	Length	Company	Credits	Cast	Notes
Bonnie Mary (aka *Bonnie Mary O' Argyle*)	1918	UK	5,000	Master Films	A. V. Bramble (d); Herbert Pemberton, Eliot Stannard (w.)	Miriam Ferris, Lionel Belcher, Arthur M. Cullin	'In Scotland, a feud between a laird and a farmer ends when their children marry.' IMDb. Filmed in the Highlands – and in Edinburgh and London – and taken from a popular song. "The Real Thing at Last. A Film Taken Amidst the Glories of the Western Highlands". (Advertisement in *The Bioscope*) '[T]he plot is sufficiently strong to stand without the aid of a popular title, although this, as well as the additional advantage of a suggested musical accompaniment, certainly enhances its value.' *The Bioscope*
Bonnie Prince Charlie	1923	UK	7,000	Gaumont	Charles Calvert (d.), Alice [Alicia] Ramsey (w.)	Ivor Novello, Fay Compton	Shot in Culloden and in Arran. The romance of the Pretender and Flora MacDonald, his defeat at Culloden, and escape to France, despite treachery and betrayal. 'Here is an opportunity to appeal to your Scottish patrons... Bagpipes, even in an English town, always attract a considerable amount of attention... Try to get as much cooperation as possible from dealers in Scottish goods, such as tweeds, Scotch shortbread, Scotch whisky, etc.' *The Bioscope* on exploitation.
Bonnie, Bonnie Banks of Loch Lomond, The	1912	USA	985	Éclair American	Henry J. Vernot (as Henri Vernot) (d.)	Barbara Tennant, Alec B. Francis, Guy Hedlund	Clara, a Highland maiden, is hired by tourists to look after their children and is taken from her Highland home. Later, she is accused of stealing a phonograph, but all she wanted was to listen to the song of the Bonnie Banks which reminds her of home.
Bonnie, Bonnie Lassie, The (aka *Auld Jeremiah*)	1919	USA	6,000	Universal	Tod Browning (d.); Tod Browning, Violet Clark, Waldemar Young (w.)	Mary MacLaren, Spottiswoode Aitken, David Butler	Drawn from a magazine story. 'Ailsa leaves Scotland for America, where she hopes to earn her living. Here an old friend asks her to marry his nephew. She meets him painting sign boards, becomes his assistant and, little knowing he is the nephew, falls in love with him.' *The Bioscope*

Title	Year	Country of origin	Length (ft) where known	Production company	Director/ producer/ writer	Actors	Summary
Bonny Prince Charlie	1912	France	1,800	Film d'Art			Fantasy romance of Prince Charlie, who is caught between his attraction towards Lord Fingal's wife, Dora, and the faithful love of Blind Angus's daughter, Mary. Dora is killed at Culloden, the broken-hearted Prince escapes to France, and Mary dies of shock.
Borrowed Plumage	1917	USA	5,000	Triangle	Raymond B. West (d.); J. G. Hawks (sc.)	Bessie Barriscale, Arthur Maude, Dorcas Matthews	Madcap Nonie, a kitchen wench in a castle off the Scottish coast, is found to be the former sweetheart of a pirate in John Paul Jones's crew. In 'an action full of thrills and surprises', he risks his neck to be near her, and she saves him. *Moving Picture World*
Bravo Kilties!	1914	UK	1,100	Barker	F. Martin Thornton (d.); Rowland Talbot (story)		'In Belgium a soldier defends a post office until Highlanders arrive.' IMDb. 'At the moment when our Scottish regiments are exciting universal admiration any film recording their prowess on the battlefield is certain of success . . . There is plenty of wholesome excitement, and also a certain amount of humour, and we make no doubt that the film will prove much to the taste of the public.' *The Bioscope*
Bride of Lammermoor, The: A Tragedy of Bonnie Scotland	1909	USA	540	Vitagraph	J. Stuart Blackton (d.) from Walter Scott	Annette Liberman, Maurice Costello	Adaptation of Walter Scott's novel. Forced into a marriage to a Duke she does not love, and the apparent betrayal by her lover, leads to Lucy's madness. She stabs the unwanted Duke, discovers that her lover has been true to her after all, and stabs herself. Romance on an operatic scale.
Bride of Lammermoor, The (aka *Lucia di Lammermoor*)	1910	Italy	980	Cines	Mario Caserini (d.) from Walter Scott		Adaptation of Walter Scott's novel. As above, except that Lucy dies of a broken heart.

Title	Year	Country	Length	Production	Credits	Notes
Bride of Lammermoor, The	1914	USA	3,000	Kennedy Features	from Walter Scott	Constance Crawley, Arthur Maude, Horace B. Carpenter	Adaptation of Walter Scott's novel. As above, except that the film ends with Edgar, the young lover, overcome by grief, walking into the quicksands of Kelpie's Flow.
Brother Jim	1916	USA	1,000	Universal	Calder Johnstone (sc.)	Thomas Jefferson, Lina Basquette, Frank Newburg	An American family melodrama of a prodigal son restored to the family by the loyalty of his child sister. The only Scottish connection is that the *Moving Picture World* review makes the point that the father is of Scottish descent, which seems to emphasise his decency.
Bunty Pulls the Strings	1921	USA	7,000	Kennedy Features	Reginald Barker (d.); J. G. Hawks, Charles Kenyon (w.) from Graham Moffat's play	Leatrice Joy, Russell Simpson, Raymond Hatton	Adapted from the comedy by the Scottish writer Graham Moffat, which was a success in London and on Broadway. Bunty Biggar, the sister of Rab and Jeemy, and daughter of Tammas, a strict Presbyterian elder in a small Scottish village, pulls the strings with all three, cuts through their troubles, and eventually marries Weelum.
Call of the Pipes, The (aka *Bonnie Banks of Loch Lomond, The*)	1917	UK	5,000	Regal Films	Tom Watts (d.); H. Grenville-Taylor (w.)	Ernest A. Douglas	The Highland laddie leaves his sweetheart and his blind father and comes to London. Hearing the bagpipes, he enlists, wins the Victoria Cross, before returning to his childhood home, his father and his sweetheart. 'All Scotch – Produced on the Bonnie Banks of Loch Lomond. Not an American idea of Scottish Scenery and Character, but the "Real Mackay."' Press advertisement
Calvinist Martyr, A	1913	France	2,112	Pathé	Adrien Caillard (d.); from the novel by Honoré de Balzac	Léon Bernard	Adapted from Balzac's *The Calvinist Martyr* (1851), the third in a series of novels about Cathérine de Medici. Marginal for Scottish interest other than it is another tale involving Mary Queen of Scots

Title	Year	Country of origin	Length (ft) where known	Production company	Director/ producer/ writer	Actors	Summary
Cameron of the Royal Mounted	1921	Canada	5,000	Winnipeg Productions	Henry MacRae (d.); Ralph Connor (story), Faith Green (w.)	Gaston Glass, Irving Cummings, Vivienne Osborne	'A young Scottish immigrant to Canada becomes a member of the Royal Canadian Mounted Police. He finds himself framed on a forgery charge, but before he can clear himself he must capture a gang of train robbers and stop a band of marauding Indians.' IMDb
Campbells Are Coming, The	1915	USA	3,937	Universal	Francis Ford (d.); Grace Cunard (screenplay)	Francis Ford, Grace Cunard, Ervin Denecke (and John Ford as Jack Ford in undetermined role)	Based on Whittier's poem 'The Pipes at Lucknow', it adds a love story to the relief of Lucknow in the Indian Mutiny of 1857. Helen Maclean, a Scotch lassie who leaves her native glens to join her father, a schoolmaster in India, is reunited to her Highland lover, who is among the first to enter the Residency with the relief forces.
Case of Scotch, A	1927	USA	2,000	Universal	Francis Corby (d.); Sidney Smith (cartoon)	Joe Murphy, Fay Tincher, Billy Butts	A Gumps comedy, with a picnic outing for Andy Gump's Scottish Society, a bevy of bathing beauties, and high jinks at the beach carnival.
Caught in a Kilt	1915	UK	1,036	Cricks and Martin	W. P. Kellino (d.); Reuben Gillmer (w.)	W. P. Kellino	Questionable. 'A jealous man tries to catch his wife flirting with a neighbour.' IMDb. No mention of Scottish theme in *The Bioscope* review of a farce involving infidelity and an Italian restaurant, but the title suggests something is going on.
Chieftain's Revenge, The (aka Tragedy in the Highlands of Scotland, A)	1908	USA	415	Vitagraph			'The Chieftain's Revenge' tells a thrilling story of Scottish life in earlier days, when lawlessness and violence swayed.' *Moving Picture World*

Title	Year	Country	Length	Company	Credits	Cast	Notes
Chirgwin Plays a Scotch Reel	1896	UK	40	R.W. Paul		G.H. Chirgwin	'The "White Eyed Kaffir" performs a sword dance with tobacco pipes.' IMDb. Chirgwin was a British music hall black-face minstrel star billed as 'the White-Eyed Kaffir'.
Christie Johnstone (aka Christina Johnstone)	1921	UK	5,000	Broadwest	Normand McDonald (d.); W.C. Clifford (w.); from the novel by Charles Reade	Gertrude McCoy, Stewart Rome, Clive Brook	'Bored nobleman acts as fairy godmother to rustic lovers – Clever acting in artistic production of early Victorian romance – Delightful Scottish settings and good photography.' *The Biograph*. Filmed in the East Coast village of Auchmithy.
Clancarty	1914	UK	1,780	London Film Company	Harold M. Shaw (d.); from Tom Taylor play, 'Lady Clancarty' (1870)	Lillian Logan, Walter Gay, Charles Rock	'A banished Lord saves the King (William III) from Jacobites.' IMdB.
Comrade's Treachery, A	1911	UK	580	British & Colonial Kinematograph Company	H. O. Martinek (d.)	Fred Paul	'In India, a private shot in the back by a rival is saved from death by a Highlander.' IMDb
Courage	1921	USA	2,444	Sidney A. Franklin Productions	Sidney Franklin (d.); Sada Cowan, Andrew Soutar (story)	Naomi Childers, Sam De Grasse, Lionel Belmore, Adolphe Menjou	Inventor wrongly imprisoned for murder of Scots steel mill owner. 'Can any Wife's love prevail through Life-Long Separation from her Husband? [*Courage*] is a wonderful story of romance, of tragedy, of pathos and happiness, with some very human sidelights in bonny Scotland thrown in for good measure . . . A gripping drama of lofty purpose.' Advertisement for the York Cinema, Adelaide, 1921
Cycle of Fate, The	1916	USA	5,000	Selig	Marshall Neilan (d. & w.)	Will Machin, Edith Johnson, Bessie Eyton	An early serial in which two orphaned children, one of whom strays into urban gangland, are looked after by old Sandy, their Scotch grandfather, who is 'thrifty'.

Title	Year	Country of origin	Length (ft) where known	Production company	Director/producer/writer	Actors	Summary
Daughter of Belgium, A	1914	UK	1,350	Barker	F. Martin Thornton (d.); Rowland Talbot (story)		A girl avenges the deaths of her father and lover and is saved by Highlanders.' IMDb
Daughter of France, A	1914	UK	2,000	Crusade Films			'A wounded soldier gives his life to save a French girl, who then fetches Highlanders to save her village.' IMDb
Daughter of MacGregor, The (aka *Jean o' the Heather*)	1916	USA	5,000	Famous Players	Sidney Olcott (d.); Valentine Grant (story)	Valentine Grant, Sidney Mason, Arda La Croix	Jean, the victim of a malicious lie, leaves her Highland home, and accepts the rough life of a Florida lumber camp. Her Scottish lover finds her and restores her to happiness and home. 'Certainly contains one of the best dog actors ever seen upon the screen. There are some beautiful scenic effects, and some vivid and convincing glimpses of village life in Scotland.' *The Bioscope*
Effects of Too Much Scotch, The	1903	UK	160	Gaumont	Alf Collins		'A drunken Scot undresses and his clothes come alive.' IMDb
Eighteen Penny Lunch, The	1905	UK	190	Warwick Film Company			'A Scotsman's sausage changes into a dog.' IMDb
Execution of Mary Queen of Scots, The	1895	USA	325	Edison			A very early re-enactment. [Available online at the Moving Image Archive (NLS)]
Fair Maid of Perth, The	1923	UK	6,000	Anglia Productions	Edwin Greenwood (d.), from Walter Scott's novel	Russell Thorndike, Sylvia Caine, Tristram Rauson, Lionel d'Aragon	The Duke of Rothesay attempts to carry Catherine off by force. The attempt is frustrated by the citizens of Perth, and, in a battle of the clans, Gow is victorious and is rewarded by the love of Catherine. *Bioscope*'s verdict is: 'Purely a title booking that may get over with suitable music and effects'. According to *Motion Picture News*, it was 'filmed in the authentic locations in Scotland'.

Title	Year	Country	Footage	Company	Crew	Cast	Notes
Faith	1920	USA	5,000	Fox	Howard M. Mitchell (d.); Joseph Anthony Roach (w.)	Peggy Hyland, J. Parks Jones, Edward Hearn	'A Scottish romance of imposture, love and the power of Faith in Providence – Appealing characterisation by Peggy Hyland in somewhat slender story – Quaintly beautiful settings, well photographed – Lavish production.' *The Bioscope*
Fate of a King, The	1913	UK	1,964	Anglia Productions	A. E. Colby (d.)		'The history of the poet-king James I of Scotland, and how he was murdered at the hands of traitors. The scene opens on a barren moor, and goes on and describes his majesty's arrival at Perth Castle.' *The Bioscope*
Favourite of Mary Stuart, The (aka *Rizzio*)	1912	France	1,250	Éclair	Victorin-Hippolyte Jasset (d.)	Paul Guidé, Mlle Sergins	To the dismay of the Scottish nobles, Rizzio, a strolling minstrel, wins the favour of Mary Queen of Scots, and becomes her confidential secretary. Darnley stabs Rizzio, and Mary discovers the dead body.
Felix Scoots through Scotland	1926	USA	1,000	Pat Sullivan Cartoons	Otto Messmer (d.)		'Felix is accidentally crated up and sent to Scotland, where he meets Angus, a "thrifty" Scotsman, and makes a deal with him to use his tail as a golf club. Angus, however, also wants to use Felix's nose as a golf ball.' IMDb
Finn and Haddie	1915	USA	1,000	Lubin	Percy Winter (d.); Denman Maley and Frank Moulan (sc.)	Frank Moulan, Denman Maley, Ada Charles	No clear reference to Scots or Scotland in *Moving Picture World* review, but title and character called Fergus Haddie, attempting to be a vaudeville star and caught up in theft mayhem, suggests a connection.

Title	Year	Country of origin	Length (ft) where known	Production company	Director/producer/writer	Actors	Summary
Flying Scots, The	1900	UK	200	Warwick Film Company		The Three Missouris	'Comic acrobats dressed as Scotsmen in their scene "More Rosin"'. IMDb
Football Daft (aka 'Fitba' Daft)	1921	Scotland	2,165	Broadway Cinema Productions	Victor W. Rowe (d.); James Milligan (sketch)	Jimmy Brough	Developed from a music hall sketch, a domestic comedy of football-lovers and failed temperance reformers. Filmed in Ibrox, Rouken Glen and Sauchiehall Street, and 'never has a better representation of a Glasgow tenement single end been seen on the screen'. *The Bioscope*.
Fortune of Christina McNab, The	1921	UK	6,000	Gaumont-Westminster	W. P. Kellino (d.); Paul Rooff (w.) from the novel by Sarah McNaughton	Nora Swinburne, David Hawthorne, Francis Lister	'The emergence of the shy and inexperienced, yet strong-minded Christina from a remote and humble Scottish home into the dazzling high-lights of the social world is just the sort of tale that is suited to the screen . . . One feels, too, that this is the kind of British film they want in the States.' *The Biograph*
Fourteenth Man, The	1920	USA	5,000	Paramount	Joseph Henabery (d.); Walter Woods (w.) from play by F. Anstey	Robert Warwick, Bebe Daniels, Walter Hiers	The comedy opens in Scotland where Captain Gordon makes the mistake of striking a superior officer and has to flee to New York. Through a series of mistaken identities, Gordon, in order to prevent thirteen at the dinner table, becomes the fourteenth man. Farce ensues. Adapted from a stage play.
Genevieve of Scotland (aka Ginevra di Scozia)	1910	Italy	820	Itala			'A well-staged story of the time of King Duncan of Scotland, historically true, with a good plot.' *The Bioscope*
Get Your Man	1921	USA	5,000	Fox	George W. Hill, William K. Howard (d.); John Montague, Alan Sullivan (story)	Buck Jones, W. E. Lawrence, Beatrice Burnham	Spurned Scots mine owner Jock McTier goes to Canada and becomes a Mountie

Gipsy and the Laird, The	1912	France	645	Gaumont			A Laird assists Gipsy, who falls in love with him, and stabs him to death when she learns that he is true to his sweetheart. Gipsy repents and confesses. Not identified as Scottish in review, but title and the settings suggests Scottish Laird.
Golden Chance, The	1913	UK	1,110	London Film Company	Percy Nash (d.) St Aubyn Millar (sc.)		Mistaken identities in the inn at Gretna Green lead to eloping couples in double marriage.
Great Scot on Wheels	1911	UK	450	Clarendon	Percy Stow		'A fat man on roller skates' IMDb
Gretna Green	1909	UK	690	Walterdaw			'Parents pursue elopers to Scotland, but arrive too late.' IMDb
Gretna Green	1912	UK	700	Heron Films	Andrew Heron (d.); Mark Melford (w.)	Mark Melford	'Father chases elopers but arrives at the smithy too late.' IMDb
Gretna Green	1915	USA	4,000	Famous Players	Thomas N. Heffron (d./w.); from the play by Grace Livingston Furniss	Marguerite Clark, Arthur Hoops, Helen Lutrell	Set in early nineteenth century. '[T]he romance of a girl who unwittingly becomes the wife of an earl, then falls in love with him in time to prevent the acceptance of a divorce decree . . . The Scotch marriage law is the pivot of the plot.' *Moving Picture World*
Gretna Green Wedding, A	1899	UK	230	R. W. Paul			'A girl's father arrives late at church.' IMDb
Guy Mannering	1912	USA	2,000	Reliance Film Company	Adapted from novel by Walter Scott	Hector Dion, Julia Hurley, Irving Cummings	'A rattling good story of Scotch smugglers, Gypsies, a lost heir and charming women.' Reliance advertisement, *Moving Picture World*

Title	Year	Country of origin	Length (ft) where known	Production company	Director/producer/writer	Actors	Summary
Harp King, The	1920	Scotland	5,000	Ace Films	Max Leder (d. and w.)	Nan Wilkie, W. R. Bell	Scottish romance, with scenes from Bearsden and Rouken Glen, with Highland dances and harvest scenes. Publicity appealed to national sentiment – 'Written in Scotland. Played in Scotland. Filmed in Scotland.' But not well received by press, and appearances were few and far between.
Harry Lauder	1921	USA	560	Kellum Talking Picture Company		Harry Lauder	Harry Lauder talking and singing sketch, with an early version of synchronised sound.
Harry Lauder and Neil Kenyon Golfing (aka *Golfing*)	1913	UK	900	Hewitt Films	G. Fletcher Hewitt	Harry Lauder, Neil Kenyon	'[A] thousand foot subject showing the famous Scotchman and Neil Kenyon, his only rival in his line, now playing at the Colonial at a huge salary, in a comedy golf match taken less than a month ago at Wembley Park, near London.' *Moving Picture World* (Kenyon was a Scottish comedian and singer, born in Greenock).
Harry Lauder in a Hurry	1908	UK	325	Gaumont	Alf Collins	Harry Lauder	'Scots star takes his time despite callboy, commissionaire, and stage manager.' IMDb
Harry Lauder Singing and Talking Pictures	1914	USA		Selig	William Morris	Harry Lauder	Series of seventeen short films of Lauder's performances recorded for the Selig Polyscope sound synchronisation system. Shot in February 1914 at Selig's Chicago studios, during one of Lauder's American tours.
Hazel Kirke	1912	USA	1,000	Majestic	Oscar Apfel (d.) from play by Steele MacKaye	Mabel Trunnelle, Herbert Prior, Edward P. Sullivan	Set on border between Scotland and England, dependent on 'peculiar Scotch marriage law, and turns on whether the Boar Head's Inn, where the marriage took place, is really in Scotland or south of the line'. Hazel Kirke is the 'pretty daughter of an old Scotch miller'. *Moving Picture World*

Title	Year	Country	Length	Studio	Director/Writer	Cast	Notes
Hazel Kirke	1916	USA	5,000	Wharton	Louis J. Gasnier, Leopold Wharton, Theodore Wharton (d., p.) from play by Steele MacKaye	Pearl White, Allan Murnane, Riley Hatch	Remake of Steele MacKaye play. 'The best loved play of the last thirty years with a truly wonderful cast headed by Pearl White.' Pathé advertisement
Hear the Pipers Calling	1918	UK	5,000	Grenville-Taylor	Tom Watts (d.); H. Grenville-Taylor (w.)	Hilda Oldfield	Tempted from home by a London adventuress, a young Scotsman's path is dogged by misfortune in London. Redeemed by the 'call of the pipes', he enlists and becomes a hero. Listed separately by IMDb but seems likely to be re-release of *The Call of the Pipes*.
Heart of Midlothian, The (aka *Jeanie Deans*)	1914	UK	5,000	Hepworth	Frank Wilson (d.); Blanche McIntosh (w.) from novel by Sir Walter Scott	Flora Morris, Violet Hopson, Alma Taylor, Stewart Rome, Warwick Buckland	'A Literal Photoplay Version of Sir Walter Scott's Immortal Novel. A Story Full of the Deepest Human Interest.' Hepworth advertisement. 'The atmosphere of those exterior scenes supposed to be laid in Scotland is well suggested, and the studio settings throughout are remarkable for their solidity and perfection of detail.' *The Bioscope*
Hearts and the Highway	1915	USA	5,000	Vitagraph	Wilfrid North (d.); Jasper Ewing Brady (w.) from the novel by Cyrus Townsend Brady	Lillian Walker, Darwin Karr, Donald Hall	The Earl of Clanranald is arrested and his death warrant is dispatched to Edinburgh. Lady Katherine, the Earl's daughter, dresses up as a highwayman and holds up the King's messenger. Her courage secures the release of her father. IMDb
Highlander, The	1911	UK	600	Natural Colour Kinematograph			'A girl weds an engineer while her Scottish fiancé is serving abroad.' IMDb

Title	Year	Country of origin	Length (ft) where known	Production company	Director/producer/writer	Actors	Summary
Highlander's Defiance, The	1910	USA	625	Selig	William Nicholas (d.)	Alvyn Wyckoff	Two Scots lads go to Boer War. At Spion Kop, Hector writes the Highlander's defiance: 'To h..l with you, the Gordons never surrender'. Both lads are killed, earning the admiration of the enemy and the grief of their sweethearts at home.
Hills Are Calling, The	1914	UK	1,150	Hepworth	Cecil M. Hepworth (d.); Reginald Hargreaves (sc.)	Tom Powers, Alma Taylor, Henry Vibart	'Away in London, the young Scotsman soon becomes indifferent to his first love and the victim of an adventuress. The latter almost ruins his career as a violinist, but a vision of the Highland lassie appears and his playing becomes rhapsodic. He discards the unworthy and hastens back to the hills, where his first love still awaits him.' (Manfacturer's synopsis)
His Highness	1916	Scotland	2,000	Club Comedies	Mr Foote (d.)		According to Scottish correspondent of *The Bioscope*, this is one of a series of films produced in a studio in Glasgow. Production facilities are described, but no detail of film and no evidence of where (or if) it was exhibited.
His Last Bachelor Night	1922	Scotland	2,000	Arc Film Company	Max Leder (p.)		One of three two-reel 'Delightful, Refined, All-Scottish Comedies', produced by Max Leder after the failure of *The Harp King* and *The Referee's Eye*. Apparently seen in Dundee with some approval by *The Weekly News*, but lambasted in *The Bioscope*, and disappeared without much trace.
His Mother	1911	USA	900	Vitagraph	Genevieve Baird (story)	Mary Maurice, Maurice Costello, Mabel Normand	A melodrama of mother and son separated and then miraculously finding each other in America. Released by Vitagraph in 1911 with original setting in Scotland and son travelling to America to study medicine. A new version is released by Kalem in 1912, with original setting in Killarney and son travelling to New York to be a musician.

Title	Year	Country	Length	Company	Credits	Cast	Notes
Hoot Mon!	1919	USA	1,000	Rolin Film	Hal Roach (d.)	Stan Laurel	A 'knock-out comic' with Stan Laurel. Set in Scotland and 'carefully costumed', with Stan as an American who has bought an inn.
Hoot Mon!	1926	USA	2,000	Christie Film Co.	Harold Beaudine (d.); Sig Herzig (story)	Bobby Vernon, Frances Lee, Jack Duffy	'More laughs are extracted from this novel comedy in Scotland than from all the Scotch jokes strung end to end for the last ten years. Bobby Vernon selling flivvers to the Scotchmen and getting messed up with the rival clans is a wow!' Christie trade advertisement. Looks like remake of the Hal Roach film.
Hot Cookies	1927	USA	1,000	Jack White (as Cameo Comedies)	Nate Watt (d.)	George Davis, Wallace Lupino, Toy Gallagher	Again poking fun at 'the Scotch' this interprets the adventures of Sandy McNabb, who shares 'the weakness of the Scot for pretty women', in restaurants and boarding house with food as motif of comedy. *Motion Picture News*
Huntingtower	1927	UK	7,000	Welsh Pearson	George Pearson (d.); Charles E. Whittaker (w.) from novel by John Buchan	Harry Lauder, Vera Voronina, Patrick Aherne	'A retired grocer and Gorbals boys save a Russian prince from Bolsheviks.' IMDb. With Harry Lauder as Dickson McCunn and six local Boy Scouts as the Gorbals Diehards. Shot in Cricklewood Studios and Bamburgh Castle.
In Fear of His Past	1914	USA	2,000	Majestic		Jack Conway, Spottiswoode Aitken, Mary Alden	'A two-part story of a villainess who contrives to get a man sent to prison for a theft she commits.' Spottiswoode Aitken plays an 'aristocratic Scotch codger . . . a character freshly conceived, amusing and well drawn' who provides much of the interest of the play. *Moving Picture World*

Title	Year	Country of origin	Length (ft) where known	Production company	Director/ producer/ writer	Actors	Summary
In His Grip	1921	UK	6,000	British Screencraft	Charles Calvert (d.); Paul Rooff (w.) from the novel by David Christie Murray	Cecil Morton York, David Hawthorne, Netta Westcott	Shot on Loch Lomond and St Vincent Street, Glasgow. Study of a 'strong man's struggle with his conscience'. *The Bioscope*. Sir Donald MacVeigh is tempted to realise capital on parcel of diamonds, but is accidentally discovered by his daughter and rescued from shame.
In Search of the Castaways (aka *Les enfants du capitaine Grant*)	1914	France	5,800	Éclair	Victorin-Hippolyte Jasset, Henry Roussel, Joseph Faivre (d. and p.); Michel Verne (w.) from the novel by Jules Verne	Josette Andriot, Denise Maural, Michel Gilbert	Lord Glenarvan and his wife are cruising in their yacht, *Duncan*, off the coast of their native land – Scotland. They discover a message in a bottle in the stomach of a whale that refers to Captain Grant who lost his ship and is stranded off the coast of South America. Thus begins a Patagonian adventure which begins in Scotland and reflects Verne's fascination with the country which is the setting for three of his novels.
Keep to the Left	1922	Scotland	1,000	Arc Film Company	Max Leder (p.)		One of three 'Delightful, Refined, All-Scottish Comedies' produced by Max Leder after the failure of *The Harp King* and *The Referee's Eye*. A one-reeler. Not much evidence of wide release in cinemas.
Kidnapped	1917	USA	4,000	Edison	Alan Crosland (d.); Charles Sumner Williams (sc.) from the novel by Robert Louis Stevenson	Raymond McKee, Joseph A. Burke, Ray Hallor	Stevenson's classic story of the travels of David Balfour through the Highlands, in unlikely alliance with the Jacobite Alan Breck Stewart, following the Appin murder of 1752. "The writer of the scenario has acquitted himself admirably, and preserved much of the spirit, and most of the essential points of the work.' *Moving Picture World*

Kilties	1927	USA	2,000	Jack White	Norman Taurog (w. & d.)	Dorothy Devore, Al Thompson, Henry Murdock	'[A] young lassie's adventure in a Scottish manse. [. . .] the first time we can recall comedy characters running around clad in the kilts and plaids of the Scotch [. . .] The titles proceed to poke fun at the supposed thriftiness of the Scotch and Dorothy does a burlesque with the bagpipes and other things associated with the inhabitants of the Northern part of Great Britain.' *Motion Picture News*
Kilties Three	1918	UK	7,000	Gaiety	Maurice Sandground (d.); Bernard Merivale (w.)	Bob Reed, Rowland Hill, Robert Vallis	Filmed in Edinburgh and Burns Country, Ayrshire. 'In Edinburgh a foundry owner weds a German spy's widow who becomes a nurse.' IMDb. Burns appears in one sequence, anticipating Sandground's *Bonnie Scotland Calls You* (1924). Ad in *Bioscope* notes: 'A NEW NOTE STRUCK IN FILM PRODUCTION. Characters in Fiction mingle with present day Realities.' Further information in PhD thesis by Caroline Merz.
Kitty Mackay	1917	USA	5,000	Vitagraph	Wilfrid North (d.); A. Van Buren Powell (sc.) from play by Catherine Chisholm Cushing	Lillian Walker, Jewell Hunt, Charles Kent, Donald Cameron, William Shea	Comedy: 'a pretty story of Scottish character in a dainty nineteenth-century setting'. *The Biograph*. Kitty is taken from the Highland cottage of the cruel McNabs to London, identities are mistaken and she finally marries Lord Engleheart's son. 'Like all Scotch comedies, character parts abound'. *Moving Picture World*
Lady from Hell, The	1926	USA	6,000	Stuart Paton Productions	Stuart Paton (d.); J. Grubb Alexander (adaptation), J. Grubb Alexander (screenplay), from story by Norton S. Parker	Roy Stewart, Blanche Sweet, Ralph Lewis	Sir Robin Carmichael, 'Scotch' officer of Highland regiment, the 'Ladies from Hell', becomes foreman of ranch in the West. The owner is killed by his son, Billy Boy, with Carmichael's gun. Carmichael returns to Scotland to marry Lady Darnley, but is arrested for the crime and brought back to America. Saved from the noose at last minute when Billy Boy confesses.

Title	Year	Country of origin	Length (ft) where known	Production company	Director/ producer/ writer	Actors	Summary
Lady of the Lake, The	1912	USA	2368	Vitagraph	J. Stuart Blackton (d.); Eugene Mullin (scenario) from Walter Scott's narrative poem	Harry T. Morey, Ralph Ince, Edith Storey	'Late one summer I was in the neighbourhood of Loch Katrine, had more than one glimpse of the lake and surrounding scenery and I can praise with authority as well as sincerity the choice of exteriors'. *Moving Picture World*. 'We believe the picture was taken in America, but, had it all been done actually in Scotland, one does not fancy that it would have gained artistically.' *The Biograph*
Lady of the Lake, The	1913	USA	3,000	Whitman Features Co.	from Walter Scott's poem		'It seems to be more an attempt to picturize the poem than to use the work as a basis for a drama. There are a vast number of titles – so many that the production loses its strength . . . There is a lack of cohesiveness or centralization of interest. *Moving Picture World*
Laird O'Knees, The	1916	USA	990	American Film Manufacturing Co.	Orral Humphrey (d.)	Orral Humphrey, John Gough, Gladys Kingsbury	'The advertising Highlander for a tobacconist loses his job. A music-hall comedian out of work puts on the kilts and is taken for a Scotch baronet and is royally entertained by a wealthy widow until the tobacconist and the comedian's landlady turn up and spoil his plans. Quite an amusing farcical comedy.' *The Bioscope*
Laird of McGillicuddy, The	1913	USA	996	Essanay		Augustus Carney, Billy Mason, Ruth Stonehouse	'A young lady breaks her engagement with her sweetheart, telling him she wants a titled husband. The sweetheart's chums evolve an idea by which the local milkman attends a ball as a Scotch nobleman. The young lady is enamoured of him at first, but his manners disgust her, and she is glad to return to her former sweetheart.' *The Bioscope*

Title	Year	Country	Length	Company	Credits	Cast	Synopsis
Laird's Daughter, The	1912	USA	1016	Selig	Richard Garrick (d.) Emmett Campbell Hall (sc.)	Allen Mathes, Adrienne Kroell, Walter Roberts	'A drama of the bonnie Scottish heather.' Selig advertisement. Airleen McGregor is prevented from marrying her poor sweetheart by her father. Sweetheart goes to America and becomes rich, eventually returning to his childhood village in time to marry his first true love.
Lass o' Killiecrankie, The	1915	USA	1,950	Victor		Elsie Albert, P. W. Nares, Isabel Vernon	The finding of a mate for Laurie Killiecrankie. Father favours Laird MacNott, mother favours Laird MacNabb, and Laurie favours Tammy, 'a poor stalwart lad'. With the aid of her grandfather, Laurie wins.
Last MacGregor, The (aka Stranger of the North; also Big Timber)	1924	Canada	5,556	Maritime Motion Picture Company of Canada	John W. Noble (d.)	Richard Travers, Ruth Dwyer, Charles Graham	Ferguson, the young Scot, enlists the help of members of his old regiment, to overcome the conniving foreman and marry Mary, the last MacGregor. 'A rather long-drawn-out story, but the picture possesses undoubted points of appeal.' The Bioscope
Last of the Stuarts, The	1909	Italy	902	Cines	Mario Caserini (d.)		The flight of the Young Pretender after the Battle of Culloden, mainly centred on his escape, disguised as a woman, with the aid of Flora MacDonald.
Law of His Kind, The	1914	USA	2,000	Rex	Frank Lloyd (d.); Phil Walsh (w.)	Herbert Rawlinson, Cleo Madison, Rex De Rosselli	'When the stern old Scotsman finds that his second wife is but an adventuress he ends his life. The woman tries to implicate his nephew, but Fate places poison in her way and a tragic ending follows.' The Bioscope
Lie, The	1914	USA	1,967	Gold Seal	Allan Dwan (d); Jeanie Macpherson (sc.)	Murdock MacQuarrie, Pauline Bush, William Lloyd, Lon Chaney	'A skilfully handled story, in which a hardened old Scotsman, brought up to regard a lie as a crime, is finally forced to admit that such a thing can be justified when it comes to saving his own daughter from a murder trial, taken in order to save her brother.' The Bioscope

Title	Year	Country of origin	Length (ft) where known	Production company	Director/ producer/ writer	Actors	Summary
Life of Robert Burns, The	1926	Scotland	7,600	Scottish Film Academy	Maurice Sandground (d.)	George Campbell, Wal Croft (and other well known Scottish actors)	'Suitability: For Scottish audiences anywhere where Scottish music and vocalists are employed . . . A jumbled up concoction of incidents in the life of Scotland's national bard, interspersed with some splendid examples of Scotland's beauty spots, and inserts illustrating some of the poet's well-known poems and songs.' *The Bioscope*. 'The picture could be considerably improved by cutting out fully fifty per cent of the celluloid and then setting fire to the other fifty.' Burns expert quoted in *The Bioscope*.
Life of Walter Scott, The	1926	Scotland	7,600	Scottish Film Academy	Maurice Sandground (d.)		Released from compilation, *Immortals of Bonnie Scotland*, apparently constructed along similar lines to *The Life of Robert Burns*. Further information in PhD thesis by Caroline Merz.
Lilac Sunbonnet, The	1922	UK	5,000	Burcher's Progress	Sidney Morgan (d.); from S.R. Crockett novel	Joan Morgan, Lewis Dayton, Nell Emerald, Forrester Harvey	Adapted from 'kailyard' novel, a sweet love story of Ralph Peden and Winsome Charteris and their attempts to marry in the context of a narrow and bigoted 'Narrow Kirk of Scotland'.
Little Gypsy, The	1915	USA	5,000	Fox	Oscar Apfel (d.); Mary Murillo (sc.), from the novel by J. M. Barrie	Dorothy Bernard, Thurlow Bergen, Raymond Murray	Replete with the strike of the weavers at Thrums, Babbie, 'a little gypsy' and a priggish young minister, this is clearly another adaptation of *The Little Minister*, though this is not mentioned in the *Moving Picture World* review.

Little Minister, The	1913	USA	3,000	Vitagraph	James Young (d.); James Young (sc.) from the novel by J. M. Barrie	Clara Kimball Young, James Young, Mrs. E. M. Kimball	'The first of five adaptations of J. M. Barrie's *The Little Minister* before 1923, Babby, posing as a gypsy, supports the striking weavers of Thrums, overcomes the outrage of the little Minister, and marries him twice: once in a Gypsy ceremony, and once in the 'Auld Licht Kirk'.'
Little Minister, The	1915	UK	3,920	Neptune Film Company	Percy Nash (d.); from the novel by J. M. Barrie	Joan Ritz, Gregory Scott, Henry Vibart, Dame May Whitty	'A Lord's fiancée poses as a gypsy and falls in love with the new minister.' IMDb
Little Minister, The	1921	USA	6,000	Famous Players	Penrhyn Stanlaws (d.); Edfrid A. Bingham (w.) from the stage version of the novel by J. M. Barrie.	Betty Compson, George Hackathorne, Edwin Stevens	'Before Sir James Barrie proved to possess an instinctive sense for the stage, a very excellent comedy was adapted from his delightful novel "The Little Minister", which enjoyed a remarkable success when produced at the Haymarket Theatre... Since then the play has had great success in America.' *The Bioscope*
Little Minister, The	1922	USA	6,000	Vitagraph	David Smith (d.); C. Graham Baker, Harry Dittmar (w.), from the stage version of the novel by J. M. Barrie.	Alice Calhoun, James Morrison, Henry Hebert [Albert E. Smith – presenter]	'When one remembers Mr. J. J. Bell's recent success as a screen author in *Wee McGregor's Sweetheart* to say nothing at all about the adaptations of Barrie's *Little Minister*, *Beside the Bonnie Brier Bush* and *The Lilac Sunbonnet*, it must be admitted that Scottish authors are keeping Caledonia's banner flying on the standard all right.' *The Bioscope*
Little Miss Nobody	1923	UK	5,750	Carlton Films	Wilfred Noy (d.); from the play by John Grahame	Flora le Breton, John Stuart, Ben Field	'The caretaker of a Scottish castle tries to trick his aunt into believing that some of the guests are aristocrats.' Wikipedia

Title	Year	Country of origin	Length (ft) where known	Production company	Director/ producer/ writer	Actors	Summary
Livingstone	1925	UK	6,000	Hero Films	M. A. Wetherell (d.)	M. A. Wetherell, Molly Rogers, Henry Walton	'This remarkable British enterprise, which involved a journey of 25,000 miles, represents an attempt to produce a picture combining the qualities of travel film and human document. The attempt may be said to have succeeded in both respects. Certainly no better subject could have been found than the life and travels of the famous missionary with whose career it deals.' *The Bioscope*. Re-released in 1927 in seven chapters. Evidence suggests that childhood in Scotland was filmed in England.
Lochinvar	1909	USA	790	Edison	J. Seale Dawley (d./w.) from poem by Sir Walter Scott	Marc McDermott, Mary Fuller, Harold M. Shaw	'Sir Walter Scott's romantic story of the love that laughed at more than locksmiths, and to which even castle walls and haughty barons were no bar, is told by the Edison Company with a wealth of scenic vesture and old Scottish atmosphere that brings out all its picturesque details.' *The Bioscope*
Lochinvar	1915	UK	2,100	Gaumont	Leslie Seldon-Truss (d./w.); from the poem by Sir Walter Scott	Godfrey Tearle, Peggy Hyland	From Scott's longer poem *Marmion* (1808). 'A Laird abducts his beloved on the eve of an enforced marriage.' IMDb
Loves of Mary Queen of Scots, The (aka *Mary, Queen of Scots*)	1923	UK	7,680	Ideal	Denison Clift (d./w.)	Fay Compton, Gerald Ames, Ivan Samson	'A romantic screen summary of outstanding events in the life of Mary, Queen of Scots. Special Features: The fact that much of the action was staged in the original locations, including several famous castles; the historical interest and pictorial beauty of these and other settings; the magnificent costumes; the performance of Fay Compton in the leading role.' *The Bioscope*. The castles included Edinburgh, Holyrood, Loch Leven and Stirling.

Lowland Cinderella, A (aka *Highland Maid, A*)	1921	UK	6,000	Progress British Photoplays	Sidney Morgan (d.); from novel by S. R. Crockett	Joan Morgan, Mary Carnegie, Mavis Clair, Nell Emerald, George Foley	'This is a pretty little story suggested by that most popular of all fairy tales, Cinderella, with a stately duchess as Fairy Godmother, and a handsome young Highland chief in the role of Fairy Prince . . . The settings, many taken in Scotland, are pretty, and the photography is consistently good.' *The Bioscope*. Filmed on location in the Highlands and in Shoreham Beach Studio in Sussex.
Lucy of Lammermoor (aka *Lucia di Lammermoor*)	1909	Italy	880	Itala	From novel by Sir Walter Scott		Another Italian adaptation of Walter Scott's novel *The Bride of Lammermoor*. Lucy, compelled to marry the wrong man, plunges a dagger into his heart, dies of grief, and her lover throws himself from a cliff.
Macbeth	1908	USA	850	Vitagraph	J. Stuart Blackton (d.); from Shakespeare's play	William V. Ranous, Louise Carver, Paul Panzer [Florence Lawrence and Florence Turner as Banquet Guests]	'When the film was screened at the Chicago exhibition, it was censored by the police. The scenes showing the duel between Macbeth and McDuff, and the stabbing of King Duncan and the brandishing of the bloody dagger, were ordered to be cut out.' IMDb Trivia
Macbeth	1909	France	1,000	Pathé	André Calmettes (d.); Michel Carré (adaptation), from Shakespeare's play	Paul Mounet, Jeanne Delvair	French adaptation of Shakespeare's tragedy.

Title	Year	Country of origin	Length (ft) where known	Production company	Director/producer/writer	Actors	Summary
Macbeth	1909	Italy	1,500	Cines	Mario Caserini (d.); from Shakespeare's play	Dante Cappelli, Maria Caserini, Amleto Palormi	Italian adaptation of Shakespeare's tragedy.
Macbeth	1911	UK	1,400	Co-operative Cinematograph	From Shakespeare's play	Frank R. Benson, Constance Benson, Murray Carrington	Adaptation for the Stratford Memorial Theatre Company, running for approx. 14 minutes.
Macbeth	1913	Germany	4,500	Industrie Gesellschaft, Heidelburg	Arthur Bouchier (d.), from Shakespeare's play	Arthur Bouchier, Violet Vanburgh	Filmed at Castle of Heidelberg, with English lead actors. 'Weather conditions would render good results almost an impossibility . . . a film has been secured which will be well worthy of a place as a permanent record of a great Shakespearian production long after it has ceased to interest a pleasure-saturated public.' *The Bioscope*
Macbeth	1915	France	3,230	Éclair	From Shakespeare's play	Séverin-Mars, Georgette Leblanc-Maeterlinck	Played to wounded Belgian soldiers in the West End Cinema in April 1915. As well as *Macbeth*, programme included Maeterlinck's *Pelleas and Melisande* (1913), both plays starring Maeterlinck's wife.
Macbeth	1916	USA	7,500	Reliance Film Company	John Emerson (d./w.); Anita Loos (intertitles), from Shakespeare's play	Herbert Beerbohm Tree, Constance Collier, Wilfred Lucas	'There has been much talk about preserving the art of great actors through motion pictures, but slight accomplishment, either because the players were lost in the new medium, or because the subjects were unwisely selected. Here we have a happy combination of actor and play, also a director competent to handle a great tragedy.' *Moving Picture World*

Title	Year	Country	Length	Company	Credits	Cast	Notes
Macbeth	1922	UK	1,175	Master Films	H. B. Parkinson (d.); Frank Miller (adaptation), from Shakespeare's play	Russell Thorndike, Sybil Thorndike	'First release in the "Tense Moments from Great Play" series.' IMDb
Macbeth	1922	Germany	1,000	Elel-Film	Heinz Schall (d.), from Shakespeare's play	Eugen Klöpfer, Albert Steinrück	German adaptation of Shakespeare's tragedy. thirty-minute adaptation in 1922.
MacDougal's Aeroplane	1915	UK	530	Phoenix Film Agency	James Read (d./w.)	James Read	'A Scotsman builds an aeroplane but it explodes.' IMDb
MacNab Visits the Comet	1910	France	900	Lux			'The dream of a man who is comet mad. It permits the introduction of a pretty ballet, and an enchanting fairy vision in a diaphanous gown. Aside from these features it has no particular interest.' *Moving Picture World*
MacNab's Visit to London	1905	UK	300	Alpha Trading Company		Arthur Melbourne Cooper	'MacNab, a comic caricature Highlander, arrives in London to visit his cousin. After a display of 'characteristic' Scottish meanness in failing to tip the station attendants, he arrives at his cousin's house where, within moments, he proceeds to destroy the drawing room with a golf club.' Available online at Moving Image Archive (NLS)
Maid o' the Storm	1918	USA	6,000	Paralta Play, Inc.	Raymond B. West (d.); J. Grubb Alexander (w.), Fred Myton (w.)	Bessie Barriscale, George Fisher, Herschel Mayall	'Bessie Barriscale is seen in the role of a little waif in a fishing village in Scotland, whose destiny is shaped by the falling of an aeroplane from the sky. How the little girl falls in love with the young aristocrat who is injured in the crash, and how she follows him to London, where she becomes the idol of that great city, presents Miss Barriscale in one of the most convincing roles in which she has appeared.' Paralta advertisement, *Moving Picture World*

Title	Year	Country of origin	Length (ft) where known	Production company	Director/ producer/ writer	Actors	Summary
Mairi: The Romance of a Highland Maiden	1913	Scotland	1,000	Andrew Paterson	Andrew Paterson (d., p., w.)	Evelyn Duguid	Filmed in North Kessock, near Inverness, an amateur production using local actors. A young girl in love with a Revenue Officer is caught up in a fight to catch smugglers. Believed to be one of the earliest story films made in Scotland, it is also the only one to survive. Available online at Moving Image Archive (NLS)
Man and the Moment, The	1918	UK	5,850	Windsor	Arrigo Bocchi (d.); Kenelm Foss (w.), from the novel by Elinor Glyn	Manora Thew, Hayford Hobbs, Charles Vane	'An American heiress weds a Scots lord to fulfill a will, leaves him for Italy, but returns after her baby's death.' IMDb
Man Beneath, The	1919	USA	5,000	Haworth Pictures Corporation	William Worthington (d.); L. V. Jefferson (sc.) from the novel by Edmund Mitchell	Sessue Hayakawa, Helen Jerome Eddy, Pauline Curley	Sessue Hayakawa as Hindu surgeon with 'the knowledge that the Hindus seem to have of magic and drugs'. Set in Scotland, India and Italy. 'Mr Hayakawa's speech, made at the University of Scotland . . . Is one of the most touching scenes he has ever enacted.' *Moving Picture World*
Man from Glengarry, The	1922	Canada	6,000	Ernest Shipman	Henry MacRae (d.); Faith Green (adaptation), Kenneth O'Hara (w.) from the novel by Ralph Connor	Anders Randolf, Warner Richmond, Harlan Knight	Drama of Gaelic-speaking and Presbyterian Highlanders led by MacDonald More ('Big Mack'), Irish and French in the Canadian lumber-camp. From a novel by Canada's best known early nineteenth-century novelist.

Maria Stuart	1927	Germany	7886	National-Film	Friedrich Feher, Leopold Jessner (d./w.); Anton Kuh	Magda Sonja, Fritz Kortner, Walter Janssen	Based on Schiller's drama of Mary Queen of Scots, with Bothwell, Darnley, Leicester and John Knox. Said to be directed by Jessner, but, according to Kuh, he was on the set only for one afternoon. Critics accused it of being 'a spoken drama presented on the screen' with the actors acting 'as if they were on the stage instead of the screen'. *New York Times*
Mary Stuart	1908	France	840	Pathé	Albert Capellani (d.); Michel Carré	Jeanne Delvair, Jacques Grétillat, Henry Krauss	'A star release, showing one of the most prominent periods in English history, ending with the execution of the fair Queen at Fotheringay'. *The Bioscope*. A 'beautifully colored picture'. *Moving Picture World*
Mary Stuart	1913	USA	3,000	Edison	Walter Edwin (d.); J. Searle Dawley (sc.), from Schiller's play	Mary Fuller, Marc McDermott, Bigelow Cooper	'It is difficult to remember a picture bearing fuller evidence of unsparing pains to ensure perfection of detail and scholarly regard for historical facts ... Often an historical play is acted as though everyone were participating in some solemn and pompous ritual, and much credit is due to the Edison players that they succeed in presenting "Mary Stuart" without any pretentious trickery.' *The Bioscope*
Mary, Queen of Scots	1912	France	910	Gaumont			'Try to give a provincial audience a word picture of medieval Scotland, for instance, and you will quickly find that it is an almost hopeless task ... But send them to a picture theatre and show them Gaumont's *Mary, Queen of Scots*, and in less than half an hour they will have a true and accurate knowledge of a rather difficult subject, and a knowledge which will remain an ineffaceable memory to serve them for future reference.' *The Bioscope*
Mary, Queen of Scots	1922	UK	1,000	British & Colonial Kinematograph Company	Edwin Greenwood (d.); Eliot Stannard (w.)	Cathleen Nesbitt, Reginald Bach	From British and Colonial series, 'Romance of British History', which included *Mary, Queen of Scots*, *Seadogs of Good Queen Bess*, *The Story of Amy Robsart*, *The Threefold Tragedy* and *The Last King of Wales*.

Title	Year	Country of origin	Length (ft) where known	Production company	Director/ producer/ writer	Actors	Summary
Mary, Queen of Tots	1925	USA	2,000	Hal Roach Studios	Robert F. McGowan (d.); Hal Roach (story), H. M. Walker (titles)	Charles A. Bachman, May Beatty, Joe Cobb	'Charming fantasy. Four dolls come to life and their adventures are most entertaining and interesting.' *The Bioscope*. The Scottish connection may only be in the title.
Master of Grays, The	1918	UK	5,000	Monarch Film Corporation	Tom Watt (d./w.)	Athalie Davis, Harvey Clifford, Ethel Douglas Ross, Ernest A. Douglas	A blending of two ballads, "The Master of Grays' and 'Auld Robin Gray', the ancient curse of the first part carried out in the second. 'The romantic scenery of Scotland is beautifully produced, together with picturesque interiors of the castle and the church. To those who revel in sentiment of the gloomy order this film may appeal.' *The Bioscope*
McFadden's Flats	1927	USA	7,800	Aher-Small-Rogers for First National	Richard Wallace (d.); Jack Jevne Charles Logue, Rex Taylor, Jack Wagner (adaptation) from Gus Hill's novel	Charles Murray, Chester Conklin	'A clever and amusing study of the friendship of a reckless and improvident Irishman and a cautious, thrifty Scotsman, and how they achieve fortune together. A very entertaining study of character.' *The Bioscope*
Modern Lochinvar, A	1913	USA	950	Thanhouser		William Russell	'His family tree contained proof that Percy Lochinvar was descended from the bold Scotchman who won his sweetheart despite all opposition. But Percy was shy, his mother was an "ardent suffragist", and his rival was a smart New York lawyer. But "what one Lochinvar had done... another would do", and he started out to make history repeat itself.' *Moving Picture World*

Moral Courage	1917	USA	5,000	Peerless Productions	Romaine Fielding (d.); Stanley Dark (story)	Muriel Ostriche, Arthur Ashley, Edward Elkas	The heroine is 'Scotch, clever enough to turn the tables on her father-in-law when he attempts to separate her from her newly wed husband.' She accepts a bribe of $100,000 from her father-in-law to divorce her husband, then applies 'a Scotch trick' and promptly remarries him. *Moving Picture World*
Now We're in the Air	1927	USA	6,000	Paramount	Frank R. Strayer (d.); Monte Brice (story); Thomas J. Geraghty	Wallace Beery, Raymond Hatton, Russell Simpson, Louise Brooks	'It's burlesque with a vengeance. Some of it borders on the vulgar . . . The comics put on kilts and have a lot of fun with the Scotch national dress. They are represented as Americans bent upon getting the wealth of their Scotch grand-dad – an oldtimer with a yen for aviation. So they take to the air. And the fun begins.' *Motion Picture News*. With Beery, Hatton and, notably, Louise Brooks.
Oh! Mr Macpherson	1912	UK		Hepworth		Billy Williams	Filmed sketch of music hall monologue performed by Billy Williams (1877–1915). http://monologues.co.uk/musichall/Songs-O/Oh-Mister-Macpherson.htm. Chorus: 'Macpherson was a Scotchsman [*sic*], and he courted bonnie Mary. He went and joined the navy, left the hills of old Glengary.'
Oh! You Scotch Lassie	1913	USA	500	Crystal Film Company	Phillips Smalley (d.)	Pearl White, Chester Barnett, Joseph Belmont	Pearl 'masquerades as a Scotch lassie, and wearing the regulation kilts, is the admiration of the entire assemblage.' A jealous fight ensues, is stopped by Chester, the policeman, who promises not to arrest her if she will become his girl. *Moving Picture World*

Title	Year	Country of origin	Length (ft) where known	Production company	Director/ producer/ writer	Actors	Summary
On the Banks of Allan Water	1916	UK	4,000	Clarendon	Wilfrid Noy (d.) Reuben Gillmer (w.) adapted from the song	Basil Gill, J. Hastings Batson, Roy Byford, Violet Graham, Grania Gray	'Many of the scenes are enacted on the banks of Allan Water, and the photography is excellent all through. The sad ending of the song is slightly altered, and the soldier hero arrives in the nick of time to rescue the "miller's lovely daughter", and the audience is left to decide for themselves whether the false soldier and his lovely bride find the happiness the song-writer denied them.' *The Bioscope*. For lyrics, see http://sangstories. webs.com/banksofallanwater.htm
Patriotism	1918	USA	6,000	Paralta Play, Inc.	Raymond West (d.); Julian La Mothe (sc.); Jane Holly, R. B. Kidd (story)	Bessie Barriscale, Arthur Allardt, Herschel Mayall, Joseph J. Dowling	American survivor of a ship sunk by German submarine is cared for at home of Robin who has her home in Scotland converted to a hospital. She discovers German spy sending anthrax to soldiers in shaving brushes, exonerates the young American, and arranges to marry him after his return from the front. 'patriotic subject, suitable for propaganda work'. *Moving Picture World*
Peggy	1916	USA	5,500	Triangle	Charles Giblyn, Thomas H. Ince (d.); C. Gardner Sullivan (w.)	Billie Burke, William H. Thompson, William Desmond	Peggy, under protest, goes from New York to Scotland to visit her uncle. 'There ensues a succession of comedy scenes showing Peggy in conflict with the sour Scots. She tells the children fairy tales, drives her car at breakneck speed, dresses in her cousin, Colin's, clothes, and scares the village drunkard out of his wits.' *Moving Picture World*. In the end, she is persuaded to stay, and probably marries the minister.
Peter's Rival	1912	UK	325	Cricks and Martin	Edwin J. Collins		'Two rivals vie for a girl who loves a Scotsman.' IMDb

Title	Year	Country	Length	Company	Credits	Cast	Notes
Pie-eyed Piper, The	1918	USA	1,000	Universal	William Beaudine (d.); C. B. Hoadley (w.)	Zasu Pitts, Billy Franey, Milburn Morante	Another Young Lochinvar. Ellen's parents are forcing her into a marriage with her cousin: 'young Lochinvar and Ellen dance, and as they reach the door they both escape. He carries the girl to his car, puts the cousin's out of action, and makes a successful elopement. Engaging little piece.' *The Bioscope*
Pimple in the Kilties	1915	USA	910	Folly Films	Fred Evans, Joe Evans (d. & w.)	Fred Evans	'Best described as a topical "comic", this release, with Pimple a member of the Scottish, provides a medium for many deeds of heroism, Pimple all but securing mention in despatches. Sub-titled in an amusing way, and, although a little overdrawn, quite upon a par with previous issues.' *The Bioscope*
Pimple's Humanity	1914	UK	690	Folly Films	Fred Evans, Joe Evans (d. & w.)	Fred Evans	'A Scots Jew fights his faithless friend.' IMDb
Pride of the Clan, The (aka *Lass of Killean*)	1917	USA	2,100	Mary Pickford Company	Maurice Tourneur (d.); Elaine S. Carrington, Charles E. Whittaker (sc.); Clarence Brown (ed.)	Mary Pickford, Matt Moore, Warren Cook, Leatrice Joy	On the death of her father, Mary becomes chief of the clan on a remote Scottish island. Her sweetheart turns out to be the abandoned child of a fashionable lady. This is an obstacle, but love conquers all. 'The fact that "America's darling" has selected a story of bonny Scotland as her next vehicle is hailed with delight among sons and daughters of the heather in this country.' *Moving Picture World.* Available on DVD.
Prince Charlie	1914	USA	1,000	Crystal Film Company	Joseph A. Golden (d.)	Charles De Forrest	No information. Charles De Forrest has a series of Crystal Comedies circa 1914 in which he features as a comedy character, Charlie. Not clear whether there is any Scottish reference, so its status is uncertain.

Title	Year	Country of origin	Length (ft) where known	Production company	Director/ producer/ writer	Actors	Summary
Putting Pants on Philip	1927	USA	2,000	Hal Roach Studios	Clyde Bruckman (d.); Leo McCarey (story), H. M. Walker	Stan Laurel, Oliver Hardy, Charles A. Bachman	'Pompous J. Piedmont Mumblethunder, greets his nephew from Scotland, who arrives in kilts. He is immediately taken to a tailor for a pair of proper pants.' IMDb
Quentin Durward	1910	France		Pathé	Albert Capellani; from the novel by Walter Scott		Quentin Durward is an archer, who has left behind poverty in Scotland to join Louis XI's Scottish Guard, and, standing in the way of treachery, earns the love of Isabelle de Croye.
Quentin Durward	1912	France	1,270	Pathé	Adrien Caillard (d.); Louis Mauzin (adaptation) from the novel by Walter Scott	René Alexandre, Claude Garry, Henri Étiévant	'It is pleasant to find a part of Scott's stirring romance visualised by the cinematograph, more especially as the particular part shown has been in the right hands for adaptation. It is that part of the story where Quentin Durward finds himself in France and rescues Isabelle de Croye from William de la Marck, as she is fleeing from her uncle, the powerful Duke of Burgundy, to throw herself on the protection of Louis XI.' *The Bioscope*
Rajah's Hatred, A (aka The Indian Mutiny)	1912	USA	604	Vitagraph	Frederick A. Thomson (d.) Marguerite Bertsch (sc.)	James Morrison, Lillian Walker, Harry Northrup	Beatrice, visiting her brother in India, is sought in marriage by an Indian prince. She refuses, the Sepoys mutiny and Beatrice is abducted, only to be saved by the Gordon Highlanders. "The Prince is taken prisoner and his followers surrender . . . Beatrice throws her arms about her brother's neck, and extends her gratitude to the captain of the Highlanders.' *The Bioscope*

Title	Year	Country	Length	Company	Credits	Cast	Notes
Real Thing at Last, The	1916	UK	2,000	British Actors' Film Company	L. C. MacBean (d.); J. M. Barrie (w.) adapted from Shakespeare	Edmund Gwenn, Nelson Keys, Godfrey Tearle, Gladys Cooper, Ernest Thesiger	A burlesque by J. M. Barrie on *Macbeth* satirising the American film producer, with Rupert K. Thunder as the impresario, Earl Macbeth, King Duncan as a comic Scot and Lady Macbeth encouraging his murder: 'Dear Macbeth, the king has gotten loud and silly. Slay him. Yours sincerely, Lady M.' 'Although it is somewhat lacking in subtlety, and is, in a few respects, unnecessarily ungenerous to the cinema, *The Real Thing at Last* makes a merry novelty.' *The Bioscope*
Referee's Eye, The	1921	Scotland		Ace Films	Max Leder (p.)		'A most laughable story of a Football, a Pudding, and an Amateur Detective.' 'Distributed, like *The Harp King* by J. C. Barker, the film flickered even more briefly across the pages of the trade press, before disappearing from view, its only impact being to taint the reputation of Scottish productions that followed.' Trevor Griffiths, *Cinema and Cinema-going in Scotland, 1896–1950*
Relief of Lucknow, The	1912	USA	985	Edison	J. Searle Dawley (d.)	James Gordon, William R. Randall, Ben F. Wilson	Preceding *The Campbells Are Coming*, but possibly inspired by the same Whittier poem, this is the story, though apparently without the romantic element, of the Sepoy mutiny and the relief of Lucknow by the heroic Highlanders.
Revenge of the Silk Masks	1912	USA	1,000	Éclair	Étienne Arnaud (d. & w.)	John Troyano, George Larkin, Muriel Ostriche, Dorothy Gibson	Scottish connection is tenuous and is not highlighted in reviews. However, the still from *Moving Picture World*, from the final court scene, shows one of the three lead female characters wearing full Highland dress, evidence, perhaps, of the continuing popularity of Highland dress as fancy dress. See also the masquerade ball in Chaplin's *The Idle Class* (1921). See http://www.archive.org/stream/movingpictureworl2newy#page/314/mode/2up.

Title	Year	Country of origin	Length (ft) where known	Production company	Director/producer/writer	Actors	Summary
Richard the Lion-Hearted (aka The Talisman)	1912	Italy	2,043	Cines	From Walter Scott's novel The Talisman		'A dramatic series of pictures illustrating the climax of Walter Scott's famous novel The Talisman ... It will charm the small boy, and he should be given a chance to see it. It will instruct him too. It will also entertain and instruct the small boy's parents.' Moving Picture World. Sir Kenneth of Scotland upholds his honour and defeats the Duke of Montserrat in mortal combat, for which he is given the hand of Edith Pantagenet by Richard, the Lion-Heart.
Richard the Lion-Hearted (aka The Talisman)	1923	USA	7,500	Allied Producers	Chester Withey (d.), Frank E. Woods (w.) from Walter Scott's novel The Talisman	Wallace Beery, Charles K. Gerrard, Kathleen Clifford, John Bowers	'Here we have a picture which in some respects may be called a sequel to Robin Hood in that it discloses the adventures of King Richard in the Holy Land. The colorful character of the English King is here depicted in all his glory by the same actor who interpreted him in Robin Hood. Wallace Beery's Richard is a swaggering monarch.' Moving Picture World. Retains the key role of Kenneth of Scotland.
Rob Roy	1911	Scotland	2,500	United Film Ltd	Arthur Vivian (attributed d.); James Bowie (p.), from Pocock's dramatisation of Walter Scott's novel	John Clyde, Theo Henries, Durward Lely	'The Scottish drama, produced by Scottish actors on Scottish ground by the Scottish Firm.' Advertisement in The Bioscope. The first three-reel film in Britain, produced by Glasgow-based company United Films. Filmed in Aberfoyle, with John Clyde and his company in 'the National Drama'. Greeted with great excitement by Scottish trade press. Though it certainly reached Australia and New Zealand, there is not much evidence that it was shown widely in the UK or the USA. A full account is given by Caroline Merz in Chapter 7, questioning Vivian's role as director.

Rob Roy (aka *An Adventure of Rob Roy*)	1911	USA	995	Gaumont		'Taken in Macgregor's Country on the actual spots in Perthshire and Argyllshire, by kind permission of His Grace the Duke of Argyll.' Gaumont advertisment in *The Bioscope*. This version, based on a single tale rather than on Scott's novel, was released within months of the United Film's *Rob Roy*, filmed on similar locations. Advertisements suggest quite ruthless competition, and may partially account for United's showing at the box office.
Rob Roy	1913	USA	2,950	Éclair	Henry J. Vernot (d.), from Walter Scott's novel	Jack W. Johnston, Nancy Avril, Robert Frazer	'It must have been a particularly difficult task to carry out such a production in America, and it says a great deal for the Eclair Company's scholarly, painstaking methods that they have caught the spirit both of the country and of the period quite perfectly, in points of detail as well as in general effect. Indeed, did one not know the contrary to be the case, one would have said that the picture could only have been made in Scotland by Scottish artistes.' *The Bioscope*
Rob Roy	1922	USA	6,000	Gaumont	W. P. Kellino (d.); Alicia Ramsey (story)	David Hawthorne, Gladys Jennings, Simeon Stuart, Wallace Bosco	'As Mrs. Ramsey is careful to explain at the opening of the film, this is not an adaptation of Sir Walter Scott's novel, but the story of the principal events in the life of the famous outlaw from his early youth in his mountain home at Inversnaid, up to a period some considerable time before his death.' *The Bioscope*. Shooting of market scenes was planned in Oban, and Kellino travelled to Oban to reconnoitre; but, according to *Oban Times*, filming was abandoned due to bad weather.

Title	Year	Country of origin	Length (ft) where known	Production company	Director/producer/writer	Actors	Summary
Robert Bruce (aka Robert Bruce, épisode des guerres de l'indépendance écossaise)	1911	France	1,336	Pathé	Albert Capellani	Louis Ravet, Paul Capellani, Henri Étiévant	Bruce's rivalry with the Red Comyn for the throne of Scotland and his eventual victory in the cause of independence. Extract from a nitrate fragment found in Netherlands Audiovisual Archive and available on site at Moving Image Archive (NLS).
Robinson Crusoe	1927	UK	6,500	M. A. Wetherell Productions	M. A. Wetherell (w.), from novel by Daniel Defoe	M. A. Wetherell, Fay Compton, Herbert Waithe	Although this is mainly set on Crusoe's desert island, 'British Studios Today' in *The Bioscope* reports on filming of *Robinson Crusoe* in Largo, Fife. No mention is made of this in the review of the film. It seems likely, however, that there were flashbacks to Crusoe/Selkirk's home life, explaining the allusion to the 'slight love interest, but this is merely to mark the lapse of time and to accentuate the loneliness and home sickness of the exile'. *The Bioscope*
Romance of Annie Laurie, The	1920	UK	2,000	Lancashire Film Studios	Gerald Somers (d.); Alfred Denville (play)	Joan Gray, Allan McKelvin	'In Scotland a Laird's bastard child elopes with a laird who is wed to a mad woman.' IMDb
Romany Lass, A (aka Rilka: or, The Gypsy Queen)	1918	UK	7,000	Harma Photoplays	F. Martin Thornton (d.); Reuben Gillmer (w.)	James Knight, Marjorie Villis, Bernard Dudley	'Advertising Phrases: Gypsy Queen Helps Make Man out of Son of Scottish House. Advertising Angles: Play up the Scotch atmosphere. In communities where there is a colony of Scots make a heavy play for their patronage. Tell them the scenes were pictured in the Highlands; that they may some of them see the very neighbourhood from whence they came ... Have a man in kilts in front of your theatre.' *Moving Picture World*

Title	Year	Country	Length	Company	Director/Writer	Cast	Synopsis
Romany, The	1923	UK	5,700	Welsh Pearson	F. Martin Thornton (d.); Eliot Stannard (w.)	Victor McLaglen, Irene Norman, Harvey Braban, Peggy Hathaway	'How a Romany chief chivalrously shelters a runaway Scottish maid from an importunate suitor and thereby incurs the superstitious wrath of his followers and the jealousy of his gipsy sweetheart forms the subject of the story.' *The Bioscope*. Filmed in Dalnaspidal, Buckie, Carnoustie and Glen Tilt. 'Rarely, if ever, has the characteristic atmosphere of Scotland been so faithfully interpreted in screen pictures.' *The Bioscope*. '"I've learnt to do the eightsome reel and the sword dance," says [Victor McLaglen], "and now only need to learn the bagpipes to complete the picture."' *The Bioscope*
Sandy	1918	USA	5,000	Famous Players	George Melford (d.); Edith M. Kennedy (sc.) from the novel by Alice Hegan Rice	Jack Pickford, Louise Huff, James Neill	'Sandy Kilday, a Scotch lad, comes to this country as a stowaway in search of his fortune.' *Moving Picture World*. Goes to Kentucky in pursuit of Ruth, becomes adopted son of Judge Hollis, and rescues Ruth's brother from crime. All ends well. From a novel by the author of *Mrs. Wiggs of the Cabbage Patch*
Sandy at Home	1916	UK	600	Transatlantic	Will Page (d. & w.)	Will Page, Betty O'Neill, Dan Hendy-Clarke	'A Scot is left in charge of his wife's and sister's babies.' IMDb
Sandy McPherson's Quiet Fishing Trip	1908	USA	430	Edison			'Sandy, a Big Brawny Scot determines on a fishing trip. For coolness arrays himself in Highland costume, kilts, bonnet, philibeg, et al. Not forgetting a bottle of "Mountain Dew" … Mosquitoes find Sandy, his bare legs a harvest … Does a Highland-fling. The Bad Boys: Two country lads discover Sandy … Imagine a wrathy, fiery Scot trying to fish. Fight mosquitoes, "cuss" in choice Gaelic, and attend to two mischievous boys, at the same time.' *Moving Picture World*

Title	Year	Country of origin	Length (ft) where known	Production company	Director/ producer/ writer	Actors	Summary
Sandy's New Kilt	1912	UK	820	British & Colonial Kinematograph Company	Dave Aylott	William Gladstone Haley	'One by one a family shortens the father's kilt.' BFI
Scotland for Ever	1914	USA	994	Vitagraph	Harry Lambart (as Harry Lambert) (d.); Charles Brown (story)	Hughie Mack, Templar Saxe	'The "twa braw Hieland laddies" land in New York, engage in a merry comedy, in which the question of trousers and kilts predominates. The kilts receive a warm welcome in the end.' *The Bioscope*
Secret of the Hills, The	1921	USA	5,000	Vitagraph	Chester Bennett (d.); E. Magnus Ingleton (w.) from the novel by William Garrett	Antonio Moreno, Lillian Hall, Kingsley Benedict	'In London, an American correspondent rescues a girl in danger and finds himself involved in a mystery complete with secret codes, creepy old mansions, counterfeiting, buried treasure and murder.' IMDb. Adapted from William Garrett's novel which places the treasure in Scotland, belonging to King James III.
Sentimental Tommy	1921	USA	8,000	Famous Players	John S. Robertson (w.); Josephine Lovett (w.) from the novel by J. M. Barrie	Malcolm Bradley, Harry Coleman, Kate Davenport	From Barrie's novel about Tommy, a young lad of Thrums (Barrie's own town of Kirriemuir), adrift in London, and remaining a boy at heart. Often considered autobiographical.

Title	Year	Country	Length	Studio	Credits	Cast	Notes
Shepherd Lassie of Argyle, The	1914	UK	3,000	Hepworth	Larry Trimble (d.); Hector Dion (w.)	Florence Turner, Clifford Pembroke, Rex Davis	'A shepherd's daughter is struck dumb when her dog frustrates an attack on her by a laird's mad brother.' IMDb 'By far the most notable feature of this excellent film is its extraordinary beauty from a scenic point of view. The whole production has been staged amidst the mountains and forests of Scotland and much of the very finest of that country's scenery has been selected.' *The Bioscope*. Filmed 'under the shadow of Ben Nevis'.
Shon, the Piper	1913	USA	1,965	Bison	Otis Turner (d.)	Robert Z. Leonard, Joseph Singleton, John Burton, Lon Chaney	'Disguised as a piper, a wealthy Scotsman wins the hand of a peasant girl.' IMDb 'Feature of Highland life; the lover, a Duke disguised as a piper, and differences which lead to a terrible battle of the clans.' *Entertainer and Scottish Kinema Record*
Skirl of the Pibroch, The	1908	UK	140	Walturdaw	Dave Aylott		'A boy plays the bagpipes and makes everybody dance.' IMDb
Snowballs	1901	UK	70	Mitchell & Kenyon			Although there is very little information on this sketch, the BFI identifies it as having been commissioned by Green's and possibly shot in Scotland. [Available on BFI Player]
Soldiers Three (aka When Scotch Soldier Laddies Went in Swimming)	1911	USA	810	Vitagraph	George D. Baker (d.)	John Bunny, William Shea (born Dumfries), Sidney Bracey	'"Three laddies ask and obtain a leave of absence for a day to visit their aged mother. On their way to the old home, they call on three Highland lassies.' Mishaps occur, including the loss of their kilts while bathing, and consequent court martial, but it ends with a "Flora de Perfecto" which they light and complacently smoke with relish.' *Moving Picture World*
Sporting Venus, The	1925	USA	7,000	Metro-Goldwyn-Mayer	Marshall Neilan (d.); Thomas J. Geraghty (w.) from story by Gerald Beaumont	Blanche Sweet, Ronald Colman, Lew Cody	Blanche Sweet as 'the reckless daughter of a reckless Scotch nobleman' and Ronald Coleman 'as the upper-class "commoner"'. 'A big appeal of this picture will be the clothes worn by Miss Sweet.' 'Has exteriors from Scotland, England, Spain and France: "The Continental flavor . . . adds tone to its atmosphere – and makes the characters appear genuine.' *Motion Picture News*

Title	Year	Country of origin	Length (ft) where known	Production company	Director/ producer/ writer	Actors	Summary
Tam O'Shanter	1915	USA	3,000	Universal	Murdock MacQuarrie (d.); Harry G. Stafford (sc.) from the poem by Robert Burns	Murdock MacQuarrie, Eva Thatcher, William White	'This pictures the scenes described in the famous poem by Robert Burns. Mr. MacQuarrie makes a good character part of Tam, the genial Scotch tippler, who is finally cured of his drunkenness by a meeting with the devil in a country church yard . . . 'The atmosphere of Scotland is only fairly well suggested. At the close Tam swears off and is happily reunited with his wife and daughter.' *Moving Picture World*
Tam O'Shanter's Ride	1912	Scotland		B.B. Films	Bert Foulger (producer or sponsor)		Shot in Ayr, using local scenes and actors, sponsored locally by Bert Foulger for B.B. Films, and shown locally, but not widely distributed. 'The scenes are indelibly fixed in the imagination, and the deil, the witches, and all the weird things mentioned seem to become realities. Each evening the audience has shown its appreciation in no half-hearted manner, and the fact that the film has been taken locally added to the enjoyment.' *Ayr Post*
Tee for Two (aka The Highland Swing)	1925	USA	2,000	Mack Sennett Comedies	Edward F. Cline (d.); Felix Adler, Al Giebler (titles)	Alice Day, Raymond McKee, William McCall	Alice Day 'as a Scotch girl recently come to this country and enmeshed in a romance with a wealthy youth whom she met on the steamer . . . The golf links where this ancient and royal sport is perpetrated proves the battleground on which this Scotch Peg triumphs over her rival for the consent of the father to a marriage.' *Motion Picture News*
Thou Fool	1926	UK	5,100	Stoll Picture Productions	Fred Paul (d.) from the novel by J. J. Bell	Stewart Rome, Marjorie Hume, Mary Rorke	'A Scots shopkeeper ruins his ex-employer, whose daughter marries a man made rich by her father's tips.' IMDb. From the author of *Wee McGregor* and set in the (fictional) Scottish village of Kilbran.

Till the Bells Ring	1926	UK	British Sound Film Productions	2,500	Graham Moffat (d & w)	Graham Moffat, Margaret Moffat, Winifred Moffat	An 'amusing trifle' in the 'true vein of Scottish humour', a 'kirk elder' mistakenly marries an 'old maid' believing she has money. Set in Ladywell, Glasgow, in the nineteenth century 'when that spot still possessed some rural amenity'. Adapted by Graham Moffat from his 1923 play, the film is significant as an early use of the phonofilm: 'Movement and sound are perfectly synchronised, and after the listener becomes accustomed to the phenomenon of screen figures appearing to talk and the ear attunes itself to the sounds, there is no difficulty in catching the spoken word.' *The Scotsman*
Twa Hieland Lads (aka *Weary Willie and Tired Tim in the Army*)	1910	USA	Vitagraph	633			'"Two Highland laddies, one seven feet four; the other five feet five, tired of farm work and every other kind of work' are persuaded to enlist in the 'awkward squad of the "Kilties"'. *Moving Picture World*. Not natural soldiers, they are subjected to practical jokes, but they get their revenge.
Two of Scotch Hot	1914	UK	R. Films	473			'A merry little British comic, dealing with the courtship of a mischievous "flapper" by two burlesque Frenchmen, who attire themselves as Highlanders in an effort to win her favour. Fast, knockabout humour – without any subtleties, of course, but in its way quite well done.' *The Bioscope*
Vanishing Dagger, The (aka *Thirteenth Hour, The*)	1920	USA	Universal	18 episodes, each 2,000	Edward A. Kull, J. P. McGowan, Eddie Polo (d.); Jacques Jaccard, Hope Loring, Milton Moore (story), George W. Pyper (sc.)	Eddie Polo, Thelma Percy, C. Norman Hammond	An Eddie Polo adventure serial: 'The story is a wild and whirling melodrama, dealing with a triangular contest for the possession of a jewelled dagger, originally the property of a wicked Indian prince-hypnotist … Varied British backgrounds, such as the Liverpool Docks, Lime Street, and Euston railway stations, Glasgow shipyard and Port Dundas Canal, invest the picture with special interest for British audiences.' *The Bioscope*

Title	Year	Country of origin	Length (ft) where known	Production company	Director/ producer/ writer	Actors	Summary
War Bride's Secret, The (aka *War Mother, The*)	1916	USA	6,000	Fox	Kenean Buel (d.); Mary Murillo (sc.)	Virginia Pearson, Walter Law, Glen White	'A powerful Scottish drama of the present day. An echo of the war amidst the fragrance of the heather.' *The Bioscope* advertisement. 'The backgrounds are Scotch and are astonishingly suggestive of the real Scotch country. Robert Burns' poems are used liberally in the sub-titles and the characters also help in the illusion.' *Moving Picture World*
Wee MacGregor's Sweetheart	1922	UK	6,000	Welsh Pearson	George Pearson (d.), from J. J. Bell story	Betty Balfour, Donald Macardle, Nora Swinburne	'Our Own Mary Pickford. The best work Betty Balfour has ever done . . . I do not think anyone realised until *Wee MacGregor's Sweetheart* was shown this week what a close rival Miss Balfour is to Mary Pickford . . . A direct challenge to "the world's sweetheart". We know too that Miss Balfour does not need to rely on any particular "type" for success. There is nothing but praise to be said for *Wee MacGregor's Sweetheart*.' *Evening News*, quoted in *The Bioscope*
What Every Woman Knows	1917	UK	5,100	Barker-Neptune	Fred W. Durrant (d.); from the play by J. M. Barrie	Hilda Trevelyan, A. B. Imeson, Maud Yates	Maggie's family agrees to educate John, a poor Scottish student, if he will marry her. He goes to London to become an MP, and is distracted by the possibility of marrying rich and sophisticated Lady Sybil. But Maggie knows better . . .
What Every Woman Knows	1921	USA	6,000	Famous Players	William C. de Mille (d.); Olga Printzlau (w.) from the play by J. M. Barrie	Lois Wilson, Conrad Nagel, Charles Ogle	'Maggie (splendidly played by Lois Wilson) is, in fact, a wonderful person, epitomising the greatness of the Scotch character in her quiet patience and deep sagacity. Conrad Nagel's John Shand seems a trifle more of a prig than he was made by Gerald du Maurier . . . Although the British atmosphere is not over-emphasised – mainly by a sedulous elimination of the ordinary film Americanisms – to satisfy any British audience.' *The Bioscope*

Where the Heather Blooms	1915	USA	1,847	Nestor	Al Christie (d. & w.)	Eddie Lyons, Betty Compson, Lee Moran	'Eddie Lyons inherits Glengarry Castle on the condition that he marries Lady Mary. Lady Mary persuades her mother to take her place while she poses as an innocent Scotch lassie. The MacDougal tells Eddie that the castle is haunted, and he takes the Lady Mary for a portrait come to life and falls in love with her. A pretty fanciful play, well produced and acted. A very good feature.' *The Bioscope*
Whist!	1910	USA	530	Essanay	Tom Ricketts	Augustus Carney, J. Warren Kerrigan	'A game of whist is continually interrupted by musical diversions. Finally, Sandy, "a short stout Scotsman", interrupts with his version of "Blue Bells of Scotland". All is resolved when the host is pacified with a "glass of Scotch in one hand, the bottle in the other, and 'Ip-i-yaddy-i-ay' on his lips".' *Moving Picture World*
White Circle, The (aka *Pavilion on the Links, The*)	1920	USA	5,000	Paramount	Maurice Tourneur (d.); John Gilbert, Jules Furthman (w.) adapted from Robert Louis Stevenson's story *The Pavilion on the Links*	Spottiswoode Aitken, Janice Wilson, Harry Northrup	Takes place on a deserted part of the Scottish coast. 'Weirdness and effects may be carried to extreme and in one incident, at least, we think the wizard Tourneur has gone a bit too far ... We refer to the scene in which he shows a goat gradually swallowed up in a bed of quick sand. A dummy may have been used but that doesn't mitigate the unpleasant feeling the sight gives.' *Motion Picture News*

Title	Year	Country of origin	Length (ft) where known	Production company	Director/ producer/ writer	Actors	Summary
White Heather, The	1919	USA	6,000	Maurice Tourneur Productions	Maurice Tourneur (d.); Charles E. Whittaker (w.) from the play by Cecil Raleigh and Henry Hamilton	Holmes Herbert, Ben Alexander, Ralph Graves, Mabel Ballin	Adaptation of a well-known Drury Lane melodrama. Scotland is the background for part of the story, but main action is in London. However, it involves someone called the 'Duke of Shetland' and the plot depends on the legitimacy of a 'Scotch marriage', the proofs of which are in a wreck at the bottom of the sea off Scotland. The film is 'said to be the first instance of a motion picture being actually directed on the ocean floor'. *Moving Picture World*. Underwater scenes filmed in Los Angeles harbour.
William Ratcliff (aka Guglielmo Ratcliff)	1909	Italy	765	Cines	From play by Heinrich Heine		From play by Heinrich Heine, or opera by Pietro Mascagni. 'William Ratcliff ... is hospitably entertained at MacGregor's castle, and falls in love with Mary, MacGregor's daughter, but is repulsed by her. In revenge he swears to kill any man who dares to betroth himself to her, which he does, in a duel with the first one. He then goes again to Mary, but is again refused, and shortly after he kills another who had become betrothed to her. Then returning to the castle he stabs Mary and shoots himself.' *The Bioscope*
William Ratcliff	1922	Austria		Astoria Films	Heinz Hanus (d.); Paul Dengler (w.)	Oscar Beregi Sr, Leo Dubois, Manja Keller	An Austrian version of Heine's play.

Wolf, The	1919	USA	5,000	Vitagraph	James Young (d.); Paul Sloane (sc.) from the play by Eugene Walter	Earle Williams, Brinsley Shaw, George Nichols, Jane Novack	The 'Wolf far from wife and family 'preys on females of special attraction in the trapper country of Canada'. Hilda McTavish has been 'led from infancy to believe that her soul is black', and her 'cruel father . . . typifies well the traditional Scottish male parent'. *Moving Picture World*
Woman Thou Gavest Me, The	1919	USA	6,000	Famous Players	Hugh Ford (d.); Beulah Marie Dix (w.) from the novel by Hall Caine	Fritzi Brunette, Katherine Griffith, Jack Holt	Mary is the 'daughter of a ruthless old Scotchman, Daniel McNeil, whose accidentally acquired wealth enables him to satisfy an old grudge against the Raa family by marrying Mary to young Lord Raa, which he does in full knowledge that the latter is a rake and spendthrift'. *Moving Picture World*. The plot revolves around Mary finding true love in London, and is set in India, Egypt, France, London and Scotland.
Woman's Triumph, A	1914	USA	4,000	Famous Players	J. Searle Dawley (d.); from Sir Walter Scott's novel *The Heart of Midlothian*	Laura Sawyer, Betty Harte, George Moss	'The inspiring tale of a woman's sacrifice for truth and her ultimate triumph and reward . . . The impressive story of the suffering heart and noble soul of a courageous woman.' Advertisement in *Moving Picture World*. The exteriors were shot in Cuba.
Ye Banks and Braes	1919	UK	5,000	Regal Films	Tom Watts	Ethel Douglas Ross, John Jenson, Daisy Jackson	'A Scots girl follows a nobleman to London and returns after discovering he is already married.' IMDb 'The Picture that will Sweep Scotland' 'The Greatest Scottish Song' 'Biggest Box Office Attraction ever offered to Scottish Exhibitors.' Advertisement in *The Bioscope*

Title	Year	Country of origin	Length (ft) where known	Production company	Director/ producer/ writer	Actors	Summary
Young Lochinvar	1911	USA	1,000	Thanhouser	From Walter Scott's poem	William Russell, Marguerite Snow	'This chap Lochinvar wanted a certain lady to be his partner for life. Things didn't break well for him, and the night of her marriage to another man arrived. Did Lochinvar figure it was all over? No, Siree! Did he just give up and lose? No, he took a chance at the last second, and – be dum-squizzled if he didn't win out, at that!' Thanhouser advertisement in *Moving Picture World*
Young Lochinvar	1923	UK	6,000	Stoll Picture Productions	W. P. Kellino (d.); Alice Ramsey (w.) from the poem by Sir Walter Scott	Owen Nares, Gladys Jennings, Dick Webb	'The exterior settings are beautiful, and include some fine specimens of old Scottish architecture, the interior sets being admirably in keeping.' *The Bioscope*. Shot in Aberfoyle. 'Special char-a-bancs ran to the location near Glasgow, and sight-seers came from miles and miles around to watch us at work, but they behaved in a wonderful manner.' Nelson Ramsay, actor, quoted in *The Bioscope*

Bibliography

Primary Sources – Printed and Manuscript

Cinema Museum, Lambeth

Aberdeen Picture Palaces, Ltd.
James F. Donald (Cinemas), Ltd.
The Queen's Room Cinema Syndicate, Ltd.
Torry Cinemas, Ltd.

Glasgow City Archives, Mitchell Library, Glasgow

D-OPW 61/5, List of Premises Licensed under the Cinematograph Act, 1909, and the Accommodation therein.

In the Possession of Mrs Rita Connelly

Diaries of Ms C. McGinniss, Diary for 1929.

National Library of Scotland, Moving Image Archive, Glasgow

5/4, Poole Family Collection.
5/7, Miscellaneous Film Material.
5/8, George Green, Ltd.
5/11//17, Cinematograph Exhibitors' Association, Edinburgh and East of Scotland Section, Minute Book.
5/22, Glasgow Picture House, Ltd.

National Records of Scotland, Edinburgh

BT2/7704, The United Films, Ltd.
BT2/8946, The Vocal Cinema Co., Ltd.
CS46/1912/1/85, Decree for Payment, Cines Co. otherwise called Societa Italiana 'Cines' Rome against The United Films Limited.
CS46/1926/12/60, Court of Session, Second Division, 1 April 1926. Reclaiming Note for Pursuer in Causa William McIlwain against The Arcadia Picture House (Glasgow), Ltd.

GD289/1/1, Playhouse Cinema, Edinburgh, Profit and Loss Ledger, 1929–68.
GD289/1/3, Palace Cinema, Edinburgh, Profit and Loss Ledger, 1925–55.
HH1/1981, Scottish Home Dept., Cinemas, Extended Notes of Proceedings in Paisley Cinema Disaster.
HH30, Military Service Appeal Tribunal Records (Lothians and Peebles).
IRS21, Scottish Charities.

Shetland Museum and Archives, Lerwick

D1/92, Wet copy Letter Book 1915, North Star Cinema, Lerwick.

The National Archives, Kew

COPY 1/556/340, Photograph (cinematograph) of Henry VIII as played by Sir Herbert Tree and Company.
COPY 1/559/172, Photograph Films (for Cinematographs) of the Play of 'Rob Roy' as actually produced at Aberfoyle.
COPY 1/565/150, Photograph Films (for Cinematographs) of the play of 'Rob Roy' as actually produced at Aberfoyle.
HO 45/20876, Entertainments, Cinema Operators, Age and Qualifications.
LAB 83/3315, Musicians in Cinemas: Scotland.

University of Stirling, Special Collections

Musicians' Union Archive
MU/1/2, *The Musicians' Report and Journal*.
MU/1/4, *Musicians' Journal*, Monthly Reports.
MU/4/2, Musicians' Union, Glasgow branch, General Meeting Minutes.

Official Publications

Parl. Papers 1919, xi (359), Coal Industry Commission, Interim Reports.

Newspapers and Periodicals

Aberdeen Evening Express.
Aberdeen Daily Journal.
Aberdeen People's Journal.
The Advertiser (Adelaide).
The Arbroath Herald and Advertiser for the Montrose Burghs.
Auckland Star.
The Ayrshire Post.
The Bioscope.
The Bo'ness Journal and Linlithgowshire Advertiser.
Campbeltown Courier.

The Cinema.
The Courier and Argus (Dundee).
Dominion.
The Entertainer, Theatrical, Vaudeville, Musical, Social and Athletic (later *The Entertainer and Scottish Kinema Record,* and *Scottish Kinema Record*).
The Era.
The Evening Post (Dundee).
The Evening Telegraph (Dundee).
The Fife Free Press and Kirkcaldy Guardian.
Forward.
The Glasgow Herald.
The Glasgow Programme.
Glasgow Weekly Programme.
The Hawick News and Border Chronicle.
Kinematograph Weekly.
Kirkintilloch Gazette, Lenzie and Campsie Reporter.
Kirkintilloch Herald and Lenzie, Kilsyth, Campsie and Cumbernauld Press.
The Motherwell Times and General Advertiser.
Moving Picture World.
The Oban Times and Argyllshire Advertiser.
Otago Daily Times.
Poverty Bay Herald.
Radio Times.
Scottish Cinema.
The Scotsman.
The Shetland News.
The Shetland Times.
To-Day's Cinema.
Wanganui Chronicle.

Published Works

Adair, Judith, 'Calendar Customs', in *The Individual and Community Life* (Vol. 9, *Scottish Life and Society: A Compendium of Scottish Ethnology*), eds John Beech, Owen Hand, Mark A. Mulhern and Jeremy Weston (Edinburgh: John Donald, 2005), 118–29.

Allen, Robert C., 'Reimagining the History of the Experience of Cinema in a Post-moviegoing Age', in *Explorations in New Cinema History: Approaches and Case Studies*, eds Richard Maltby, Daniel Biltereyst and Philippe Meers (Chichester: Blackwell, 2011), 41–57.

———, 'Relocating American Film History: The "Problem" of the Empirical'. *Cultural Studies* 20, no. 1 (2006): 48–88.

———, *Vaudeville and Film, 1895–1915: A Study in Media Interaction* (New York: Arno, 1980).

———, 'Vitascope/Cinématographe: Initial Patterns of American film Industrial Practice', in *Film before Griffith*, ed. John L. Fell (Berkeley and Los Angeles: University of California Press, 1983), 144–52.

Ardill, Thomas, and revised by Matthew Imms, 'Tour of Scotland for Scott's Poetical Works 1831', in *J.M.W. Turner: Sketchbooks, Drawings and Watercolours*, ed. David Blayney Brown (London: Tate, 2012).

Bailey, Peter, 'A Community of Friends: Business and Good Fellowship in London Music Hall Management, c.1860–1885', in *Music Hall: The Business of Pleasure*, ed. Peter Bailey (Milton Keynes: Open University Press, 1986), 33–52.

Bakker, Gerben, *Entertainment Industrialised: The Emergence of the International Film Industry, 1890–1940* (New York: Cambridge University Press, 2008).

Balázs, Béla, *Theory of the Film: Character and Growth of a New Art* (New York: Dover Publications, 1945).

Ball, Robert Hamilton, *Shakespeare on Silent Film: A Strange Eventful History* (New York: Theater Arts Books, 1968).

Benjamin, Walter, *The Arcades Project* (Cambridge, MA: Harvard University Press, 1999).

Bottomore, Stephen, 'From the Factory Gate to the "Home Talent" Drama: an International Overview of Local Films in the Silent Era', in *The Lost World of Mitchell and Kenyon: Edwardian Britain on Film*, eds Vanessa Toulmin, Patrick Russell and Simon Popple (London: BFI, 2004), 33–48.

Bowden, Sue, and David M. Higgins, 'Short-time Working and Price Maintenance: Collusive Tendencies in the Cotton-spinning Industry, 1919–1939', *The Economic History Review* 51, no. 2 (1998): 319–43.

Bowers, Judith, *Glasgow's Lost Theatre: The Story of the Britannia Music Hall* (Edinburgh: Birlinn Ltd, 2014).

———, *Stan Laurel and Other Stars of the Panopticon* (Edinburgh: Birlinn Limited, 2007).

Briggs, Asa, 'The End of the Monopoly', in *British Television: A Reader*, ed. Edward Buscombe (Oxford: Oxford University Press, 2000), 63–91.

Bromhead, A. C., 'Reminiscences of the British Film Trade', *Proceedings of the British Kinematograph Society* 21 (11 December 1933).

Brooker, Jeremy, 'The Polytechnic Ghost', *Early Popular Visual Culture* 5, no. 2 (2007): 189–206.

Brown, Julie, 'Framing the Atmospheric Film Prologue in Britain, 1919–1926', in *The Sounds of the Silents in Britain*, eds Julie Brown and Annette Davison (Oxford: Oxford University Press, 2013), 200–21.

Brown, Julie, and Annette Davison, eds, *The Sounds of the Silents in Britain* (Oxford: Oxford University Press, 2013).

Brown, Richard, 'The Missing Link: Film Renters in Manchester, 1910–1920', *Film Studies* 10 (2007), 58–63.

Brown, Richard, and Anthony Barry, *A Victorian Film Enterprise: The History of the British Mutoscope and Biograph Company* (Trowbridge: Flick Books, 1997).

Bruce, Frank, *Showfolk: An Oral History of a Fairground Dynasty* (Edinburgh: National Museum of Scotland, 2010).
Burns, Robert, 'Journal of a Tour in the Highlands Made in the Year 1787', in *The Oxford Edition of the Works of Robert Burns. Volume I*, ed. Nigel Leask (Oxford: Oxford University Press, 2014).
Burrows, Jon, *Legitimate Cinema: Theatre Stars in Silent British Films, 1908–1918* (Exeter: University of Exeter Press (Exeter Studies in Film History), 2003).
———, 'Penny Pleasures: Film Exhibition in London during the Nickelodeon Era, 1906–1914', *Film History* 16, no. 1 (2004), 60–91.
———, 'Penny Pleasures II: Indecency, Anarchy and Junk Film in London's "Nickelodeons", 1906–1914', *Film History* 16, no. 2 (2004), 172–97.
Burrows, Jon, and Richard Brown, 'Financing the Edwardian Cinema Boom, 1909–1914', *Historical Journal of Film, Radio and Television* 30, no. 1 (2010), 1–20.
Casetti, Francesco, 'Filmic Experience', *Screen* 50, no. 1 (1 March 2009), 56–66.
Caughie, John, 'Broadcasting and Cinema 1: Converging Histories', in *All Our Yesterdays: 90 Years of British Cinema*, ed. Charles Barr (London: BFI, 1996), 189–205.
Chanan, Michael, *The Dream That Kicks* (London, Boston and Henley: Routledge & Kegan Paul, 1980).
Cinematograph Exhibitors' Diary, (London: S. Presbury & Co., 1928).
Cloy, David, 'Scottish Film Production in the Silent Period', in *Scotland in Silent Cinema*, ed. Janet McBain (Glasgow: Scottish Screen, 1998).
Colwell, Stacie A., '*The End of the Road*: Gender, the Dissemination of Knowledge and the American Campaign against Venereal Disease in World War 1', in *The Visible Woman: Imaging Technologies, Gender and Science*, eds Paula Treichler, Lisa Cartwright and Constance Penley (New York: New York University Press, 1998), 44–82.
Cook, Patricia, 'Albany Ward and the Development of Cinema Exhibition in England', *Film History* 20 (2008), 294–307.
Crawford, Robert, 'Country Lear', *Times Literary Supplement*, 6 November 2009.
Daney, Serge, 'La Remise en scène', in *La rampe: cahier critique 1970–1982* (Paris: Gallimard, 1983).
Davison, Annette, 'Workers' Rights and Performing Rights: Cinema Music and Musicians prior to Synchronized Sound', in *The Sounds of the Silents in Britain*, eds Julie Brown and Annette Davison (Oxford: Oxford University Press, 2013), 243–57.
Devine, T. M., *The Scottish Nation, 1700–2000* (London: Allen Lane, 1999).
Dickinson, Margaret, and Sarah Street, *Cinema and State: The Film Industry and the British Government, 1927–84* (London: British Film Institute, 1985).
Diggle, Elizabeth, 'Journal of a Tour from London to the Highlands of Scotland, 19 April – 7 August 1788', n.d. Manuscript Collection ms. gen. 738. Glasgow University Library.

Dolin, Tim, 'The Great Uncredited: Sir Walter Scott and Cinema', *Screening the Past*, 34 (August 2012).

Ehrlich, Cyril, *The Music Profession in Britain since the Eighteenth Century: A Social History* (Oxford: Clarendon Press, 1988).

Emerson, Ralph Waldo, 'Tribute to Walter Scott on the One Hundredth Anniversary of His Birthday, 15 August 1871', in *The Works of Ralph Waldo Emerson*, Vol. 4 (New York: National Library Company, 1905).

Freer, Walter, *My Life and Memories* (Glasgow: Civic Press Limited, 1929).

Fried, Michael, *Absorption and Theatricality: Painting and Beholder in the Age of Diderot* (Chicago, London: University of Chicago Press, 1988).

Gaudreault, André. *Film and Attraction: From Kinematography to Cinema* (Urbana: University of Illinois Press, 2011).

Gaudreault, André, and Philippe Marion, 'A Medium Is Always Born Twice . . .', *Early Popular Visual Culture* 3, no. 1 (2005): 3–15.

The Ghost on the Fairground, National Fairground Archive, 2007. http://www.nfa.dept.shef.ac.uk/history/miscellaneous_articles/article15.html.

Gifford, Denis, *The British Film Catalogue Vol. 1, Fiction Film, 1895–1994*, 3rd ed. (London: Fitzroy Dearborn, 2001).

Griffiths, Trevor, *The Cinema and Cinema-going in Scotland, 1896–1950* (Edinburgh: Edinburgh University Press, 2012). 'Sounding Scottish: Sound Practices and Silent Cinema in Scotland', in *The Sounds of the Silents in Britain*, eds Julie Brown and Annette Davison (Oxford: Oxford University Press, 2013), 72–91. http://public.eblib.com/choice/publicfullrecord.aspx?p=3055628.

———, 'Work, Leisure and Time in the Nineteenth Century', in *A History of Everyday Life in Scotland, 1800 to 1900*, eds Trevor Griffiths and Graeme Morton (Edinburgh: Edinburgh University Press, 2010), 170–95.

Gunning, Tom, 'Pictures of Crowd Splendor: The Mitchell And Kenyon Factory Gate Films', in *The Lost World of Mitchell & Kenyon: Edwardian Britain on Film*, eds Vanessa Toulmin, Simon Popple and Patrick Russell (London: BFI, 2004), 49–58.

Hanssen, F. Andrew, 'Revenue Sharing and the Coming of Sound', in *An Economic History of Film*, eds John Sedgwick and Michael Pokorny (London: Routledge, Taylor and Francis Group, 2005), 86–120.

Hardie, James Keir, *The Common Good: An Essay in Municipal Government* (Manchester: National Labour Press, 1910).

Hardy, Forsyth, *Scotland in Film* (Edinburgh: Edinburgh University Press, 1990).

Hiley, Nicholas, '"Nothing more than a 'craze'": Cinema Building in Britain from 1909 to 1914', in *Young and Innocent? The Cinema in Britain, 1896–1930*, ed. Andrew Higson (Exeter: University of Exeter Press, 2002), 111–27.

How to Run a Picture Theatre: a Handbook for Proprietors, Managers, and Exhibitors (London: Heron, 1914).

Hutchison, J. H., *The Complete Kinemanager, Etc.* (London: Kinematograph Publications, 1937).

Iversen, Gunnar, 'Norway', in *Nordic National Cinemas*, eds Tytti Soila, Astrid Söderbergh Widding and Gunnar Iversen (London: Routledge, 1998), 102–41.
Johnson, Samuel, and James Boswell. *A Journey to the Western Islands of Scotland*, ed. Peter Levi (Harmondsworth: Penguin, 1984).
Kember, Joe, *Marketing Modernity* (Exeter: University of Exeter Press, 2009).
King, Elspeth, *Scotland Sober and Free* (Glasgow: Glasgow Museums and Art Galleries, 1979).
The Kinematograph Year Book (London), 1921.
Kissell, Jack, 'Cinema in the By-ways', *Educational Film Bulletin* 33 (1946), 22–31.
Kuhn, Annette, *Cinema, Censorship and Sexuality, 1909–1925* (London: Routledge, 1988).
Lebas, Elizabeth, *Forgotten Futures: British Municipal Cinema, 1920–1980* (London: Black Dog Publishing, 2011).
Lee, Clive H., 'Scotland, 1860–1939: Growth and Poverty', in *The Cambridge Economic History of Modern Britain. Volume II: Economic Maturity, 1860–1939*, ed. Roderick Floud and Paul Johnson (Cambridge: Cambridge University Press, 2004), 428–55.
Lindstrom, J. A., 'Where Development Has Just Begun: Nickelodeon Location, Moving Picture Audiences, and Neighborhood Development in Chicago', in *American Cinema's Transitional Era: Audiences, Institutions, Practices*, ed. Charlie Keil and Shelly Stamp (Berkeley: University of California Press, 2004), 217–38.
Lloyd, John, *Light & Liberty: A History of the EETPU* (London: Weidenfeld and Nicolson, 1990).
Low, Rachael, *The History of the British Film 1906–1914* (London: Allen & Unwin, 1949).
Maloney, Paul, *Scotland and the Music Hall 1850–1914* (Manchester: Manchester University Press, 2003).
Maltby, Richard, Melvyn Stokes and Robert C. Allen, eds, *Going to the Movies: Hollywood and the Social Experience of Cinema* (Exeter: University of Exeter Press (Exeter Studies in Film History), 2007).
Marwick, Sir James David, *List of Markets and Fairs Now and Formerly Held in Scotland* (London, 1890).
Maver, Irene, 'Leisure Time in Scotland during the Nineteenth and Twentieth Centuries', in *Scottish Life and Society: The Individual and Community Life*, Vol. 9, *A Compendium of Scottish Ethnology*, ed. John Beech, Owen Hand, Mark A. Mulhern and Jeremy Weston (Edinburgh: John Donald, 2005).
McArthur, Colin, ed., *Scotch Reels* (London: BFI Publishing, 1982).
McBain, Janet, 'Green's of Glasgow: "We Want 'U' In"', *Film Studies* 10 (Spring 2007): 54–7.
———, 'Mitchell and Kenyon's Legacy in Scotland: The Inspiration for a Forgotten Film-making Genre', in *The Lost World of Mitchell & Kenyon*, eds Vanessa

Toulmin, Simon Popple and Patrick Russell (London: BFI, 2004), 113–21.

———, 'Scotland in Feature Film: A Filmography', in *From Limelight to Satellite*, ed. Eddie Dick (Glasgow and London: Scottish Film Council and British Film Institute, 1990), 233–53.

McKernan, Luke, 'A Girl Cinematographer at the Balkan War', *The Bioscope*, 27 May 2007. https://thebioscope.net/2007/05/27/a-girl-cinematographer-at-the-balkan-war/.

———, 'Lives in Film, no. 1: Alfred Dreyfus – part 3', *The Bioscope*, 14 March 2010. https://thebioscope.net/2010/03/14/lives-in-film-no-1-alfred-dreyfus-part-3/.

———, *Topical Budget: The Great British News Film* (London: BFI Publishing, 1992).

McNeill, Carol, *Kirkcaldy Links Market* (Kirckcaldy: Fife Council Central Area Libraries and Museums, 2004).

Moretti, Franco, *Distant Reading* (London: Verso, 2013).

Musser, Charles, *The Emergence of Cinema: The American Screen to 1907* (*History of the American Cinema*, vol. 1) (New York: Scribner, 1990).

Oakley, C. A., *Fifty Years at the Pictures* (Glasgow: Scottish Film Council/BFI, 1946).

Pennant, Thomas, *A Tour in Scotland and Voyage to the Hebrides, 1772* (1776) (Edinburgh: Birlinn, 1998).

Pierce, David, *The Survival of American Silent Feature Films, 1912–1929*, CLIR Publication, no. 158 (Washington, DC: Council on Library and Information Resources and The Library of Congress, 2013).

Pocock, Isaac, *Rob Roy Macgregor; or, 'Auld Lang Syne;' a National Operatic Drama Extended with an Intr. & C. by a Glasgow Playgoer* (Glasgow, 1868).

Porter, Laraine, 'Women Musicians in British Silent Cinema prior to 1930', *Journal of British Cinema and Television* 10, no. 3 (2013), 563–83.

Pryluck, Calvin, 'The Itinerant Movie Show and the Development of the Film Industry', in *Hollywood in the Neighborhood*, ed. Kathryn Fuller-Seeley (Berkeley: University of California Press, 1983), 37–52.

Rigney, Ann. *The Afterlives of Walter Scott: Memory on the Move* (Oxford: Oxford University Press, 2012).

Rossell, Deac, 'A Slippery Job: Travelling Exhibitors in Early Cinema', in *Visual Delights: Essays on the Popular and Projected Image in the Nineteenth Century*, eds Simon Popple and Vanessa Toulmin (Trowbridge: Flick Books, 2000), 50–60.

Rubin, Miri, 'What Is Cultural History Now?', in *What Is History Now?*, ed. David Cannadine (London: Palgrave Macmillan, 2002), 80–94.

Rushton, Richard, 'Early, Classical and Modern Cinema: Absorption and Theatricality', *Screen* 45, no. 3 (2004), 226–44.

Scannell, Paddy, 'Public Service Broadcasting: The History of a Concept', in *British Television: A Reader*, ed. Edward Buscombe (Oxford: Oxford University Press, 2000), 45–62.

Scrivens, Kevin, and Stephen Smith, *The Travelling Cinematograph Show* (Tweedale: New Era, 1999).
Scullion, Adrienne, 'Geggies, Empires, Cinemas: The Scottish Experience of Early Film', *Picture House* 21 (1996), 13–19.
———, '"The Cinematograph Still reigns Supreme at the Skating Palace": The First Decades of Film in Scotland', in *Moving Performance: British Stage and Screen, 1890s–1920s*, ed. Linda Fitzsimmons and Sarah Street (Trowbridge: Flicks Books, 2000), 80–100.
Shail, Andrew, 'Intermediality: Disciplinary Flux or Formalist Retrenchment?', *Early Popular Visual Culture* 8, no. 1 (2010): 3–15.
Skinner, James Scott,. *My Life and Adventures* (Aberdeen: City of Aberdeen, Arts and Recreation Division in association with Wallace Music, 1994).
Street, Sarah, *British National Cinema* (London, New York: Routledge, 1997).
Swallow, Johnnie, *Round-a-bout Scotland* (Largs, c. 1986).
Tom Johnston: Man of His Century (Kirkintilloch: Strathkelvin District Council, 1985).
Toulmin, Vanessa, 'Cuckoo in the Nest: Edwardian Itinerant Exhibition Practices and the Transition to Cinema in the United Kingdom from 1901 to 1906', *The Moving Image* 10, no. 1 (2010), 51–79.
———, *Pleasurelands* (Hastings: National Fairground Archive / The Projection Box, 2003).
———, 'Telling the Tale: The Story of the Fairground Bioscope Shows and the Showmen who Operated Them', *Film History* 6, no. 2 (1994), 219–37.
———, '"Within the Reach of All", Travelling Cinematograph Shows in British Fairgrounds 1896–1914', in *Travelling Cinema in Europe: Sources and Perspectives* (*KINtop Schriften* 10), ed. Martin Loiperdinger (Frankfurt am Main and Basel: Stroemfeld Verlag, 2008), 18–33.
Toulmin, Vanessa, Simon Popple and Patrick Russell, eds. *The Lost World of Mitchell & Kenyon: Edwardian Britain on Film* (London: BFI, 2004).
Toulmin, Vanessa, Patrick Russell, and Tim Neal. 'The Mitchell and Kenyon Collection: Rewriting Film History', *The Moving Image* 3, no. 2 (2003): 1–18.
Trevelyan, G. M., 'Autobiography of an Historian', in *An Autobiography and Other Essays* (London: Longmans, Green, 1949), 1–51.
'The Triumph of the Animated Picture', in *Stage Year Book 1908*, 47–9.
Twain, Mark, *Life on the Mississippi* (Harmondsworth: Penguin, 1985).
Vélez-Serna, María, 'Preview Screenings and the Spaces of an Emerging Local Cinema Trade in Scotland', *Historical Journal of Film, Radio and Television* 36, no. 3 (2016), 285–304.
———, 'Showmanship Skills and the Changing Role of the Exhibitor in 1910s Scotland', in *Performing New Media, 1890–1915* (*Early Cinema in Review: Proceedings of Domitor*), eds Kaveh Askari, Scott Curtis, Frank Gray, Louis Pelletier, Tami Williams and Joshua Yumibe (Bloomington and New Barnet: Indiana University Press and John Libbey, 2014), 105–14.

Victoria, and David Duff, *Queen Victoria's Highland Journals* (London: Hamlyn, 1997).

Walker, Graham, 'Johnston, Thomas (1881–1965)', in *The Oxford Dictionary of National Biography*, eds H. C. G. Matthew and B. Harrison (Oxford: Oxford University Press, 2004).

Walker, William M., *Juteopolis: Dundee and Its Textile Workers, 1885–1923* (Edinburgh: Scottish Academic Press, 1979).

Waller, Gregory A., 'Introducing the "Marvellous Invention" to the Provinces: Film Exhibition in Lexington, Kentucky, 1896–1897', *Film History* 3, no. 3 (1989), 223–34.

Walsh, Peter, 'Standards of Practice in Transition: The Showmanship of Jasper Redfern as It Emerged', in *Performing New Media, 1890–1915* (*Early Cinema in Review: Proceedings of Domitor*), eds Kaveh Askari, Scott Curtis, Frank Gray, Louis Pelletier, Tami Williams and Joshua Yumibe (Bloomington and New Barnet: Indiana University Press and John Libbey, 2014), 95–103.

Wordsworth, Dorothy, *Recollections of a Tour Made in Scotland*, ed. Carol Kyros Walker (New Haven: Yale University Press, 1997).

Wordsworth, William, 'Memorials of a Tour in Scotland, 1803. VII. Stepping Westward', in *Complete Poetical Works* (London: Macmillan and Co., 1888).

Wright, Valerie, 'Juteopolis and After: Women and Work in Twentieth-century Dundee', in *Jute No More: Transforming Dundee*, eds Jim Tomlinson and Christopher A. Whatley (Dundee: Dundee University Press, 2011), 132–62.

Unpublished Sources

Bohlmann, Julia, 'Regulating and Mediating the Social Role of Cinema in Scotland, c.1896–1933', PhD thesis, University of Glasgow, 2015.

Merz, Caroline, 'Why Not a Scots Hollywood?: Scottish Fiction Film Production in Scotland, 1911–1928', PhD thesis, University of Edinburgh, 2016.

Websites

The Bioscope. https://thebioscope.net

Early Cinema in Scotland Research Project, 'Early Cinema in Scotland 1896–1927'. http://earlycinema.gla.ac.uk/

Media History Digital Library. http://mediahistoryproject.org/earlycinema/

National Library of Scotland Moving Image Archive. http://movingimage.nls.uk

News on Screen, British Universities Film and Video Council. http://bufvc.ac.uk/newsonscreen/

Pickard's Papers Project. http://pickardspapers.gla.ac.uk

Royal Commission of the Ancient and Historical Monuments of Scotland, Canmore database, https://canmore.org.uk/

A Vision of Britain through Time. http://visionofbritain.org.uk
Who's Who in Glasgow in 1909, Glasgow Digital Library. http://gdl.cdlr.strath. ac.uk/eyrwho0331.htm

DVD Collection

The O'Kalem Collection: 1910–1915 (Dublin: Irish Film Institute, 2015).

Index

Notes: **bold** indicates figure; the filmography is not indexed

Aberdeen, 8, 19, 21–2, 27, 29, 33–4, 42–3, 53, 62, 64, 78, 134–5, 140, 160, 168, 181
Aberdeen Picture Palaces, 45, 177, 180
Aberdeen Trades Council, 71
Aberdour, 19
Aberfoyle, 114–15, 117–19, 122, 161
adaptation, 113, 158–60, 162
Airdrie, 8, 140
Albin, A. S., 175
Allen, Robert. C., 15, 21, 24–5
Alloa, 96
Amalgamated Engineering Union, 179
Ancaster, Charles, 175
Ancient Shepherds, 20
Annie Laurie (song), 149
Arbroath, 28, 161
Arcades Project, The, 143
Argosy Films, 47
Arran, 161
Associated British Cinemas, 174
Atholl, 161
Auchmithie, 161
Auld Robin Gray (song), 149, 158
Aveling, Edward, 95
Ayr, 49, 160, 166
  Ayr Races, 17
Ayr Post, 142

Bairnsfather, Bruce, 74
Baker, Jack Carlton, 48
Balkan Wars (1912–13), 57, 132
Bálazs, Béla, 1
Ballachulish, 61
Balzac, Honoré de, 159
Banff, 62

Banks, Joseph, 153
Bannockburn, 76
Barker, Will, 113–14, 132
Barker Motion Photography Company, 48, 112, 114, 124, 150
Barrie, J. M., 150
B.B. Films Services, 141
B.B. Pictures, 35–6, 45–8, 62, 76, 137
Beerbohm Tree, Sir Herbert, 113
Bendon, 'Prince' (William), 26, 48
Bendon Trading Films, 48
Benjamin, Walter, 143
Bennell, J. J. (John Joseph), 27, 36, 40, 46, 137, 140–1
Benson Shakespearean Company, 111
Bermondsey Borough Council, 91
Bernstein, Sidney, 68, 170
Bestalk (sound system), 176
Biddall, George, 16
Biddall, Victor, 140
Bioscope, The, 8, 43, 47, 57–8, 69, 74, 77, 93, 115, 118, 139, 141, 149, 152, 160–2, 166, 170, 172, 174–5, 182
Bioscope Annual, 34, 48
Blairgowrie, 22
block-booking, 4, 131
Boer War, 26, 57, 132
Bo'ness, 40, 54–5, 58–9, 63, 134, 180
  Bo'ness Children's Festival, 63, 137
Bo'ness Journal, 163
Bonnie Brier Bush (play), 122
Bonnie Prince Charlie, 61
Borders Kinematograph Company, 136
  Borders Newsreels, 136
Borthwick, Jessica, 132
Bostock, E. H., 45

INDEX

Boswell, James, 153
Bottomore, Stephen, 133
Boucicault, Dion, 113
Bowie, James, 48, 111–12, 114, 122
Boxer Rebellion (1898–1901), 57
Braemar, 22
Brahan Estate (Dingwall), 24
Brechin, 62
British Acoustic, 167, 182
British Board of Film Censors (BBFC), 7–8
British Broadcasting Corporation (BBC), 108, 130–1, 181
British Film Institute, 131
British International Pictures (BIP), 173–4
British Talking Pictures, 176
Bromhead, A. C., 25
Brown, Richard, 35, 42, 44
Broxburn, 76
Buchanan, Captain Angus, 168
Buchanan, R. C., 45
Buchanan, Robert, 169
Buckie, 8, 45
Buckstone, Walter, 112–14
Burnette, Fred Randall, 138
Burns Hall (Dunedin, New Zealand), 125
Burns, Robert, 150, 153
Burntisland, 76
Burrows, Jon, 34–5, 44
Byron, Lord (George Gordon), 153

Calder, Robert, 21–3, 33–4, 55, 57, 132, 135
   Robert Calder's Famous Cinematograph and Pictorial Concert Party, 56
Caledon Pictures Limited, 75
Calvert, Charles, 161
Calverto, J. F., 26–7
Campbeltown, 6, 22, 54, 56–8, 60, 63–4
Campbeltown Courier, 132, 134, 138
Casetti, Francesco, 1, 10, 143
Chalmers' Cinematograph, 26
Chaplin, Charles, 4, 61, 68, 163, 177
Chaplin, Syd, 74
Cheltenham Echo, 80
Chief Constable Ross (Edinburgh), 65
Chief Constable Thom (Hawick), 65

Church, 10–11, 55–6, 65–6
   Baptist Church, 65
   Church of Scotland, 54
   Presbyterian Church, 6, 56, 64
   Free Church, 55, 64–5, 93
   United Free Church, 66
   United Presbyterian Church, 55
cinema
   'alternative', 91
   'cinema of attractions', 134, 142
   cinema orchestra, 69–71, 77, 79, 80–1, 167, 178–81
   purpose-built, 3–4, 10, 35, 40, 53, 131, 135–6, 142
Cinema Commission, 102
cinemas and venues
   Alhambra (Stirling), 80
   Alhambra Winter Zoo (Aberdeen), 27
   Annfield Halls (Glasgow), 36
   Arcadia Picture House (Glasgow), 76, 83
   Argyle Electric Theatre, 138
   Black Bull Cinema (Kirkintilloch), 103–4, 106–7
   Britannia Panopticon (Glasgow), 25, 40
   Burgh Halls (Pollockshaws, Glasgow), 124
   Cinema de Luxe (Lochgelly), 137, 174
   Cinema House (Edinburgh), 79
   Cinema House (Glasgow, later Regent Cinema), 69–71, 73
   Cinema House (Kilbirnie), 76
   Coliseum (Aberdeen), 137
   Coliseum (Glasgow), 166, 172, 175, 178–9
   Corn Exchange (Kirkcaldy), 27
   Crosshill Picture House (Glasgow), 172
   Elder Picture House (Glasgow), 75
   Electric Cinema (Bo'ness), 59
   Electric Theatre (Charing Cross, Glasgow), 40
   Empire (Edinburgh), 24
   Empire (Motherwell), 71
   Empire Picture House (Montrose), 95
   Gaiety Theatre (Ayr), 124
   Gaiety Theatre (Clydebank), **73**
   Gathering Hall (Oban), 61
   Gathering Hall (Portree), 64

cinemas and venues (*cont.*)
  Glen Cinema (Paisley), 78
  Globe Cinema (Aberdeen), **182**
  Grand Central Picture House (Aberdeen), 77
  Grand Theatre (Glasgow), 68
  Green's Playhouse (Glasgow), 3
  Grosvenor Cinema (Glasgow), 137
  Hengler's Circus (Glasgow), 40
  Hillfoot Picture House (Alva), **72**
  Hillhead Picture Salon, 79, 137
  Hippodrome (Bo'ness), 58–9, 72, 79, 84, 137, 180
  Hippodrome (Hamilton), 45
  Imperial Picture House (Glasgow), 179
  King's, The (Hawick), 59
  King's Cinema (Aberdeen), 74–5
  King's Cinema (Perth), 76
  Kinnaird Picture House (Dundee), 74
  La Scala (Aberdeen), 79, 137
  La Scala (Paisley), 75
  La Scala (Saltcoats), 73, 138
  Lewis Picture House (Stornoway), 64
  Lyceum (Edinburgh), 168
  Lyceum (Glasgow), 75–6
  Municipal Cinema (Burgh Hall, Montrose), 79, 95
  Municipal Cinema (Town Hall, Kirkintilloch), 97, 99, 102, **105**, 106
  New Caley Picture House (Edinburgh), 178
  New Picture House (Edinburgh), 79–80, 172
  New Savoy (Glasgow), 172
  New Victoria (Edinburgh), 181
  North Star (Lerwick), 58, 60–1, 63, 138
  Palace (Edinburgh), 168–9, 172–3, 176–7, 181
  Palace (Rothesay), 136
  Pavilion (Bo'ness), 59
  Pavilion (Dunoon), 94
  Pavilion (Hawick), 58–9
  Pavilion (Motherwell), 71
  Pavilion Picture House (Kirkintilloch), 97–9, 102, 104, **105**, 106–7
  Picture House (later Star Cinema, Bo'ness), 59, 180
  Picture House (Campbeltown), 58, 138
  Picture House (Dalkeith), 78–9
  Picture House (Denny), 76
  Picture House (Dunoon), 94
  Picture House (Falkirk), 76
  Picture House (Glasgow), 40, 44, 75, 124, 168
  Picture House (Kilmaurs), 76
  Picture House (Oban), 58, 61, 64
  Picture House (Paisley), 178
  Picture House (Wishaw), 79
  Picture Palace (Ayr), 141
  Picture Pavilion (Largs), 76
  Playhouse (Aberdeen), 178
  Playhouse (Edinburgh), 172–3, 175, 177–81
  Poole's Synod Hall (Edinburgh), 74, 79, 168–9, 172, 174, 178
  Pringle's Picture Palace (Edinburgh), 71
  Pringle's Picture Palace (formerly Queen's Theatre, Glasgow), 27, 44
  Queen's Hall (Edinburgh), 35
  Queen's Picture House (Kilmarnock)
  Regent Picture House (Edinburgh), 175
  Regent Picture House (Glasgow), 74–5, 77, 80, 176–7, 179
  Rialto (Glasgow), 178
  Rialto (Kirkcaldy), 74
  Rutland (Edinburgh), 181
  St Andrew's Halls (Glasgow), 22, 40
  St Andrew Square Picture House (Edinburgh), 169
  St George's Picture Theatre (Paisley), 111, 123–4
  Silver Kinema (Edinburgh), 168
  Skating Palace (Glasgow), 25
  Star Palace (formerly Bridgeton Town Hall, Glasgow), 36
  Star Picture Palace (Aberdeen), **182**
  Temperance Hall (Kirkintilloch), 101
  Theatre, The (Croft Road, Hawick), 59
  Theatre de Luxe (Rothesay), 138
  Town Hall (Bo'ness), 59
  Town Hall (Clydebank), 124
  Volunteer Hall (aka Drill Hall, Bo'ness), 59
  Wellington Palace (Glasgow), 22, 27, 35–6, 46
  Whitevale Theatre (Glasgow), 36

INDEX 253

Cinema Exhibitors Diary, 131
Cinema Service, 68
Cinematograph Act (1909), 7, 28, 93
Cinematograph Exhibitors Association
    (CEA), 7–8, 71, 77–8, 80–2, 94–5,
    166, 173, 174, 177, 179, 181–2
Cinés Company, 126
Clements, Emily, 84
Clyde (River), 157
    shipbuilding, 5, 157, 162
    Red Clydeside, 11, 70
    Falls of Clyde, 156
Clarendon Speaking Pictures, 169
Clyde, John, 112–15, 121–3, 126
Clydebank, 92
Coatbridge, 8, 45, 76, 96
Coborn, Charles, 26
Cock, Gerald, 130
Codona, Henry, 16
Codona, William, 19
Comin' Through the Rye (song), 150
Common Good, The, 95–6
Conciliation Board, 82
Cook, Thomas, 157
Covenanters, 54, 66
Cramond Brig (play), 122
Crawford, Robert, 53
Cruikshank, S., 175
Cullen, Matt, 125
cultural series, 14

Deablitz, K., 79
De Banzie, Edward, 122
Dent, Arthur, 101
Devine, Tom, 54
Dickens, Charles, 150, 160
Diggle, Elizabeth, 153
Dickson, Louis, 59, 72, 84, 137, 180
Dixon (Glasgow), 46
Duchess of Argyll, 55
Duke of Argyll, 117
Dumas, Alexandre, 150
Dumfries and Galloway Military Appeal
    Tribunal, 77
Dunbar, 45
Dunfermline, 19
Dundee, 5, 19, 22, 27, 33–4, 41–2, 45–6,
    49, 53, 60, 122, 135, 140, 160

Dunoon, 19, 92
    Dunoon Town Council, 94
Durris House (Aberdeenshire), 23

Edinburgh, 19, 28, 34, 42–6, 53, 78, 122
Edinburgh College of Cine-Operators, 85
Edinburgh Film Guild, 181
Edison Kinetophone, 168
Educational Film Bulletin, 112
Edzell, 22
Electrical Trades Union (ETU), 77
Elgin, 29, 176
Elite Entertainments Syndicate
    (Aberdeenshire), 45
Emerson, Ralph Waldo, 150
Empire Kinematograph and Grand
    Concert Party, 57
Entertainer, The, 70, 80, 137
Entertainments Tax, 180
Era, The, 25
Evans, Edwin, 166
everyday, 130–2, 136, 139, 142–3, 164
exhibition, 15, 33, 45, 91, 130–1
    charity benefits, 76
    in fixed-site venues, 29, 33, 37
    in drill halls, 37, 41
    in former skating rinks, 37
    in music halls, 24, 26–7, 36–7
    in public halls, 16, 20–1, 27
    in estates and country houses, 23–4
    in permanent cinemas, 28, 33–5
    by private companies, 35
    in purpose-built venues, 36–7, 40
    as 'treats', 6, 55–6
    'pictures-only' programme, 58, 61
    'runs system', 43
    standardisation of exhibition, 3, 58
exhibitors, 4, 26, 42, 45, 81–2, 134, 139,
    167, 174, 180, 182
    travelling, 15, 27, 33, 41–2

Fabian Society, 95
'factory gate' films, 133–4
fairground, 1, 4, 14, 17, 20, 33, 131, 135,
    141
    fairground season, 16
    fairground entertainers, 33
Falkirk, 22

Fallen Heroes Fund, 76
Famous Players–Lasky, 101
Feathers, Peter, 21, 33, 135
   Feathers' Animated Panorama, 135
Film Theatres' Act (Norway), 92
films
   Ae Fond Kiss (2004), 158
   Andrée at the North Pole (1897), 56
   Annie Laurie (1913), 158
   Annie Laurie (1916), 158
   Annie Laurie (1927), 74, 158, 175
   Arrival at Whitehart Hotel, Campbeltown (1914), **144**
   Arizona Cat Claw, The (1919), 104
   Arrah-na-Pogue (1911), 113
   Arrival of the Davaar *at Campbeltown Pier* (1900), 57
   Auld Robin Gray (1910), 158
   Auld Robin Gray (1917), 158
   Battle of the Ancre and the Advance of the Tanks (1917), 168
   Beloved Blackmailer, The (1918), 104
   Better 'Ole, The (1926), 74
   Birth of a Nation (1915), 65
   Blackmail (1929), 172
   Blackpool: the Wonderland by the Waves (1912), 133
   Bonnie Annie Laurie (1918), 158
   Bonnie Prince Charlie (1923), 62, 148, 161
   Bottle Imp, The (1917), 159
   Britain Prepared (1916), 168
   Britain's Call (1914), 168
   British Troops at the Balkans (1917), 102
   Bravo Kilties! (1914), 163
   Broadway Babies (1929), 172
   Broadway Melody, The (1929) 172
   Broken Coin, The (1915), 102
   Bunco Bill's Visit (1914), 99
   Call of the Pipes, The (1918), 163
   Calvinist Martyr, A (1913), 159
   Campbells Are Coming, The (1915), 163
   Christie Johnstone (1921), 161
   Chu Chin Chow (1923), 169
   City Lights (1931), 177
   Colleen Bawn, The (1911), 113
   Comin' Through the Rye (1916), 158
   Comin' Through the Rye (1923), 158
   Coronation Parade, Broxburn (1910), 136
   Crossing the Great Sahara (1924), 168
   Curse of War, The / Maudite soit la guerre (1914), 99
   Daughter of McGregor, A (1916), 149
   Dawn (1928), 8
   Dreyfus Trial, The – Scene at the Verdict (1899), 56
   Dr Jekyll and Mr Hyde (1920), 159
   Elephants Stacking Timber (1903), 56
   End of the Road, The (1918), 7–8
   England Awake (1932), 177
   Epic of Everest (1924), 168
   Exploits of Elaine (1915), 102
   Fair Maid of Perth, The (1923), 148
   Fife and Forfar Light Horse (1899), 56
   Fight for the Flag in Transvaal (1900?), 57
   Fitba' Daft (1921), 9, 162
   Fox Hunting (1911), 112–13
   Frau im Mond (1929), 173
   Girl-Shy Cowboy (1928), 175
   Glimpses of North Scotland (1918), 153
   Grand Hotel (1932), 177
   Great Golf Match – Vardon v. Park (1899), 56
   Great Railway Smash in England (1906), 56
   Great Western Road (1915), 136
   Great Western Road (1922), 136, **144**
   Greater Riches, The (1920 – not completed), 160–1
   Henry VIII (1911), 113–14, 118, 123–5
   Highland Brigade at Lochaber, The (1899), 56
   Highland Waterfalls (1913), 156
   Huntingtower (1928), 162
   Idle Class, The (1921), 10, 62
   In His Grip (1921), 161
   Jack and the Beanstalk (1913), 99
   Jeanie Deans (proposed by United, but not made), 111, 115, 119
   Julian, the Tank Bank (1918), 141
   Kidnapped (1917), 159
   Kintyre Cattle Show, The (1900), 57
   Land of Burns (1912), 141–2
   Lady Lauder in Rothesay (1922), 136

Laying the Foundation Stone at Kirkintilloch Parish Church (1913), 136
Les Misérables (1917), 62
Life of Christ, The (1912), 7, 25
Little Minister, The (1915), 161
Little Minister, The (1921), 159
Lochgelly at Work and Play (1922), 133, 136
Lochgelly Old Age Pensioners' Drive to Crook o' Devon (1928), 137, **144**
Lord Roberts and Our Troops (1900?), 57
Love Story of Aliette Brunton, The (1924), 173
Maria Stuart (1927), 159
Master of Grays, The (1918), 158
Mata Hari (1931), 177
Merry Widow Waltz (1908), 80
Messina Earthquake (1909), 56
Nanook of the North (1922), 105
Nell Gwyn (1926), 74
None but the Brave (1928), 175
Nostromo (1926), 59
Open Road, The (1926), 157
Passion de Jeanne d'Arc, La (1928), 173
Peggy (1916), 149
Peg o' my Heart (1922), 62
President Kruger in his Carriage (1898), 56
Pride of the Clan, The (1917), 149
Prince of Wales in Edinburgh, The (1899), 56
Quo Vadis (1924), 62
Red Saunder's Sacrifice (1912), 99
Rob Roy (United, 1911), 9, 11, 48, 110–27, **116**, **120**
Rob Roy (later, *An Adventure of Rob Roy*, Gaumont, 1911), 115, 117, 160–1, 163, 183
Rob Roy: the Highland Rogue (Disney, 1953), 119
Robinson Crusoe (1927), 161
Romany, The (1923), 161
Sandy McPherson's Quiet Fishing Trip (1908), 10
Sapho (1913), 7
Scenes at Mr. Gladstone's Funeral (1898), 56

Scenes in the Land of Bonnie Prince Charlie (1912), 153
Scottish Grand National, The (1919), 141
Showboat (1929), 172
Singing Fool, The (1928), 166, 170, 172, 178–9
Sortie de l'Usine (Lumière, 1895), 133
Some Garden Flowers (1914), 99
Street Scene in Johannesburg (1898), 56
Suicide Club, The (1914), 159
Tam O'Shanter's Ride (1912), 141–2
Tayport to Dundee in Front of an Engine (1901), 136
Taxi Dancer, The (1927), 175
Their Son / Sensation im Wintergarten (1929), 173
Thief of Bagdad, The (1924), 59
Till the Bells Ring (1926), 169
Treasure Island (1912), 159
Trey of Hearts (1915), 62
Trip to Samoa, A (1905), 56
Vanishing Dagger, The (1920), 162
Way Down East (1920), 79–80
White Heather (1919), 161–2
Why Girls Leave Home (1921), 104
William Ratcliff (1909), 159
William Ratcliff (1922), 159
Wolf, The (1919), 162
Woman's Triumph, A (1914), 162
Young Lochinvar (1924), 158–9
First World War (1914–18), 3, 33–4, 41, 58, 68, 76, 78, 81, 113, 132, 138
Forfar, 19
Forres, 62, 161
Forward, 96
Foulger, Bert, 141
Fraserburgh, 19, 34, 57
Freer, Walter, 22, 92
Friese-Green, Claude, 157

Gaelic, 6, 61, 154
Galashiels, 19
Gaumont, 25–6, 48, 116–18, 133, 140, 150
Gaumont–British Picture Corporation, 174, 180
Gaumont Graphic, 132
Gaylor, David, 136
Gaylor, W. P., 136

Geographical Information Systems, 2
German, Sir Edward, 113
'ghost shows', 16
Gibson, Bailie (Kirkintilloch), 98, 107
Gillespie, James, 136
Gisborne (New Zealand), 117
Glasgow, 3, 5, 19, 22, 34–5, 41–4, 46, 49, 52–3, 78, 93, 122, 140, 162, 166, 180
　Corporation, 5, 22–3, 91–5
　Education Authority, 8
　Glasgow Fair, 19
Glencoe (Argyll), 156
Glendale (Isle of Skye), 64
Glendaruel (Argyllshire), 55
globalisation, 3, 58
Glover, William, 122
Good Templars, 20, 27, 36, 46
Gorbals (Glasgow), 36
Gordon Castle (Aberdeenshire), 23
Govan (Glasgow), 19, 46, 96
Gray, Joe, 134, 137
'Great Disruption' (1843), 54
Green family, 141
　Green, Bert, 141
　Green, Fred, 141
　Green, George, 17, 19, 36, 47, 141
　Green, Susan, 138
Green's Film Service, 45–8, 61–2, 68, 137–8, 141
Green's British Moving Picture News, 141
Green's Scottish Moving Picture News, 137, 141
Greenock, 19, 40, 96, 140, 169
Grierson, John, 108
Griffiths, Trevor, 3, 9, 22, 35, 125
Grosvenor Topical News, 137
Gunning, Tom, 133

Haddington, 45
Haddo House (Aberdeenshire), 27
Haddon, Thomas, 46
Hamilton, 43
Hardie, Keir, 95
Hardy, Forsyth, 115
Harris, Jack, 140
Hart, James, 137
Hawick, 54, 58–60, 63, 65
Hawick News, 65–6

Hayward's Pictures (Wnaganui, New Zealand), 125–6
Heart of Midlothian, The (novel), 162
Heine, Heinrich, 159
Henderson, H., 123
Highlands, 2, 10, 112, 149, 153, 162–4
　Highlands and Islands, 6, 64–5
Hiley, Nicholas, 35, 40–1
Hillswick, 64
Hollywood, 58, 131, 150, 164, 167, 173, 177, 182
How to Run a Picture Theatre, 139
Hubner, Arthur, 25
Hugo, Victor, 150
Huntly, 45
Hutchison, T. D., 101

Ideal, 48
Iff, Herr, 79
Independent Labour Party (ILP), 92, 95, 107
Industrial Council, 82
Inveraray, 55
Inverness, 8
Ireland, 5, 9, 52, 162
Irvine, Malcolm, 175
Ivanhoe (novel), 150

Jacobite, 61, 66, 110, 121, 159
James F. Donald (Cinemas) Litd., 77
Jeanie Deans (play), 122
Johnson, Samuel, 153, 156–7
Johnston, Thomas, 92, 95–6, 101, 103, 107
Johnstone, 92
Jury's, 46, 48, 139

Kalem Company (and O'Kalems), 9, 113, 162
Kean, William, 25
Keith, 45
Kelso, 19
Kemp family, 20
　Kemp, George ('President'), 137
　Kemp, Harry, 137–8
Kilmarnock, 19, 166
Kinema Managers' Association, 75
Kinematograph Weekly, 48, 131, 140
Kinematograph Year Book, 34, 70

Kineto, 150
King, A. B., 181
King, Elspeth, 23
King's Theatre (Wellington, New Zealand), 125
Kinning Park (Glasgow), 46
Kingston (Glasgow), 46
Kirkcaldy, 16–17, 19, 22, 76, 92
Kirkcudbright, 96
Kirkwall, 6, 62
Kirkintilloch, 11, 40, 95–108
   Common Good Fund, 101
   municipal cinema, 91–108
   Municipal Pictures, **100**, 101, 104, **105**
   Muncipal Pictures Committee, 101, 106
   Town Council, 96, 98, 101, 106
Kirkintilloch Herald, 99, 101–2, **103**, 106–7
Kirriemuir, 161
Kissell, Jack, 112
Klangfilm, 175–6
Kosting, Ernest, 79

Labour Party, 95–6
Lady of the Lake (play), 122
   Lady of the Lake (poem), 150, 158
Laird, Margaret and George, 36
Langside (Glasgow), 46
Largo, 161
Lasky, Jesse, 173
Lauder, Harry, 149, 162
Laurencekirk, 62
Lebas, Elizabeth, 91
Leith, 19
Lely, Durward, 118–19, 121–3, 126
Lely's Limited Gigantic Cinematograph Carnival and Pictorial Festival, 135
Lerwick, 6, 22, 26, 54–5, 60–1, 63–4
Limbless Soldiers' and Sailors' Fund, 76
Lindstrom, J. A., 37
Linlithgow, 45
Little Minister, The (novel), 159
Lizars, 21, 23, 56, 135
local newspapers, 54–5, 132
'local topical', 2, 12, 130–9
Lochgelly, 143
Loch Katrine, 156
Loch Lomond, 157

Lost World of Mitchell and Kenyon, The, 131
Lumière brothers, 56
Lyle, James, 103–4, 106

Macbeth (play), 159
MacDonald, Flora, 153
Mackenzie, Peter Robert, 78
magic lantern, 14, 21
   lantern shows, 27
Maltby, Richard, 1
Maloney, Paul, 23–4
Manchester, 47
Mann, Arthur (North Star, Lerwick), 60–2
Marmion (poem), 150
Marsh, J. J. (Billy), 73
Maver, Irene, 19
Maxwell, John, 4, 173–4
Mayne, Walter, 28
McBride, James, 69, 72, 77
   aka 'Scotty', 112, 118–19, 124–5, 141, 160–1
McGinnis, Kitty, 170–2
McKinnon, Thomas, 111, 114
McIndoe, John, 16
Méliès, 56
Miller, Robert, 72
Mitchell and Kenyon, 131, 133, 135, 137–8, 141
Mix, Tom, 163–4
Mohaly Tone Film Apparatus, 176
Modern Marvel Company, 27, 35
modernity, 1, 11–12, 14, 63
   modernism, 53
Montrose, 53, 92, 160–1
Moretti, Franco, 147
Moss, H. E., 19, 24
Motherwell, 8, 19, 27, 45
Movietone, 175
Moving Image Archive (National Library of Scotland), 17, 133, 136–8, 164
Musicians' Union (MU), 71, 78, 80–2, 166–5, 178–81
Musselburgh, 176
Musser, Charles, 55

Nairn, 45
National Archive, The, 114

National Association of Theatrical Employees (NATE), 71, 78, 82
National Association of Municipal Cinemas (Norway), 92
National Fairground Archive (University of Sheffield), 131
Neilson, Robert, 111
New Century Pictures, 27, 46
newsreel, 132
nickelodeon, 34, 36–7
   shop-front shows, 34
Noel, Captain J. B., 168
Nordisk, 48
Normand, Mabel, 68
North Berwick, 45
Norway, 5, 52, 92

Oban, 6, 54, 58, 60–4
Oban Times, 55
OK Pictures, 97, 100
Olcott, Sidney, 113
Old Mortality (novel), 159
On the Banks of Allan Water (song), 158
Orkney, 53
Ormonde Family, 56, 135
Ormiston, Thomas, 4, 97

Paisley, 19, 40, 43
   Paisley Races, 17
Palace of Variety, 24
Paramount, 101, 173
'parish state', 54
parlour music, 14, 150, 158–9
Partoon, C. F., 160
Paterson, Dove, 27
Pathé, 48, 113, 150
   Pathé Gazette, 132
Paul, R. W., 19
Pearson, George, 113
Peebles, 27, 45
Pennant, Thomas, 153, 156
'penny gaffs', 34
Perth, 140
Philorth Estate (Aberdeenshire), 23
Phonofilm (de Forest and Case), 169
Pickard, A. E., 25–6, 126
Pickford, Mary, 149
'picture palace', 1, 40–1, 53

Pierce, David, 147
Pocock, Isaac, 119, 124
Pollokshaws, 46
Polmont, 176
Portobello, 19
Portree (Isle of Skye), 64
Powers Cinephone, 176
Prince, Sydney, 27
Prince Edward Pictures, 27
Pringle, Ralph, 27, 44
Pringle's Picture Palaces, 44
Provincial Cinematograph Theatres, 40, 43, 75

Queen Victoria, 134, 153
quota, 174

Radio Times, 130
Ratcliffe, J. S., 80
Rattter, J. D., 138
'rational entertainment', 55, 57
RCA Photophone, 178
regulation, 7, 92
Reith, John, 108
'remote reading', 148
Renfrew, 19, 92
renters, 25, 45, 48, 134, 140, 183
   Renters Association, 48
   renter-exhibitors, 48
representation, 2, 10
Rigney, Ann, 119
Rob Roy, 155–6
Rob Roy
   Sir Walter Scott novel, 110–11, 150
   theatre production, 113, 117–24, 126
Robello, Paul, 134
Roberts, Alexander, 78
Ross, James, 21
Rubin, Mira, 66
Russo–Japanese War (1904–5), 57

Saltcoats, 20, 137
Salvation Army, 20
Samuelson, G. B., 113
scenics, 2, 150
   examples of early Scottish scenic films, **151**

Schiller, Friedrich, 159
Scotch Reels, 115
Scott, George Urie, 36, 45
Scott, Sir Walter, 10, 111, 113, 122, 149–50, 153, 160
Scott, T. J., 45
Scottish Cinema and Variety Theatres, 174
Scottish Film Productions (1928) Ltd, 176
Scottish Kinema Record, 74
Scottish Moving Pictures Company, 111
Scottish Office, 6–7, 96
Scottish Secretary, 92, 96
Scottish Trades Union Congress, 71, 179
Scotsman, The, 35, 122–3
Scullion, Adrienne, 24
serials, 4, 163
Shakespeare, William, 150
Shaw, George Bernard, 95
Shetland, 53, 62, 138
    Shetland Archive, 61
Shetland News, 138
Shetland Times, 63
Shotts, 76
Showman's Year Book, 19
showmanship, 74–5, 183
showmen, 4, 15, 19, 28, 33, 134
    showpeople, 17
Simmers, Hugh, 71, 84–5
Singleton, R. V., 45
skating rinks, 37
Skinner, Scott, 134
Skye, 64
sound (conversion to), 166–83
South Wales, 47
Spanish–American War (1898), 57
Spean Gorge, 156
Springburn (Glasgow), 46
staff, 68, 178
    apprentice, 70, 78
    attendants, 68, 82
    bonuses, 77
    booking 'clerkess', 69
    booking manager, 70
    checkers, 69
    chocolate-sellers, 82
    cleaners, 68–70, 72, 82
    collective bargaining, 82
    doorman, 69
    female staff, 70, 83–5
    front-of-house, 68
    managers, 4, 11, 42, 49, 68–9, 72–7, 80
    Military Appeal Tribunals, 72, 77, 84
    money takers, 69, 82
    musicians, 68–72, 77, 82
    Music Director, 79–81, 84
    operators (projectionists), 68–9, 72–3, 77–9, 82
    outings, 76–7
    pianist, 80
    part-time, 70–2
    programme-sellers, 82
    spool winder, 69–70
    training, 77–8, 85
    ushers, 69–70, 74, 82
Stage, The, 25
Stage Yearbook, 27
star system, 4
'stars', 49, 68–9
Stationers' Company, 114
Stevenson, R. L., 150, 159
Stewart, Bob, 46
Stirling, 19
Stokes, Melvyn, 1
Stonehaven, 28, 62
Stornoway, 6, 64–5, 92–3
Strachur (Argyllshire), 55
sublime, 156–8
'super film', 57, 131
Sutton Coldfield, 47
Swallow, Peter, 17
Sweden, 5, 52
synchronised sound, 168–70

television, 130, 134
Temperance, 46, 140
Thurso, 62, 64–5
Timmons, Tommy, 137, 174
Today's Cinema, 119
Topical Budget, 102, 132
Torry Cinema Ltd (Aberdeen), 177–8, **182**
Toulmin, Vanessa, 15–17, 24

Tourneur, Maurice, 161
Trevelyan, G. B., 143–4
Turner, J. M. W., 153
Triangle, 48
Trossachs, 154
Twain, Mark, 150

Udny (Aberdeenshire), 24
United Films Limited (Glasgow), 48, 111–19, 122, 124, 126
Urban, 150

Valentine, James, 21
variety, 25, 57, 60, 174–5, 180, 183
  cine-variety, 24, 48
  concert party, 21, 27, 61
  'turns', 59, 167
vaudeville, 175
venues, 52–3
  venue, fixed-site, 1, 4, 10, 41, 58
  church hall, 53
  drill hall, 20, 37, 53
  Masonic hall, 20
  music hall, 14, 24–5, 27, 33, 43
  public halls, 14, 20, 25, 37
  temperance halls, 20, 37, 53
  town halls, 91
Verne, Jules, 150
Vinegarhill, 19, 36
Vitaphone, 175
Vivian, Arthur, 111–12, 123
Vocal Cinema Co. Ltd, 169

Walker, George W., 27–8
Walker, William, 21, 33, 56, 134–7
  Walker's Royal Cinematograph, 23, 134, 137
Wanlockhead, 157
Warwick Trading Company, 112
Waverley (novel), 159
website, 2–3
West of Scotland Electric Theatres Company, 40
West Highland Railway, 61, 65
Western Electric, 175–6
Westerns, 61, 117
West's Pictures (Adelaide, Australia), 125
Whifflet, 76
Wick, 65
Wilcox, Herbert, 74
Williamson, James, 132
  Wiliamson Kinematograph Company, 139
Wilmot, Jimmy, 17
Wilmot, John, 19
Wilson, George Washington, 21
Windsor Theatre (Auckland, New Zealand), 126
Wordworth, Dorothy and William, 153–7
world literature, 149–50
Worden, Peter, 131
Wolverhampton, 47

Yates, Frank Danvers, 112–14
Young Lochinvar (poem), 158

EU representative:
Easy Access System Europe
Mustamäe tee 50, 10621 Tallinn, Estonia
Gpsr.requests@easproject.com

www.ingramcontent.com/pod-product-compliance
Lightning Source LLC
Chambersburg PA
CBHW062124300426
44115CB00012BA/1804